Culture's Vanities

American Intellectual Culture

Series Editors: Jean Bethke Elshtain, University of Chicago,
Ted V. McAllister, Pepperdine University,
Wilfred M. McClay, University of Tennessee at Chattanooga

Culture's Vanities

The Paradox of Cultural Diversity in a Globalized World

David Steigerwald

ROWMAN & LITTLEFIELD PUBLISHERS, INC.
Lanham • Boulder • New York • Toronto • Oxford

ROWMAN & LITTLEFIELD PUBLISHERS, INC.

Published in the United States of America
by Rowman & Littlefield Publishers, Inc.
A wholly owned subsidiary of The Rowman & Littlefield Publishing Group, Inc.
4501 Forbes Boulevard, Suite 200, Lanham, Maryland 20706
www.rowmanlittlefield.com

PO Box 317
Oxford
OX2 9RU, UK

British Library Cataloguing in Publication Information Available

Library of Congress Cataloging-in-Publication Data

Steigerwald, David.
   Culture's vanities: The paradox of cultural diversity in a globalized world / David
   Steigerwald.
      p. cm.—(American intellectual culture)
   Includes index.
   ISBN 0-7425-1196-0 (alk. paper)—ISBN 0-7425-1197-9 (pbk. : alk paper)
Globalization—social aspects.   2. International relations and culture.   I. Title.
   II. Series.
   BX5995.B8H37 2004
   283'.092—dc22
                                                                2004007059

Printed in the United States of America

♾™ The paper used in this publication meets the minimum requirements of
American National Standard for Information Sciences—Permanence of Paper for
Printed Library Materials, ANSI/NISO Z39.48-1992.

For Drew,
Doubt much, but never lose faith

Then was I beside him as his craftsman,
and I was his delight day by day;
Playing before him all the while,
playing on the surface of his earth;
and I found delight in the sons of men.

Discourse on Wisdom
Proverbs 8: 30–31

Nor will their masters be better off: the earth's surface will be hideous everywhere, save in the uninhabitable desert; Art will utterly perish, as in the manual arts so in literature which will become, as it is indeed speedily becoming, a mere string of orderly and calculated ineptitudes and passionless ingenuities; Science will grow more and more one-sided, more incomplete, more wordy and useless, till at last she will pile herself up into such a mass of superstition, that beside it the theologies of old time will seem mere reason and enlightenment. All will get lower and lower, till the heroic struggles of the past to realize hope from year to year, from century to century, will be utterly forgotten, and man will be an indescribable being—hopeless, desireless, lifeless.

William Morris, *The Aims of Art* (1886)

Contents

~

Preface: The Follies of
Cultural Determinism in
an Age of Anti-Culture

Sometime in the last quarter of the twentieth century, the developed world appeared to slip from the Age of Materialism into the Age of Culture. Culture has become to our time what religion was to the early modern period and science to the Enlightenment. Economic Man of the nineteenth and early twentieth centuries has abdicated in favor of Cultural Person, and the new regime has replaced class consciousness with cultural consciousness.

At least this is true of intellectuals on the whole, among whom "cultural analysis" has been adopted practically across the board, regardless of subject or the specific discipline of the writer. Measuring everything from the accumulation of wealth to the exertion of military power against some cultural background has become more than just a way of raising interesting questions; it is now the litmus test for "cutting-edge" thought, against which most writing is measured and judged. It is not too much to say that the foremost dynamic in the so-called postmodern mind over the last generation has been the conviction, now hardened into dogma, that culture determines history.

In the United States, if not throughout the developed world, this cultural determinism has trickled down from the intellectuals and now assumes the position of common sense. Culture is the new catchall, the court of first and last appeal, the basis of public policy, the obligatory note, the place we all reside. Even a casual listener can hear Americans using culture to explain nearly everything. They wage culture wars. They pledge loyalty to cultural identities. They speak of being cultural citizens, enfranchised not in a nation-state of law but in a mystical communion of blood ties. They give a great deal more attention to their self-proclaimed cultures than to the sort of work they are increasingly forced to do. They permit themselves to be lumped into discrete groups for the purpose of exploitation because advertisers, always acutely attuned to contemporary mood, have discovered that they can use culture to organize consumer niches. Indeed, I would wager that the present conviction that individuals are fixed in distinct cultures, that their ideas, abilities, predispositions, values, likes, and dislikes are all distinct products of that culture, is far more widely and deeply held than genuine class consciousness ever was—at least in the United States.

The historical forces behind the rise of this cultural determinism must be as deep as the shift is profound. I make no claim here to having figured it all out. But it cannot be a coincidence that cultural determinism is most pronounced among people who, on the whole, enjoy material comfort well beyond what is necessary to survive and who accept with varying degrees of enthusiasm a social order based on constant technological change and consumer activity, all organized through and beneath bureaucratic regimes, both public and private. People still locked in the survival struggle are not typically given to obsessions with the nature of their cultures. This is very different, let me make unequivocally clear, from saying that poor people lack cultures; they simply have more pressing things to worry about. On the surface, then, it appears that cultural determinism is a product of generalized abundance. Perhaps it reduces to an axiom: People of general leisure and abundance have more time and wealth to create more culture, and their intellectual sensitivities follow accordingly.

If it were all that simple, there would be no sport in criticizing the new determinism, which is, after all, my intention. The fact is, in any case, that the above axiom is gravely flawed. To assume that material wealth gives rise to more culture implies that material want limits cultural achievement and that leisured classes were always more cultured than the people they sat upon. Neither of these implications bears serious scrutiny. More important, the axiom confuses intellectual obsession over culture with the creation of culture itself; it assumes that simply talking about culture creates culture and that merely seeing oneself as part of a people makes it so. In the essays that follow, I argue to the contrary that material abundance undermines the will to culture and obstructs the creation and continuity of all the things that matter most to culture. Reduced to fundamentals, the universal will to culture issues in two inclinations: first, the desire to create superfluous objects, things that are not strictly necessary to biological survival; and second, the organization of collective human ties that transcend the individual and reach across generations. Both of these essential inclinations strive toward the creation of permanent, or at least enduring, elements of life. The world we inhabit today, based as it is on constant change and the relentless consumption of goods, cannot, strictly speaking, satisfy the yearning for permanence. So instead of a simple axiom, we confront a paradox. The intellectual framework of cultural determinism has been built in a social and economic climate hostile to the creation of culture, properly understood. Rather than an Age of Culture, ours is better described as an Age of Anti-Culture. And our axiom turns on its head: The intellectual obsession with culture has intensified as the capacity of human beings to create and sustain enduring elements of life has been siphoned away.

Under such circumstances, cultural determinism becomes almost self-delusory and, in many ways, a ruse better designed to support the status quo than to criticize it. Indeed, a more specific explanation behind why the idea of culture, as distinguished from culture itself, has come to constitute the main framework for understanding human affairs is that the concept carries with it two traditions of usage that, over time, have been mangled into a set of complacent assumptions about how power works. Since Raymond Williams first called attention to the historic emergence of the culture concept in his pivotal *Culture and Society* (1958), it has been widely understood that culture carried an aesthetic meaning, as a synonym for taste, and an anthropological meaning, as in culture as a way of life. Each of these two usages has an integrity and importance of its own; and while they can and should be distinguished, they are historically linked and ultimately inseparable. Over the last half-century, as the culture concept was applied with increasing frequency and in increasingly casual fashion, each usage was corrupted. The aesthetic conception of culture was buried in the postwar flush of consumer affluence; the conviction that taste was essential to the good life because it reflected the commitment to the creation of superfluous beauty was degraded into the idea that taste boiled down to a matter of choice, the foremost value of a consumer society. At roughly the same time, meanwhile, once-marginalized racial and ethnic groups were slowly incorporated into the social orders of the developed world. As they were nudged into the system of consumer abundance and the bureaucratic structures that hold that system in place, they necessarily relinquished the patterns of life that provided them with distinct cultures in the anthropological sense. Yet members of those once-marginalized groups and their advocates resorted to the anthropological conception of culture to insist that those special ways of life remained largely intact in spite of their inclusion in a largely homogenized social system.

From these two broad corruptions of worthy traditions flowed many of the currents of thought that punctuated the 1990s. The intellectuals invented something they called "cultural agency," which, reduced to formula, held that individuals actively shape their cultural lives by the choices they make, particularly their choices as consumers. The act of consumption was invested with all manner of symbolism and, accordingly, with power. They invented something called multiculturalism and insisted not only that America was host to any number of thriving and distinct cultures but that the members of those cultures could—and should—be incorporated fully into the bureaucratic structure without impairing their distinctiveness. They developed a rhetoric of cultural diversity to gloss over the self-contradictory notion that we can have it both ways: a world of distinct cultures amid homogenized abundance or, more precisely, a world of enduring ways of life amid perpetually shifting individual choice. Here, then, are the contemporary distillations of the two traditions of cultural thought—culture as endlessly flexible choice and culture as perpetually distinct ways of life—bound together, now buttressing the status quo by ignoring material reality.

Oddly, both of these common misapprehensions rest on a view of culture as an ideal, rather than a concrete here-and-now, condition. The act of creation, after all, is at the heart of both traditions. The creation of enduring and beautiful objects depends on the execution of craft skills, and those skills are essential ingredients to distinct ways of life. The corruption of taste into choice not only ignores the importance of hard practice in mastering such skills but, more directly, ignores how thoroughly homogenized work is today. At the very moment when intellectuals in the developed world were inventing the notion that individuals expressed themselves by choosing one good over another, more and more people worldwide were being dragged out of traditional work settings into the world of mass production so that those Western illusions of choice might be satisfied. The debasement of labor, first imposed in the West a century ago, is now a global phenomenon and cannot conceivably encourage the careful production of well-made goods or sustain the traditions of skill essential to community distinctiveness. Within the developed world, meanwhile, work largely has been reduced to various tasks executed within bureaucracies, formerly well known for their capacity for grounding down human differences and leaving human beings in a state of restless alienation. Just as culture as choice can be a persuasive aesthetic ideal only if the centrality of work is dismissed, so culture as diversity can be a persuasive anthropological claim only if the fundamental nature of bureaucracies is ignored. In both cases, their persuasive power depends on the willingness to accept culture as a mere ideal, in contrast to the practical ways daily life is now led.

The more we strive to believe in the ideals, the more apparent the gap between them and material reality and the greater the temptation to recover culture as an antidote to alienation. Particularly those people recently inducted into the world of bureaucratized consumption, precisely because they are, in a real sense, new arrivals whose memories of older ways of life remain vivid and meaningful, are apt to sense that something very important is missing. The historic promise of inclusion in the mainstream—a promise that had to be fulfilled in the name of basic justice—always included the seduction that the mainstream was the road to individual fulfillment. Two generations ago, that much-abused figure, the white male, having discovered that the seduction was a cruel hoax, largely reconciled himself to a meaningless life, and he might now be enjoying the last laugh as the intellectuals convince newcomers that they can join up and still have their distinct communities. Over the last generation, members of racial and ethnic minorities have faced the paradox of winning inclusion in an alienating world. It is natural for many to react by trying to reassert roots in the form of "identity" claims. But they have had the misfortune of coming to this point amid an intellectual climate that offers them only artificial sustenance. When these new alienates grab hold of culture as their lifeline, all they have in their hands are much-debased concepts—in the forms of multiculturalism and cultural diversity—that counsel capitulation to the very system that brings on the alienation in the first place. Rather than a future of endless cultural diversity, we are much more likely to have a situation in which the descendants of once-marginalized peoples are as resigned to living lives as meaningless as that of any good WASP today. Maybe they'll even become Republicans.

Not least will this be so because the economic ruling class understands clearly what sort of game culture has become. Sensing how deeply the yearning for cultural community is among people at once increasingly deprived of roots and under the delusion that culture is what you make it, the purveyors of plastic abundance have perfected the strategy of niche marketing, a line of manipulation they have embraced because they recognize how little difference there is in the products they make. They have succeeded almost in the same sense that snake-oil salesmen succeed among people with irreversible fatal illnesses: by selling phony nostrums to desperate people. This material reality—that too much of what passes as cultural diversity is in truth cultural homogeneity—signals a deeper reality as well, a reality utterly at odds with much of what passes as cultural analysis these days. That is, the contemporary ruling classes no longer need to dictate prevailing tastes, as ruling classes in the past were apt to do. Taste itself, in the form of well-honed discriminating judgment about quality, is irrelevant to the way power operates in contemporary society. As goes taste, so goes culture: in an Age of Anti-Culture, the idea that culture is power no longer holds true.

The economic ruling class has beaten their critics at the cultural game, and the sooner progressive-minded people come to grips with that, the better. Strictly speaking, there is no longer a cultural ruling class, and yet the absence of such an animal only seems to make the control of economic and political ruling classes that much more secure.

Sun River, Oregon
August 2003

~

Acknowledgments

Books are always biographical to some extent, and they have their own biographies. This one was hatched in a period of personal gloom, a time when I was so put off by academia and so despairing of the tone and substance of American intellectual life that I was seriously considering becoming an over-the-road trucker. Luckily, fate intervened in the form of a Fulbright lectureship to Okinawa, Japan, which is, believe me, about as far away from Midwestern academia as you can get. Living in a place whose people have endured about the worst that nature and humanity can dump on anyone and who nonetheless carry themselves in great good humor provided just the right dose of distance and leisure that I needed to get my feet back beneath me. Much of my time there was spent simply sitting on the coral edge of Awase Bay watching the old women in their sun bonnets and galoshes pick their way through the tidal pools. I suppose I'm obliged to say that I wasn't wasting time but rather seeing first hand how global consumerism and delicate ways of life were colliding. But the fact of the matter is that, for the first time in many years, I had the privilege of just sitting and thinking, and doing so in a place of exquisite natural beauty. For that marvelous respite, I must thank Samuel Shepherd, Kazuko Kamimura, and their staff at the Fulbright Office in Tokyo, as well as all my colleagues at the National University of Japan–Ryukyus, and Okinawa International University.

I intend this particular book as part of a series of studies on the rise of the idea of culture in the nineteenth and twentieth centuries. In some ways, it should probably have been written last, but Steve Wrinn at Rowman & Littlefield, along with the editors of their promising series in American intellectual and cultural history, Jean Bethke Elshtain, Wilfred M. McClay, and Ted V. McAllister, offered me the chance to finish it first. There was some challenge in bringing my thinking up to date while also remaining confident of my historical judgments, but I expect that is all to the good. Among other effects of working this way, however, has been that much of the larger historical writing has been done already and has been read by a number of generous friends and critics. I hadn't asked them to read this particular manuscript, but Paul Croce, Rochelle Gurstein, and Bill Childs read so much of that other work that I must thank them here just for starters. Lynda Behan, my steadfast sounding board, patiently reads everything I throw at her with good-natured skepticism; if nothing else I have to applaud her perseverance. My friend and colleague Cemil Aydin read parts of the manuscript and offered particular advice on life at Harvard in the era of Cornel West. Most of all, I thank Raymond Haberski and Maurice Isserman for their help and comments. Finally, let me thank Bernard Murchland, editor of *Civic Arts Review* in which parts of chapters 1 and 5 first appeared.

One of the compensations to the teaching position I now hold is that many of my students are what university bureaucrats call "non-traditional," which is to say that they are grown-ups. Regardless of the particular reason for migrating to college, they invariably carry a good deal of hard-earned wisdom with them, and it is not just putting nice words together to say that I learn as much from them as they from me. So much is this true that I have entrusted several of them with bits and pieces of this book. I owe a bow to both Karyn Price and Eric Furniss, who have read extensively for me; Furniss was particularly helpful because, as an ex-radio laborer, he was able to speak with real authority on the sins of Clear Channel radio. Melissa Kaspar used her legal expertise to offer timely help on Supreme Court material. I must also thank Betsy Blankenship and her staff, whom I probably treat as my personal librarians much more than I should.

This book began in a period of personal malaise and was finished in a period of family crisis. Like a good love story, its climax ran through the tragedy of death and collapse, but ended, I'm overjoyed to say, in reaffirmation and strengthened bonds. Through these days, my family and I have been blessed with the friendship of many people whose decency always amazes me. I am lucky to be close to Tom Bray and Rebecca Butler; Tom and Bobbi Frey; Sue and Kevin Koloff; and the whole Henkel family, including Zach, who, though the only person I know who owns a chain-mail shirt, ought to remember that a good anti-modernist wouldn't drive an SUV, much less a Jag. I hope my brothers, Tom Steigerwald and Larry Woerner, understand how much we have come to depend on them and how deeply grateful we are. To Susan, Stacey, and Drew: We now know that forgiveness and redemption work. And that is an extraordinary gift.

CHAPTER ONE

~

On the Rise of Cultural Determinism in an Age of Anti-Culture

It is commonplace to say that we have been living in paradoxical times. Strengthened world markets, computer technology, and new forms of communication created an indisputably global condition during the last twenty years, and yet public life was punctuated with provincialism and fundamentalism. Coca-Cola, Kentucky Fried Chicken, Nike sneakers, and Japanese electronics came to constitute the visible ingredients of everyday life for people the world over. From the villages of northern Thailand to the cities of South America, humanity took on similar and universally recognized trappings of existence, in spite of the vast differences in language, tradition, physical distance, and, perhaps most of all, wealth. Yet globalization shared headlines daily with separatist movements of varying degrees of intensity and violence, from Quebec to Sri Lanka, from Corsica to northern India, from Chechnya to Hawaii. Not many days went by when worldwide television, one of the foremost technologies acting to knit people together, neglected to bring some display of political or cultural division. A period that began with people singing the Disney anthem "It's a Small World After All" ended, shockingly, with religious fundamentalists flying airplanes into the tallest symbols of that cheery little world.

During the 1990s, it was a rare place that could claim to be free of divisive spirits and a rarer place still that could claim to be governed by a temper of true cosmopolitanism, a spirit that draws human loyalties outward toward ends more substantive than mere economic and material gain and yet still carries memory and tradition. There were few places from which people at home in the world of their ancestors could still develop the broad sympathies—among them, the instinct of fine craftsmanship, the devotion to the constant refinement of culture, the respect for honorable traditions, the forbearance for deviations from those traditions, and the wisdom to know what traditions are inhumane—that mark humanity at its most generous. In place of a serious cosmopolitanism that might encourage us to be skeptical about the benefits of global consumerism and high technology and that, in so doing, might help us preserve the best parts of all pasts, an idealized, resurgent provincialism developed.

This provincialism was not a mere reaction to change, a cranky attempt to resist the inevitable. Rather it was the instinct most in keeping with technologies that made it unnecessary to seek creative outlets for the mastery of nature. If anything, the contemporary forms that economic and technological changes have taken undercut the material and physical bases of humane sympathies. The communications technologies that drive global change today are intrusive, and they distance human beings from the communities to which they are supposedly attached. Meanwhile, a globalizing market system, which spreads those intrusive gadgets, makes power increasingly abstract and remote. Together these two dominating forces serve less to bring the world's people together in a global village than to destroy the substantive cultures, folkways, religious traditions, and traditional methods of production of all people swept into their orbit, yet they offer no worthy substitute. Instead of the cozy global village, it is closer to the truth to say that we are falling into lives of ill-defined deracination. We are all becoming rootless.

Even as it creates universal rootlessness, the recently ascendant technological and economic status quo flatters the provincial. Advertisers, in their relentless effort to leave no potential market unexploited, have perfected the game of niche appeals; they carve up a population into categories and serve them all the same plastic goods in different packages. In the United States at least, the entire network of mass-produced consumer products now runs on the principles of niche appeal and block-by-block market research. The appeal to group differences inherently reshapes the groups themselves, gutting whatever qualities made them distinct in the first place by coaxing them into the blandest of all value systems, the system of consumption. Even the much-ballyhooed virtue of the Internet, which supposedly allows isolated people to discover others of similar tastes and habits, makes any genuine community of people impossible. The advocates of "virtual community" insist that electronic relationships are no less real than traditional face-to-face ones; physical proximity, so they say, is now irrelevant. But in the collective lives of human communities, physical proximity is not simply a matter of having everyone in one place at the same time. Geography carries with it collective memory, community connections to nature, to climate, to the earth, and therefore is home to distinct skills grown out of the engagement with specific conditions, distinct products designed to meet local needs, and myths and values born of a specific place. These are the elements of culture, properly understood, and every one of them is trampled on, discarded, or neglected in systematic and intentional ways by those who profit from mass consumption and mass communications. It is ample testimony to just how rootless we have become, how profoundly disengaged from the natural world we are, that we apparently have forgotten that roots are sunk in the earth.

This correspondence between high-tech consumerism and the provincial sensibility is the best way to explain the appearance of provincialism among the people most saturated with media and most committed to the values of consumption. During the 1990s, when virtual wealth created dreams of lim-itless ease and perpetual indulgence, when supposedly sober business analysts predicted the Dow would exceed 30,000 and well-respected scholars pro-claimed the "end of history," Americans gave themselves over to various sorts of separatism as readily as Indonesian islanders. Some, it is true, were lu-natics, such as the milquetoast Ohioan who decided to reclaim Texas as an independent republic. It is hard, or at least impolite, to say the same of the residents of Berkeley Hills, Staten Island, or the San Fernando Valley who demanded "independence" from the cities to which they have long been at-tached; and if not impolite, it was certainly impolitic to level charges of in-sanity at Hispanic proponents of a contemporary *reconquista* in the South-west or African American students who insisted on exclusive dorms so that they could feel comfortable among their own. The spirit of separatism was pronounced among suburban Christians and deaf lesbians alike. And some of the foremost advocates of provincialism in America were college administra-tors, who, in the name of a contrived diversity, stooped to harassing students and faculty into workshops where the slightest human differences were em-bellished into concrete proof of fundamental cultural distinctions. Then those champions of diversity typically climbed into their Volvos, cruised to their upscale homes, and—who knows?—maybe settled in for a dinner of nouveau California-Italian or some Thai take-out and a good Cabernet.

Against this backdrop of provincialism without consequences, it is worth recalling that Western intellectuals began the era of industrial capitalism—a time when the world was a good deal less orderly than they wanted to imagine—by defining the good life as an accumulation of widened experi-ence, the absolute first requirement of which was liberation from the village. Kant believed that humanity had a natural cosmopolitanism embodied in "our common right of possession on the surface of the earth on which, as it is a globe, we cannot be infinitely scattered, and must in the end reconcile ourselves to existence side by side." To Alexis de Tocqueville, the provincial tendencies of democracy, in particular the temptation of people in an egalitarian setting to resort to antisocial exile, had to be checked against the cosmopolitan spirit: "If men are to remain civilized or to become so, the art of associating together must grow and improve in the same ratio in which the equality of conditions is increased." John Stuart Mill had no patience with the idea that a person could be better off as a provincial than as a member of a cosmopolitan nation. "Nobody can suppose," Mill wrote in the mid-nineteenth century, "that it is not more beneficial for a Breton or a Basque of French Navarre to be . . . a member of the French nationality, admitted on equal terms to all the privileges of French citizenship . . . than to sulk on his own rocks, the half-savage relic of past times, revolving in his own little mental orbit, without participation or interest in the general movement of the world." A half-century later, poet Ezra Pound recalled Mill when he defended Modernism as a "struggle against provincialism," the "ever-damned spirit" conferred on the world by thugs such as Napoleon, whom "only a backwards hell like Corsica would have produced."[1]

At just that historic moment when the world abruptly became more homogenized and regulated than ever, when globalization turned village life into a hawkers' square and culture became the currency of shills, we saw a longing for the dusty roads of the provinces. In place of urbanity and cosmopolitanism, the 1990s saw the elevation of rusticity and insularity as public virtues. We went from Sinclair Lewis's *Main Street*, or, better still, Mary Antin's homage to the liberation of modernity in her autobiographical account of immigration, *The Promised Land*, to Clifton Taulbert's rose-colored nostalgia for life in the segregated South, *Once Upon a Time When We Were Colored*. Even the self-described radical feminist bell hooks waxed teary-eyed over life under segregation as her "homeplace," back "where we had a history."[2] Compare Mill's scorching contempt for the Basque "to sulk on his own rocks" and "revolving in his own little mental orbit" with much of what has been written on race, ethnicity, or gender by a Western academic in the last ten years, and you can grasp the sea change of intellectual attitude.

Whether the war on terrorism will throw the more blatant expressions of provincialism into disrepute remains to be seen. It is hard to deny at least a superficial similarity between the cultural fundamentalism of Americans and the violence-spawning fundamentalisms in many other places. For one thing, they share a certain artificiality, not to say phoniness. If the "Republic of Texas" guerrillas betrayed their contrived nature by following someone from

Ohio, they were not all that removed from, say, the early leaders of the radical Basque movement in Spain who did not even know the traditional language when they launched their violent efforts to recover their golden era. Osama bin Laden posed as a holy man, but he had no bona fide religious credentials. In Zacharias Moussai and other radicals reared in the West we see one of the more curious consequences of globalization: Islamic Holden Caulfields.

We must be careful, though, not to conflate American provincialism with radical separatism. There is no moral equation between Islamic radicals who fly planes into office buildings and American college administrators who employ their "diversity plans" in an effort to make minority students comfortable—however misconceived those efforts. Any conflation of the two is silly and obtuse and would have to ignore the qualitative differences in means and motives. It would also have to ignore the practical differences of causes and conditions. Whatever the motives of someone like bin Laden, whose historical point of reference is the eighth century, it is indisputable that movements like his find fertile ground because of specific circumstances. The Palestinian question serves as the lightning rod for discontent, and that popular rage is pretty easily explained by the suffocating despotisms, widespread displacement of populations, and endemic poverty of the region—to say nothing of the increasingly violent imperialism of Israel and the United States. Quite obviously, the provincialism of Americans bears no relation to such movements because it is not a reaction to desperate conditions.

This point, in essence, is precisely what catches my eye: Over the last generation, Americans embraced cultural fundamentalism in direct proportion to their material well-being. The more they spewed the "American way of life" around the world, upending and overrunning the ways of life of other people, the more they retreated into the cocoon of self-proclaimed culture. In ways unprecedented in human history, they discarded institutional commitments to faith and family, picked up and moved out of physical communities that previously defined their "homeplace," and yet claimed an ever-more-intense commitment to "their culture." With little reflection on the damage they did to the essence of culture, they liberated themselves from the confines of traditional bulwarks and intermediary institutions and joined the ranks of corporate workers. They placed themselves in the maw of a bureaucratic order and still claimed to have emerged with their "diversity" intact. With varying measures of resigned acquiescence and celebratory exuberance, they accepted the latest wave of the capitalist homogenization of labor, this time in the application of the computer to the workplace, and little was said of the importance of distinct forms of labor to genuine human diversity. More than that: Their cultural theorists decided that work no longer mattered. They could not even meet their historic obligation to ensure social justice without spinning the self-deluding myth that once-marginalized people can enter the full thrust of a homogenized society without actually becoming homogenized themselves. They invented comforting words. Diversity and multiculturalism were habitually invoked as cover-alls that excused past injustice, drew attention away from the actual cultural consequences of group inclusion, and ignored the concrete effects of economic and technological change. Where virtual prosperity made them so giddy that imagination could be detached from material realities, Americans convinced themselves that they could have the best of both worlds: a world of cheap consumer goods, which among other things necessitated the exploitation of labor in nondeveloped nations, and a secure existence in the comforting culture of their ancestors.

It is impossible to have it both ways, and the question at hand is why Americans came to believe that they could.

Some Preliminary Concessions to the Dogma of Diversity

I would like to think that this study is not just another screed against affirmative action or another snotty lament over the dismissal of Western civilization. Affirmative action remains a noble end, at least as it applies to African and Native Americans. Properly conceived, it is a guarantee of good faith, and the individual-rights claims against it strike me as inconsequential compared to the historic wrongs such programs are intended to remedy. It is a practical issue for me; affirmative action programs have proved their worth in elevating racial minorities, at least African Americans, from marginalized desperation to something very close to full participation in this society. At what point affirmative action will have accomplished its ends—Justice O'Connor has set the mark at twenty-five years—is a matter that reasonable people can debate in civil fashion. But at such a point, African Americans will still be justified in maintaining the core of such efforts: the promise made in the 1964 Civil Rights Act that discrimination will not be permitted in this society.

I am less interested in the merits and demerits of what came to pass as affirmative action than I am with the language games that came to surround the effort. In what surely is indicative of the shifting contemporary mind, programs intended to create racial and ethnic integration, plain and simple, came to be defended as "diversity plans." The main purpose of all affirmative action programs is to secure the presence of once-marginalized groups into the nation's institutional life, to integrate them in the mainstream. The nation's racial history rendered such achievements worthy on their face and necessary if the United States wanted to make justice more than just a pretense. There are always costs to such things, however, one of which was that the beneficiaries of integration would have to climb off the provincial rocks that oppression had kept them on. That this would be so ought to have been self-evident in any case, but it is an even more formidable reality when we acknowledge that integration into contemporary America means integration into a corporate-bureaucratic order that undercuts human peculiarities by imposing standardized patterns of work, living, and thought. Defenders of affirmative action lost the will to acknowledge this cost. Indeed, they fabricated a myth—a self-delusion—that minorities could be conducted into the nation's institutional order without cultural compromise. They could be integrated and yet diverse. They could have it both ways.

We should recognize that, as with any complex moment, there are many good reasons why Americans pronounced themselves committed to cultural diversity at a time of far-reaching homogenization. For one thing, it is a matter of simple common sense to think that America is more diverse than ever. In an ethnic sense, that is absolutely true. The present wave of immigration has brought a much greater diversity of peoples than the last great wave a century before. It may be that the typical American-born Anglo experienced that earlier immigration more intensely in the early twentieth century than he would today, given that the proportion of immigrants in the population was higher in 1910 than in 2000. But those immigrants were almost entirely European (even if that Anglo considered Italians and Jews to be members of other races), while today's immigrants are from everywhere. Anyone who has caught a cab, bought a newspaper, shopped in a carry-out, or paid attention to who bussed their restaurant table in any city during the 1990s had good reason to think that American culture was wonderfully diverse. A public school teacher in any metropolitan district in the country might easily have taught students born in dozens of different countries, sometimes all at once. Even Iowa, of all places, developed an "immigrant problem" during the 1990s.

Many of the corporate, academic, and governmental agents of diversity were white people who never had much experience with nonwhites. The very sort of people most likely to fill bureaucratic careers overwhelmingly tended to be middle- and upper-class whites who grew up in ethnically homogenized suburbs; they might have known a few tokens, but that was about the extent of their interaction. They never experienced the sometimes-turbulent, sometimes-harmonious ethnic and racial interaction that has always taken place among the working classes. It was a new thing to them to have a black colleague, and we should remember that the people who came to power in the 1990s, most of whom were in their fifties and sixties, were alive at the tail end of segregation, so day-to-day interaction among equals was still something to marvel at and most assuredly is not something to belittle.

For that generation, the rhetoric of diversity served two purposes. It finished out the commitment to racial integration that had been the historic burden of their generation, and once they came to control the nation's institutions they took to ramming home their diversity plans regardless of the practical reality on the ground. Second, the rhetoric governed as a sort of code of conduct, or at least a guide to proper manners, so that people still unaccustomed to one another and still uneasy in one another's presence could work together, even if in an awkward formality. Honesty and direct dealing between individuals was probably sacrificed; guidelines to proper manners were easily ridiculed as "political correctness." But there was little genuine harm in having today's American-born Anglo being polite at worst and even enthusiastic about the integration of the office. Surely it is better to have that same Anglo "celebrate diversity" in a time of substantial ethnic changes in the population than to have him scolding the "hyphenated American," reading Madison Grant's *Passing of the Great Race*, or joining the Ku Klux Klan as his great-grandfather might well have done during and after World War I.

Meanwhile, for those once-marginalized people who were swept into the mainstream—and this was most acutely true for African Americans, whose historic claims make them a special case in all such regards—the rhetoric of diversity amounted to a promise of institutional good faith, a working acknowledgment that they would be treated politely. To the extent that African Americans conceived and articulated the rhetoric, it represented their own claims to control and their own proprietary interests asserted over the institutions to which they gave themselves. Far more important to the argument I propose here, people of color clung to the rhetoric as a hedge against their own alienation, a malady particularly keen for the first postsegregation generation, now ensconced in the nation's bureaucratic life. First-generation immigrants always suffer the brunt of alienating culture shock, and in an objective historical sense, the demands for diversity programs and the like signaled attempts at political solutions to the problem of alienation. Still, it was at once a little poignant and a bit absurd that Henry Louis Gates

Jr. might try to recreate at Harvard the world of "colored people" in which he was raised.

There were also practical legal and political purposes behind multiculturalism and diversity, at least in their institutional settings. The notion that race-based programs, usually lumped together as affirmative action, are valuable because they enhance diversity was at the heart of Lewis Powell's controlling opinion in the *Bakke* decision, probably the founding document of the diversity dogma. In that famously ambivalent ruling, the court struck down the use of strict racial quotas in university admissions and still ruled that using race as an admissions factor was constitutional, so long as the state could prove a compelling interest. That interest, Powell argued, lay in the general value of intellectual diversity that theoretically correlates with racial and ethnic diversity. Everyone is better off, the argument goes, when exposed to a diversity of viewpoints, experiences, and, presumably, "cultures." While Powell's opinion was a compromise that bridged a clearly divided court, it freed affirmative action programs from merely remedial purposes. As remedies, affirmative action policies theoretically could be confined to those institutions that had actively practiced racial discrimination in the past, and while many, if not most, older colleges and universities had indeed done so, the charge could not be made against new institutions such as the University of California at Davis, which was the defendant in *Bakke*. Moreover, remedial programs are limited in time, because sooner or later past wrongs will be righted and the rationale for the programs exhausted. Powell's diversity argument—against Powell's own hopes, to be sure—made it possible to employ affirmative action programs everywhere and to do so permanently for all groups able to lay claim to bureaucratic attention.

It is easy to see that the Powell opinion made the bureaucratic commitment to diversity both inevitable and extremely appealing. It provided an almost-irrefutable argument for perpetual programs, the wish-dream of bureaucrats public and private. Broadened beyond the confines of legal argument, the set of claims implied in the Powell doctrine—that racial and ethnic integration were better understood as diversity, that this diversity benefited everyone because it inherently broadened cultural experience, and that, broadly speaking, the goal of affirmative action was not racial justice as such but the general edification—was invoked time and again to justify the creation of new bureaucratic structures in academia, government, and the corporate world, a virtual cottage industry of diversity programs, officers, and consultants. As the period's economic transformation took hold, another wrinkle was added to the Powell doctrine: that diversity is essential in both education and business because the new global economy demands an awareness of and sensitivity to other cultures. Lest they be accused of building programs for merely idealistic reasons—merely liberal ones at that—America's bureaucratic leaders insisted that to succeed in the global environment, one has to be multicultural.

The foregoing helps explain the reasons for the emergence of the diversity dogma and hints at its virtues. But it also begs the main question: How was it that Americans convinced themselves that a globalized bureaucratic and technological society would yield greater cultural diversity? Both of the general pillars of the dogma—that racial and ethnic integration created cultural diversity and that economic globalization made cultural diversity a compelling national interest—reflected this strange presumption. And the self-refuting qualities of both ought to have raised the question a long time ago.

After all, the boosterish enthusiasm with which the latter claim was usually repeated should have raised the suspicion that it is palpable nonsense, not least because it presumed that genuine cultural diversity was perfectly harmonious with an immersion in the world marketplace. Yet the market rules everyone and lays down a set of principles that all must dance to. The popping of the East Asian economic bubbles in the mid-1990s revealed that there was no "second way" to capitalist development, as many admirers of Japan and South Korea had convinced themselves. The claim that bureaucratic diversity is essential to success in a global setting betrayed an amusing naiveté among those Americans who thought they were on the cutting edge of change. If a Japanese executive would look across a table at American counterparts and see a fiftyish WASP, a lesbian Latina, a young black man, and a disabled transgendered Native American, he would see four people determined to convince him to reduce trade barriers, stop guaranteeing lifetime employment, and adopt the market model. Americans apparently expected the rest of the world to think just like them, which is to say that they expected others to believe that economic homogenization and human diversity are entirely compatible.

The other pillar of the dogma, that racial and ethnic integration is better understood as cultural diversity, is just as flawed but more deeply embedded. Its power is rooted in more than a generation of comfortable living in the confines of bureaucratic regulation. In the mid-twentieth century, the best Western intellectuals were convinced that bureaucracies of any sort were the structural implements of totalitarianism. A generation later, Westerners, but Americans probably above all, became so accustomed to living within a pervasively regulated society that they had come to think of such a life as the epitome of freedom. With few exceptions, the serious critique of bureaucracy was abandoned. Just as they convinced themselves that their multinationals could run roughshod over the world and actually increase cultural diversity, so they convinced themselves that they could be insulated with all the security of bureaucratic life, which can only function by laying down sets of uniform regulations that inherently reduce living human differences, while still maintaining their cultural integrity.

To those of us not yet prepared to relinquish materialism entirely, it is plain that the rise of diversity rhetoric and multiculturalism was a product of economic globalization. The coincidence of timing is suggestive enough. But the similarities between multiculturalist rhetoric and corporate strategy clinch the case. As David Rieff ably pointed out as early as 1993, the "treasured catchphrases" of the multiculturalists were perfect imitations of those heard in corporate planning sessions, workshops, and literature. If the professors sought "cultural diversity," the CEOs called for "product diversification"; if the professors "repudiated boundaries," the CEOs made borders irrelevant. The multiculturalists denounced "Eurocentrism" and deluded themselves into thinking that they were posing a radical challenge to the status quo, but multinational corporations had surrendered any commitment to political or cultural nationalism long before. "There is no business establishment anymore that is committed . . . to hegemonic notions of European superiority," Rieff contended. "Our corporate masters are learning to eat sushi like everyone else." Just as it was good business for the corporation to dispense with any sort of nationalism as a means for securing new consumers everywhere, so it made sense to reach out to women, ethnic minorities, and gays in order to market goods to them. That the production of the vast consumer edifice rested on the exploitation of unskilled labor and a widening income gap within the United States was the other side of the multiculturalist coin and proved that there was nothing radical about multiculturalism. What came of it all, Rieff maintained, was "the multiculturalism of the market, not the multiculturalism of justice."[3]

I share this view. At its worst, cultural determinism was a ruse that glossed over the expanding dominance of multinational corporations committed to the exploitation of people as consumers and laborers. It permitted Americans to think that they could plunge into the world of consumption and still hold on to their roots. Bad enough as a self-delusion, the dogma gave them license to think the same of the rest of the world, and that is infinitely more pernicious. While corporations "without borders" claimed more and more of the globe, Americans, who benefited most as a people from that expansion, largely absolved themselves from either responsibility or guilt by assuming that the cultures of the world would be left intact. Multiculturalism repudiated "borders" and ridiculed nationalism at the very moment when multinational corporations were dissolving the integrity of nation-states, the only institutional structures strong enough to counterbalance corporate power. Multiculturalists rejected the virtues of assimilation and integration and came to believe that deracination was impossible. So aligned, multiculturalism ought to be seen as the ideological justification for the corporate integration of much of the world.

Recent prosperity, coupled with the inclusion of racial and ethnic minorities firmly into the bureaucratized mainstream of life, created a historical moment when Americans in general were willing to accept the dominant economic and political structures. Rather than challenging either, they threw their energies into cultural assertions. And here rests the best clue as to why Americans convinced themselves they could have the best of both worlds. The 1990s was also the heyday of cultural determinism, when "culture" became the be-all and end-all of intellectual analysis and of the popular mind as well. All the foregoing considered, the most important underlying fiber in the dogma of diversity and its companion, multiculturalism, was the conviction, largely unexamined, that culture is both eternal and endlessly flexible. As such, according to the widespread misapprehension, culture can survive anything. No bureaucratic regulation threatens it. No amount of consumerism corrupts it. Even as they confused it with race and ethnicity, Americans saw culture as the principal element of contemporary life capable of absorbing the moment and changing accordingly.

The Inflation of Culture

It is hardly surprising that Americans should believe that they live amid the splendor of cultural diversity. Culture, it seems, is everywhere.

Through the 1990s, public life in America was dominated by the "culture wars," because the legislative and electoral life of the nation was consumed in "cultural politics." People lined up one way or another according to their "cultural identity." While money still meant power in Washington, at the very moment when, we now know, the accounting industry had a stranglehold on regulations that permitted some of the greatest corporate malfeasance in history, politics on the surface ran according to the conflicts between cultural interest groups. Cold War liberals used to call such political collections "status groups," motivated, they argued, by vague and irrational anxieties. By the 1990s, no one dared suggest that gay activists or their opposite number, Christian conservatives, were motivated by irrational urges; cultural conflict was assumed to be the basic fuel of legitimate political conflict. Culture, indeed, was supremely political, and politics was cultural. No wonder pundits and dispassionate scholars alike took to analyzing something they called "political culture."

If current affairs of state came to be regarded as essentially cultural matters, the same twist logically applied to the great streams of history. The rise of Western power, according to military historian Victor Davis Hanson, was not so much a matter of political strength, technological genius, or economic dynamism but of the "2,500-year tradition," running back to the Greeks, of soldier democrats. This cultural tradition, he announces, "explains not only why Western forces have overcome great odds to defeat their adversaries but also their uncanny ability to project power well beyond the shores of Europe and America. Numbers, location, food, health, weather, religion—the usual factors that govern the success or failure of wars—have ultimately done little to impede Western armies, whose larger culture has allowed them to trump man and nature alike."[4] Hanson might sound a bit too much like a cheerleader for Western imperialism, but even the sharpest and wisest critics of the spread of Western power emphasized the culture in imperialism. It was almost as if they wanted to claim that Joseph Conrad, not British weapons, had oppressed Africa; the concept of "orientialism," not the French shackling of workers to rubber trees, subjugated Vietnam. In an intellectual climate where imperialism was understood more as a function of the culture of nation-states than of the political dynamics of nation-building, it makes sense that citizenship in nation-states would become "cultural citizenship." In the face of this tilt of mind, even so staid a discipline as diplomatic history began to appeal to culture, lest it fall into utter irrelevance.[5]

That high school and college students are now as likely to read Chinua Achebe as Joseph Conrad must mean, by this reasoning, that imperialism is done for. But then we are left to scratch our heads about its reappearance in the Bush administration's unabashed enthusiasm for conquest and domination. Presumably Mr. Bush, Mr. Cheney, and Mr. Wolfowitz are all products of a "cowboy culture," as is often suggested. Or perhaps they are products of "the culture of national security," which, according to Peter J. Katzenstein, leads some foreign-policy "actors [to] respond to cultural factors" as much as, and sometimes more than, material interests—apparently it's not about the oil after all. Even *realpolitik* should be understood as cultural, contends Alastair Iain Johnston, because this hard-nosed view of international life "has persisted across vastly different interstate systems, regime types, levels of technology, and types of threat."[6] Perhaps such matters have something to do with culture, but at best abstractly, while they are much more directly related to the concrete realities of military might, short-sighted greed, and the hubris of power, all of which are universal human vices that transcend cultures and must be resisted because they run so deep and wide.

That cultural determinism is not the sole possession of the intellectual Left testifies in subtle ways that culture and politics are not the same things. As opposites so often do, conservative intellectuals seized on the same inflated notion of culture to attack their opponents. During the 1990s, Norman Podhoretz chided America for its "culture of appeasement," while Thomas Sowell and Francis Fukuyama both appealed to culture to demonstrate why some people were economically successful and others were not—so much for Marx and Lenin. David Horowitz, meanwhile, dubbed his right-wing think tank the Center for the Study of Popular Culture.[7]

Beyond Right and Left, culture captured some of America's most independent thinkers in the last generation. Stephen Carter bemoaned the nation's hostility toward religion in his The Culture of Disbelief. Robert Hughes keenly dismantled the pretensions of politicized art in The Culture of Complaint. James Davison Hunter, a theologian whose writings on the culture wars were among the most underappreciated works of the period, chalked up America's mood as a "culture of ambivalence." And Christopher Lasch's Culture of Narcissism probably stands as the model for such jeremiads.[8]

The point is not that cultural analysis is necessarily flawed or even unpersuasive. Edward Said's Culture and Imperialism is a majestic work, and Said himself was the very model of what an intellectual should be today—deeply humane, widely learned, broadly experienced, and instinctively political. In any case, it would be a bad career move, to put it lightly, for someone who considers himself an intellectual-cultural historian, as I do, to dismiss cultural analysis out of hand. What is crucial here is simply to note the incredible breadth and frequency of the resort to cultural analysis, which suggests that it became far more than mere academic fashion. Cultural analysis emerges out of the temper of the time and was the one solid piece of ground that the intellectuals shared with their fellow citizens.

After all, everybody seems to have obtained a culture of their own in recent years, which permitted them to mark their distance from others. Or, if they were liberal-minded, they could revel in a world where culture was as varied as individuals, allowing them to pick and choose from culture A or culture B as suited their tastes. Forget the debate over the literary canon or the fight over the place of Western civilization in elite universities: The better measure of culture's inflation was its influence in textbook publishing or in the 1991 proclamation of the National Science Teachers Association, which launched the group's program in "multicultural science education" on the grounds that because "our global society consists of people from many diverse cultural backgrounds[,] we should appreciate the strength and beauty of cultural pluralism." Doing so would have to grow out of the understanding, as one advocate put it, that "there is more than one way to learn science and that every student has a unique learning preference, style, and approach." Note here the conflation of "diverse cultural backgrounds" and individual "style."[9]

Health care workers were instructed to heed the cultures of their patients. Presumably we get sick not according to the universal biological nature of our bodies but according to our specific cultures. It is indisputable that different ethnic groups suffer different maladies and predispositions and in different degrees, but that is a matter of genetics, not culture. Nevertheless, exhorting her readers to surrender the "lofty contempt for people whose culture is different or seems strange," Madeleine Leininger called for a commitment to "transcultural nursing." Nursing, she insisted, "can no longer be . . . an activity based solely upon knowledge of man's physical and emotional needs." The new multicultural environment meant that "understanding the culture of an individual seeking health care is just as important . . . as is knowledge of the physiological and psychological aspects of an individual's illness." Nurses could not be mere caretakers to the ill, they had to be anthropologists as well. And these important cultural differences were not only based on the typical diversity of race and national origins. Healthy living itself constitutes a culture, according to the professionals, a helpful thing to understand when, for instance, treating drug addicts. As William L. White explained, drug addiction is "a way of life, a means of organizing one's daily existence, and a way of viewing people and events in the outside world." Addiction, in short, is a culture by anthropological definition, with its high priests, its values, its "bicultural" members. Successful treatment begins with identifying how deeply "enmeshed" the addict is in this culture and then moving them into the "culture of recovery."[10]

What once would have been considered human idiosyncrasy, a quirky habit, an off-beat hobby, or just plain weirdness can now lay claim to institutionalization as "cultures"—not, mind you, as cultural ephemera but as cultures in and of themselves. Fly fishing is no longer a peaceful pastime; its advocates insist that it is a culture in its own right. No doubt church bingo, chess in the city park, and flea markets all deserve similar elevation. Cultural studies scholar Erika Doss recently revealed her discovery of the not-so-lost world of "Elvis Culture," whose inhabitants regard Elvis Presley with all the reverence of a god; they make pilgrimages to Graceland and create shrines to him in their homes. The faithful—the true believers—do battle with the big, bad corporate types who scurry to control Elvis's image, knowing that they can rely on the "mystery and wonder" that is the eternal Elvis to help them frustrate the efforts to vulgarize his memory into a mere money machine.[11]

If Elvis fans can have a culture all their own, there is no reason why bu-reaucracies or corporations cannot. In the late nineteenth century, the hey-day of rugged individualism, the Supreme Court perverted the Fourteenth Amendment and defined corporations as legal individuals. In our age of cul-ture, corporations and other bureaucracies are defined as little worlds of their own. Whenever a major merger is announced, the stock analysts ponder whether the mix of "corporate cultures" will work, as if arranging a marriage. Since Tom Peters invoked the term to explain why some firms succeed and some fail, it has been taken as a matter of course among organizational the-orists that corporations have cultures. Corporations "have personalities too, just like individuals," intones the author of a standard collegiate text on or-ganizational behavior. It is legitimate to speak of corporate cultures, accord-ing to another, because individual firms have their distinct artifacts, symbols, values, and rituals; corporate cultures "are shared, communicated through symbols, and passed down from generation to generation of employers." Once its culture is institutionalized, the corporation "acquires immortality," because it presumably lives beyond its founders. Just look at McDonald's, "the definitive example of a powerful and successful organizational culture. . . . It's not by chance that a McDonald's meal tastes pretty much the same everywhere."[12]

When the Federal Bureau of Investigation came under fire for a rash of near-scandals in spring 2001, Iowa senator Charles Grassley, who chaired a subcommittee that oversaw the FBI, chalked the problems of mismanage-ment and investigative sloppiness up to the Bureau's "cowboy culture." Grassley's comments conjured up images of FBI agents sashayin' and swag-gerin', saving schoolmarms and orphans while giving the bad guys no quar-ter. But Grassley had in mind "a kind of a culture that puts image, public re-lations, and headlines ahead of the fundamentals of the FBI." Presumably this "cowboy culture" is different from the "cowboy culture" of Mr. Bush and Mr. Cheney. But then it is good to know that cultural diversity thrives even among cowpokes and buckaroos.[13]

One might expect some circumspection and care from National Public Radio, which presumably is devoted to noncommercial cultural program-ming, as many of its endowments insist. But its benefactors probably meant something different from the usage that has come to prevail within the net-work over the last decade. Indeed NPR has become a major culprit in the in-flation of culture.

Regular listening provides numerous examples of culture's exaggeration among reporters and subjects alike. In June 2001, for instance, as the Na-tional Basketball Association (NBA) postseason was coming to its conclu-

sion, *Morning Edition* did a story on the dramatic turnaround of the Philadelphia 76ers. The team's success, according to reporter Tom Goldman, resulted
from the willingness of Coach Larry Brown and star player Allen Iverson to
get along. Brown, Goldman, explained, was "a sixty-year-old white coach, a
traditionalist, part teacher, part disciplinarian." Iverson, by sharp contrast,
was "a twenty-five-year-old street-tough black player, an individualist who
. . . chafed at things like practice and team rules. To NBA old-timers, Iverson was public enemy number one, the head punk in the league's growing
gang of young misfits." Goldman reckoned the blossoming friendship between the two men as "a hopeful metaphor for the league's generations and
cultures coming together." How Brown could be seen as a traditionalist when
he had launched his career as a long-haired, polyester-wearing "non-
conformist" coach in the old American Basketball Association was never explained. How Brown, whose subsequent career has taken him back and forth
across the college and pro ranks in search of enormous contracts, could be
considered a part of any culture when he would never stay in one place too
long never entered into Goldman's story. It would be difficult enough to defend the proposition that the NBA has one culture all its own, much less the
claim, which Goldman casually handed down, that it has two. But instead of
seeing Brown and Iverson—the whole league for that matter—as cogs in the
corporate marketing of sports as entertainment and the manufacture of
celebrity, Goldman depicted the two men as worlds apart.[14]

Stretching culture to encompass everything, using it as shorthand for
complicated social developments, Americans have made the term meaningless. We have oversold culture. We have come to see it as far too powerful a
thing. By stretching it as we have, we have brought the concept to near-
meaninglessness, the fate of all overused words. Culture is not the most powerful realm in human affairs. Wealth and the capacity to exploit labor remain
the fuel of economic change; to these fall the privilege of setting the material conditions of life for most people. Class conflict still revolves around the
struggle over just how powerful those forces are in daily life. The state, for all
the recent changes in its parameters, remains the seat of coercion, setting the
laws by which life is regulated. The state still enjoys the monopoly on police
powers. It still largely retains the focus of public loyalties, even in those developed nations where blatant patriotism long has been considered vulgar.
The state still sends out the military to push its way against its enemies. To
say that values and ideologies, which are legitimately understood as cultural
creations, drive the economic and political realms is not incorrect, but it ab-
stracts power by investing it at a remove from its basic sources. To say that
military power is a creation of culture is not wrong, but it is still the bombs

and tanks, not a way of life, that allow one nation to crush another. Had Mao labored under the cultural determinism of our time, he would have said that power comes out of his ideas about the barrel of a gun.

On the Inflation of Culture
in an Age of Anti-Culture

The great historical question—probably the most important one we can ask of our recent intellectual history—is why the inflation of culture came about. This is different from asking why the intellectual classes became obsessed, either pro or con, with diversity. Indeed, it is not the "diversity" in cultural diversity that strikes me as out of joint; it is not the "multi" in multiculturalism that gives me pause. Rather, it is the unreflective deployment of culture as a vision of the good society that has to be explained. Why were the other emotionally charged categories of race, ethnicity, gender, and sexual orientation all subsumed under the concept of culture? Why has justice come to be defined as a matter of culture rather than of morals, ethics, or law? Why was public debate considered cultural rather than a forum for democratic disputation, a quest for power, or a competition over who gets to feed at the public trough? Why culture?

The inherently amorphous nature of what we call culture makes it all the harder to get our hands on any good answers, and any answers are inherently qualified. They are matters of degree and not absolutes. But perhaps there is much to learn by paring the concept back to its essentials.

First of all, the idea of culture—which we must distinguish from the objective material reality of what anthropologists call culture—is a relatively recent creation that dates back only to the Enlightenment. The mid-twentieth-century British critic Sir Herbert Read, a wise and tasteful man, once claimed that "the first recorded use of the word [culture] in its modern sense is 1510." Though he left us with no citation to check, he added a cryptic comment about his general dating: This was, he said, "just when capitalism began to get going." [15] We can forgive Sir Herbert his imprecision, if for no other reason than because dating intellectual developments is always an imprecise business. It is clear, nonetheless, that he was a bit early with his guess and that the idea of culture became fixed in the Western mind only in the nineteenth century, just when, indeed, capitalism had begun to get going. Here is our first clue to culture's inflation. Somehow or other, the concept appears to be joined to the birth of capitalism, and this relationship raises the immediate possibility that capitalism's expansion might well have something to do with culture's inflation.

Though its common usage is modern, the culture concept can be traced profitably back to deeper fundamentals. The English word for culture, as both Raymond Williams and Hannah Arendt taught us in the 1950s, derives from the Latin concept of cultivation. According to Arendt, while Cicero was probably the first to describe the cultivation of the mind, its initial meaning implied the cultivation of land. The term lost its agricultural connection entirely only in the nineteenth century, as it began to carry increasingly important social baggage. Yet in that original sense culture contains important insights into the human condition, ones that accord with anthropology's most important observations. Culture as the cultivation of the earth speaks to the necessity to work, and with that, it encompasses the technological capacities of a people. More important, it implies a connection to nature, perhaps even humanity's dependence on nature, and yet speaks to the human drive to master nature. Mastery over nature was to be gained through the refinement of the natural world, not through its destruction; the acquisition of such mastery promised not emancipation from nature so much as distance from nature's unforgiving demands. The refinement of nature, furthermore, required labor; the more refined the labor, the greater the mastery.

What was important in that initial association remains valuable. Culture's early association with agriculture tied the concept to necessity and yet apprehended the deep-seated human need to transcend the primitive. This is a universal need that speaks to an anthropological truth: All people create culture as a way of distinguishing themselves from the specific natural world to which they are beholden. Culture at its roots defines humanity, therefore, because though we can never escape biological need and therefore should never delude ourselves to the contrary, humanity distinguishes itself from sheer animality by distancing itself from those inescapable bonds. This tension, between necessity and the need to rise above it, makes up the essential human condition, and the tension is best maintained through the activity of creative work, broadly understood. Culture's fundamental connection with agriculture suggests that without meaningful labor there can be no meaningful culture.

The key dynamic within this basic observation rests in the meaning of cultivation, a useful synonym for which is refinement. Agricultural labor was always directed toward meeting the need for food, but it also inherently was a refinement of nature, a human improvement of the environment. While the agricultural heritage of the concept reminds us that we cannot transcend nature, nonetheless this initial connection was terribly limited in how much meaning it could convey. If agricultural labor produced only foodstuffs that were to be consumed, then it was incapable of carrying humanity very far away from the precipice of survival and making life somehow more enduring. As Arendt pointed out, for the idea of culture to mean much, it had to be abstracted away from its association with husbandry. "It is not likely," she wrote, "that great art would ever have sprung" from that limited association. After all, "it is hardly the mentality of gardeners which produces art."[16] She was right about this: The will to cultivation had to move beyond the limits of sustenance-producing labor, because such labor was too clearly a reminder of how little control people had over nature. While there was indeed mastery in turning nature itself into a human creation, the products of agriculture were still to be used to meet nature's demands. The momentum of the cultivated will had to move beyond such limits to the creation of what Franz Boas, the father of cultural anthropology, called unnecessary goods; that is, things that were unnecessary to meeting biological demands. Here, Boas believed, was the wellspring of culture. Arguably the entire infrastructure of culture—a people's art and aesthetic values, religious institutions and myths, sexual mores and taboos—emerged from the will to create beyond mere sustenance and distance human beings from biological need.

Though the pressures of mere sustenance can be eluded, nature continues to exercise ultimate dominion in its one relentless imposition, death. But even here people used culture to distance themselves from the inevitable. The products of culture were not only unnecessary, but, as Arendt famously contended, they were "durable" as well. The material goods that constituted culture, she insisted, were items created through laboriously acquired skills with the intention of lasting. There is no reason to limit this insight to the creation of physical artifacts, for spiritual systems, aesthetic principles, language, and the craft skills used to create the goods themselves, even if they seem more elementally human, should be considered "durable" in the same sense. Once they satisfy biological necessities, societies build value systems to check human nature, just as they develop certain skilled crafts as a way of shaping their environment. They develop familial structures, gender relations, child-rearing practices, and sexual taboos in order to regulate the cycle of reproduction. They take up the spiritual life as a way of accounting for nature's caprice, and from that, they create particular ways of dealing with death, the ultimate and universal reminder that nature is our master after all. If these anthropological elements are durable in the sense that Arendt meant that term—that is, not strictly immortal so much as enduring across generations and therefore capable of being stores for community values and traditions—they also share with art the important quality that they are not absolutely necessary to the biological existence of an individual. Because they are not natural elements, they can neither be consumed nor exhausted.

They serve to extend the individual life beyond mere biological existence, not only by allowing us to leave items of our making for posterity but by rooting us in traditions and community settings that precede our birth and remain after death. Collectively, anyhow, culture allows us to cheat death, and that is its elemental purpose.

If the foregoing is true, then common sense would suggest that culture has become the prevailing frame of reference in the developed world because we enjoy it in such abundance. We are up to our necks in unnecessary goods and far removed from nature's demands; toil, in the form of laborious struggle against nature, is largely behind us. Obviously, the creation of unnecessary goods always required a certain freedom from drudgery; producing art or talking with the gods are not things that starving people tend to do. If abundance and leisure time were the building blocks of culture, then the developed world as it is today ought to be the most cultured society imaginable.

Such a conclusion is seductively simple, not to say simplistic. The wellsprings of culture are not found in the distance from nature and the survival struggle but rather in the human engagement with those demanding elements. Abundance and leisure, far from producing culture, produce its antithesis, which has taken the form of a society built on the hyperconsumption of goods.

Consider leisure, the opposite of labor. If leisure were a prerequisite to cultural creation, then only leisured classes would have created cultures. But we know this is not true. The will to refinement, seen most obviously in the practices of craft skills and religious ritual, is indisputably universal, regardless of how poor people are. We now understand that even slaves always found enough time and energy to develop the elements of culture. In exerting a creative will, slaves defied their systematic dehumanization and proved that the will to culture was not the exclusive possession of leisured classes. Indeed leisured classes are not particularly good at creation because they tend to forsake labor. Slaveholders from the Greeks to Jefferson had plenty of time to think, to be sure, and their ruminations fed the stock of artifacts we now possess. But well-heeled philosophers tend to be exceptions to the rule that leisured classes find it far easier to consume than to create—something that Jefferson understood well, given his musings about the dependence of the master on the slave and the virtues of agricultural labor. The paltry contributions of leisured classes to culture indicate that leisure might provide the time for reflection and the respite from toil that can then be redirected into the creation of durable objects but cannot itself produce such objects. By definition, leisure is nonwork, the cessation of activity, and therefore is incapable of producing anything beyond the imaginary. Leisure is a better companion to consumption than to creation. It tends to create parasites rather than producers. As soon as one turns to the practical act of creation, leisure turns to labor, which must be based upon skills the very refinement of which is impossible without long and difficult practice—without work, in other words.

If leisure is by definition incapable of producing culture, the material abundance of the contemporary developed world systematically frustrates cultural creation and is, at bottom, a source of anti-culture. Because it has been spectacularly successful in producing the necessities of life, capitalism from the early nineteenth century on destabilized the delicate tensions necessary to the proper exercise of the will to refinement, first by destroying the processes by which craft skills were accumulated and then by turning everything into a temporary good to be quickly consumed and abruptly replaced. The destruction of meaningful work went hand in hand with the expansion of activities devoted to consumption. The degradation of labor brought with it an accompanying degradation of the craftsmen's sensibilities and produced a world that was, quite frankly, less and less capable of creating any refinement at all. As the capacity to produce goods of quality diminished, so did the value of the craftsman's knowledge, which always carried with it the accumulated memories of communities. In unique ways, the methods of everything from fishing to metalwork were at some point direct reflections of local conditions and therefore symbolic expressions of distinct ways of life. Where there is an everyday application of skilled work, culture is connected organically to the living reality of communities and inherently connects the present to the past through the expression of accumulated knowledge and to the future through the creation of goods intended to last.

Historically, the elimination of local skill has provided the most important sluiceway through which mass production and mass consumption have flooded into everyday life, and when these methods of human reorganization have done so, they replaced cultural activities not with new forms of culture but with commodities. Once people are moved into mass-produced settings, they become dependent on mass-produced goods to provide necessities. They may acquire material abundance, but at a steep cultural cost. For local products that might otherwise identify a distinct people slowly give way to standardization. The more they concede control of their traditions of work to the encroaching system of high-tech consumption, the more they tend to lose control of their value systems, their unique notions of the spiritual world, and even their approach to death. Both culture as refined work and culture as the collective memory of a distinct people are systematically destroyed in a world built on the constant replacement of goods. In our world, nothing lasts, intentionally so.

Though it may well have originated in the will to master nature, consumer abundance has carried those people in its midst so far from nature that the will to refinement has been eliminated as an essential part of society and lives on only in marginalized nooks and crannies. And it is vitally important to understand that the degradation of that will, which leads to the substitution of the arts and crafts with products designed for merely temporary entertainment, parallels the relentless dilution of other basic elements of culture properly understood—religious systems, sexual mores, kinship patterns, mythologies—in short, entire ways of life. Ours is an age of anti-culture, because it alienates human beings from nature, disparages refined work, and dissolves away organic connections to past and future, not least by running on a scheme that simultaneously replaces everything and destroys everything.

We come, then, to the heart of the paradox. If culture as a living, organic reality in the lives of human beings is undermined and dissolved to the extent that they embrace technologically generated patterns of consumption, then it is certainly strange that the mental obsession with culture should expand in direct correspondence to the dominance of consumer society. It appears that culture as an idea, as distinguished from culture as a material reality or an active process, came to the fore only as a consequence of culture's demise. As human beings with an instinctual will to culture, we have sought it out with mounting intensity, all the more desperate because so little of what can genuinely be called culture is to be found. And we are left with mostly the mere assertion of ideals as culture, imaginary wisps that gain credence among anxious believers who appeal to past ways of life long surrendered or, worse, who have confused their choices between product A and product B with control over their way of life.

This condition can only be understood as deracination, which should not be confused with homogenization, strictly speaking. If the world continues on the economic and technological course that has been established since the end of the Cold War, people will not be ground into bland facsimiles. They won't all become middle-class American suburbanites, no matter how many people aspire to some version of that creature of abundance. People remain thankfully stubborn about their particularities and concede them, for the most part, only grudgingly and gradually. The Cameroonian who wears a Nike T-shirt instead of traditional homespun is still a Cameroonian; CDs, MTV, and music videos arrive in India but carry Indian music, not American country-pop. But, nonetheless, local and particular ways of life are gutted when the system of high-tech consumerism arrives. For the real genius of this system is that it works more effectively by absorbing a way of life than by assaulting it; the aesthetic and spiritual values that it rests on work at such a low common denominator that it appears to harmonize with local cultures. It is a seductive bargain through which people accept the subtle degradation of traditions, the slow deterioration of delicate institutions, and other apparently acceptable compromises in exchange for chasing abundance. What this means in the last analysis is not that the world is bound to become a multihued carbon copy of the "American way of life" but that the peoples of the world will become culturally disenfranchised in their own particular way. As that happens, people will continue to make claims to cultural distinctiveness, because as the material realities of existence grow increasingly similar—as factory work under multinationals becomes common, if not the rule; as television, cell phones, and the Internet become standard issue in daily lives everywhere—abstract claims to culture are the only assertions of human difference left to make.

In the eighteenth century, the faith in reason sprang up as a secular faith and dominated the imagination of the thinking classes, even though their assumption that human affairs and the physical world were regulated by orderly nature was quite at odds with the material realities of both. In the nineteenth century, apologists for the emerging industrial order invested a similar faith in the hidden hand of the marketplace, which, they insisted, would bring material bounty, a claim contradicted by the stark poverty of the working classes the age created. In our time, culture has become the metaphysical presence that is presumed to guide human affairs, and this too is a faith out of kilter with material realities.

Notes

1. Immanuel Kant, *Perpetual Peace: A Philosophical Essay*, ed. A. Robert Caponigri, trans. M. Campbell Smith (New York, 1948), 19; Alexis de Tocqueville, *Democracy in America*, vol. 2 (New York, 1945), 118; J. S. Mill, "Nationality," (1862), quoted in E. J. Hobsbawm, *Nations and Nationalism Since 1780: Programme, Myth, Reality* (New York, 1992), 34; Pound quoted in David Hollinger, "Ethnic Diversity, Cosmopolitanism, and the Emergence of the American Liberal Intelligentsia," *American Quarterly* (December 1975); reprinted in *In the American Province* (Bloomington, Ind., 1985), 60.

2. bell hooks, *Yearning: Race, Gender, Cultural Politics* (Boston, 1990), 33–34.

3. David Rieff, "Multiculturalism's Silent Partner," *Harper's* 287 (August 1993): 66–67.

4. Victor Davis Hanson, *Carnage and Culture: Landmark Battles in the Rise of Western Power* (New York, 2001), 440–41.

5. Edward Said, *Culture and Imperialism* (New York, 1993); William V. Flores and Rina Benmayor, eds. *Latino Cultural Citizenship: Claiming Identity, Space, and Rights* (Boston, 1997); Renato Rosaldo, "Cultural Citizenship, Inequality, and Multicultur-

alism," in *Race, Identity, and Citizenship: A Reader*, ed. Rodolfo D. Torres, Louis F. Miron, and Jonathan Xavier Inda (Malden, Mass., 1999), 253–61; and Aihwa Ong, "Cultural Citizenship as Subject Making: Immigrants Negotiate Racial and Cultural Boundaries in the United States," in Torres et al., *Race, Identity, and Citizenship*, 262–96.

6. Peter J. Katzenstein, "Introduction: Alternative Perspectives on National Security," in *The Culture of National Security: Norms and Identity in World Politics*, Katzenstein ed. (New York, 1996), 3; Alastair Iain Johnston, "Cultural Realism and Strategy in Maoist China," ibid., 217.

7. Norman Podhoretz, "The Culture of Appeasement," in Gary J. Dorrien ed., *The Neoconservative Mind: Politics, Culture, and the War of Ideology* (Philadelphia, 1993); Thomas Sowell, *Race and Culture: A World View* (New York, 1994); Francis Fukuyama, *Trust: The Social Virtues and the Basis of Prosperity* (New York, 1995).

8. Stephen Carter, *The Culture of Disbelief: How American Law and Politics Trivialize Religious Devotion* (New York, 1993); Robert Hughes, *The Culture of Complaint: The Fraying of America* (New York, 1993); James Davison Hunter, *Before the Shooting Starts: Searching for Democracy in America's Culture War* (New York, 1994); and Christopher Lasch, *The Culture of Narcissism: American Life in an Age of Diminishing Expectations* (New York, 1978).

9. Quoted in Napoleon A. Bryant, Jr., "Make the Curriculum Multicultural: Act Now and Make Science an Inclusive Endeavor," *Science Teacher* 63 (February 1996): 30; Lenola Allen-Sommerville, "Capitalizing on Diversity: Strategies for Customizing Your Curriculum to Meet the Needs of All Students," *Science Teacher* 63 (February 1996): 23.

10. Madeleine Leininger, "The Culture Concept and Its Relevance to Nursing," *Journal of Nursing Education* (1967), reprinted in *Transcultural Nursing: Concepts, Theories, and Practices*, ed. Leininger (New York, 1978), 109–11; William L. White, *Pathways from the Culture of Addiction to the Culture of Recovery: A Travel Guide for Addiction Professionals* (Center City, Minn., 1996), 5.

11. Erika Doss, *Elvis Culture: Fans, Faith, and Image* (Lawrence, Kans., 1999).

12. Stephen P. Robbins and Mark C. Butler, *Organizational Behavior: Concepts, Controversies, and Applications*, 5th ed. (Englewood Cliffs, N.J., 1991), 571–74; Debra L. Nelson and James Campbell Quick, *Organizational Behavior: Foundations, Realities, and Challenges* (St. Paul, Minn., 1994), 488–94.

13. Douglas Jehl, "Senators Criticize FBI on McVeigh Papers," *New York Times*, May 14, 2001, A: 9.

14. "Analysis: Team Harmony among the Philadelphia 76ers," *Morning Edition*, June 6, 2001.

15. Herbert Read, *To Hell with Culture and Other Essays on Art and Society* (New York, 1963), 11.

16. Hannah Arendt, *Between Past and Future* (New York, 1968), 212.

CHAPTER TWO

~

The Misappropriation of Culture in the Contemporary Mind

Since linguist and anthropologist Edward Sapir first made the argument in 1924, it has been widely understood that the concept of culture has two distinct parents, aesthetics and anthropology. As with any child, the concept as it is used today is a mix of these two different traditions, and therein rests another solid clue as to culture's rise to intellectual dominance in recent years. From the aesthetic tradition, culture assumed the inherently subjective quality of taste; from the anthropological, it veered toward indefinable abstraction. Like misanthropic genes that take hold because of their flaws, these two large shortcomings—subjectivity and abstraction—have erased the considerable virtues in both traditions, and they also explain the culture concept's strength today. At least in its contemporary usage, culture has become so widely useful because it directly mirrors the nature of the contemporary structures of power, which run on their ability to cater to subjective consumer whims while at the same time homogenizing the planet's market and labor systems into abstract arrangements of hidden hands, bureaucratic management, and computer controls. Both subjective and abstract, culture shares the paradoxical nature of the present order.

Its two-part amorphousness suits culture for any number of purposes. Americans invoke culture as a means of convincing themselves that they still control their destiny, and they often speak as if culture were a collection of possessions. We define our own cultures by what sort of music we like to listen to, what sort of television we watch, what sort of clothes we buy. So we have hip-hop culture and Trekkie culture, "tweener" culture and NASCAR culture. The proliferation of culture, in this sense, is directly related to the proliferation of products, and culture is reduced, not merely to taste, as the nineteenth-century bourgeoisie conceived it, but what is worse, to mere fashion. In its profound subjectivity, oddly, culture can be imagined as eternal and unchanging. If advertisers market African American goods, then this must mean that African American culture remains intact regardless of the removal of racial barriers and the dismantling of distinctly African American ways of life. If one's culture is a matter of subjective imagination, if culture is whatever we want it to be, then alienation is impossible, save for the isolated few who want to be alienated. When culture is understood in this way, it becomes possible to remain "rooted" in an ancestral community even while abandoning all but the most superficial props of ancestry.

Meanwhile, the abstract quality of the concept—what is and what is not culture cannot be decided with any real precision—makes culture useful for all sorts of rhetorical purposes. Especially in a political system that is moved by professional managers of interest and activist groups, culture in the abstract provides a convenient way to lay claim to solidarities that hardly exist in practice. To the extent that culture has automatic resonance and touches on a fairly widespread consensus that possessing distinctiveness is a good thing, political claims to cultural integrity provide a ready-made language. Politicizing culture not only carries with it an assumption of moral ground, it creates an unanswerable argument. Who is to say, after all, that this group or that group is not genuinely united by culture and therefore more or less deserving of legal protection and political recognition?

It must be understood at the outset that these two large difficulties are embedded in the intellectual history of culture. At its point of origin, the aesthetic tradition rests on a body of thought that sought to define aesthetic judgment or, put simply, taste. Taste is inherently subjective, and no amount of quarreling, hand-wringing, or jumping up and down can change that reality. Wherever culture is reduced to taste, the concept is subjective. On the other hand, anthropology, the science of culture, has always defined the idea as "a way of life," and that conception, no matter how intense the effort to discipline it, is inherently abstract. The best thinkers in both of these traditions have recognized these inherent problems and struggled with their implications. But as the culture concept has spilled out of the hands of careful thinkers, these shortcomings have become pronounced, and curiously, have made culture an apparently irresistible word.

A Revisionist History of Taste

Snobbery is out of fashion these days. Try telling someone that "their music" is garbage, or that television, any television, is drivel. Doing so automatically elicits sneers, if not physical assaults. Snobbery has become a major faux pas, the equivalent on the social-vice hierarchy of smoking a cigarette; among the smart set, it ranks with racism, misogyny, and homophobia as a sin no polite person should commit in public. So much is this the case these days that any independently minded person ought to make a practice of turning up the nose just to spite the dogma, except that there is a grain of truth in the contemporary scorn for cultural pedantry. Snobbery is a losing proposition, at least in a philosophical sense. Beauty is in the eye of the beholder, and there's no accounting for taste.

The problem with today's anti-snobbery—what I call "cultural populism"—is that its advocates show precious little sense of where taste and culture first intersected. The standard interpretation, probably rooted in Raymond Williams's seminal *Culture and Society* (1958), is that the aesthetic tradition traces back to Matthew Arnold and his much-maligned definition of culture as "the best which has been thought and said in the world." According to Williams, Arnold's quest for perfection started the nineteenth-century bourgeoisie down the elitist path over which culture was used to define class boundaries, among other things. Williams's hope was that the emergence of "culture as a way of life" indicated the maturation of the democratic masses and was a more generous conception of what culture might be. Culture may have "been the product of the old leisured classes who seek now to defend it against new and destructive forces," Williams wrote. Now it "is the inheritance of the new rising class, which contains the humanity of the future."[1] In increasingly crass ways, Williams's work, which was very fair to Arnold, has been turned to the populist argument that any aesthetic standards, any defense of "high culture," automatically is an attempt to impose class-based standards of beauty, artistic excellence, and decorum.

Arnold and his peers come in for regular abuse because they did use culture as a generic word to encapsulate aesthetics and delicate sensibilities, and, as Williams notes of Arnold, for educating the unlettered masses. But Arnold was hardly the first thinker to raise a defense of "the best that was thought and said." For that matter, a close reading of Arnold reveals that he wasn't all that interested in aesthetics as such.

Rather, the first Westerners to begin systematically considering how one might assert and defend standards of aesthetic judgment were eighteenth-century Enlightenment philosophers. And the term they deployed to evoke refinement and cultivation was not culture but taste. It makes sense that Enlightenment thinkers should address themselves to the problem of taste, for in an age in which describing universal systems set the standard of accepted truth, so important a thing as beauty could hardly be left to mere subjective fancy or transitory whim. Beauty, like God, is inherently an ideal, impervious to objective verification and hard to pin down. Like religious faith, setting standards of beauty posed a problem: Was beauty really in the eye of the beholder, or were certain objects beautiful because some inherent quality appealed to a universal standard?

The philosophy of taste probably had its beginnings with Francis Hutcheson's *Inquiry into the Original of Our Ideas of Beauty and Virtue* (1725), but the most important thinkers to take up the problem were David Hume and Immanuel Kant. Hutcheson believed that all beauty was natural and that its appreciation was instinctual; taste was a universal human attribute. Yet the writers who succeeded him insisted to the contrary that taste and beauty, however rooted in nature, required interaction with, if not action upon, the natural world. Among Hutcheson's successors, it was widely agreed that taste judgments were profoundly human, and there was bound to be a great deal of quarrelsome conflict, therefore, whenever differences came head to head. Hume, for one, took issue with the notion that beauty was inherent in objects and insisted to the contrary that it was a subjective mental construct. Aesthetic judgment enjoyed universal agreement in theory—everyone likes beauty—and yet in practice there was "great inconsistency and contrariety" in what was considered beautiful. This inconsistency was surely not nature's fault, given that humanity tended toward the vain and the unreliable. "We are apt to call barbarous whatever departs widely from our own taste and apprehension, but soon find the epithet of reproach retorted on us," he wrote. "It is natural for us to seek a *standard of taste,*" but that did not mean that there was a natural standard. Recognizing as much, acknowledging the great gap between "reason and sentiment," Hume concluded that "to seek the real beauty or real deformity [in any object] is as fruitless an inquiry as to pretend to ascertain the real sweet or the real bitter."[2]

At least as a point of departure, Kant shared Hume's presumption that taste was subjective, which is exactly why he was absolutely obliged to take the matter up. The problem of aesthetic judgment was the same as with moral judgment to him. Here was an essential feature of reasoning humanity, and yet it was all but indefinable. As in moral claims, taste was highly subjective, and yet the simple proclamation—"This is beautiful"—begged the agreement of others and therefore required a basis in objective consensus in order to be true. In trying to set standards of beauty, one could appeal to universality so that whatever was universally considered beautiful—say a sunset—might safely be placed among the ranks of beautiful things. Or beauty might be judged by the "test-of-time" measurement, so that what lasts is what deserves to be called beautiful. Yet we like only what is agreeable to us, that which causes us pleasure, and consequently he concluded that taste was a subjective matter. "Taste lays claim merely to autonomy," Kant wrote, and it would not do, then, "to make other people's judgments the basis of determining one's own." Beauty, like truth, was in the eye of the beholder, and Kant nearly threw up his hands over the futility of venturing any objective basis for aesthetic judgment. "It is absolutely impossible to provide a determinate, objective principle of taste that would allow us to guide, to test, and to prove its judgments. . . . There is nothing we can do that would allow us to grasp it any further."[3]

Kant, being Kant, was unable to leave matters at that. Taste, he maintained, required judgment. Judgment resisted mere pleasure and embraced disinterestedness, which then presumably allowed the observer to consider how the subjective sense of beauty might become more generous. One begins by thinking for oneself, then broadens the mind to "think from the standpoint of everyone else" and thereby "overrides the private subjective conditions of his judgment, and finally ends by thinking consistently, which encourages universal communicability." By seeking that universal assent, the aesthete turned the instinctive sensation of pleasure into a disinterested principle and thus harmonized instinct with the "higher cognitive powers." Thus "taste enables us, as it were, to make the transition from sensible charm to a habitual moral interest without making too violent a leap." Once that leap was made and a taste judgment commanded universal assent, then, and only then, could "genuine taste take on a definite, unchangeable form." As though appealing to Truth or God, Kant settled on "supersensible" aesthetic judgments built on the willingness to "think from the standpoint of everyone else."[4]

In appealing to the "supersensible," Kant placed aesthetic judgment in a precarious place, because it left him fishing for a source of sound standards. He came to rely on innate genius to set standards, as his long discussion of the fine arts in the *Critique of Judgment* reveals. In his rendering, fine art was the product of reason matched with skill. Fine art was not to be confused with craft: The latter was "mercenary art" and mere labor; the former was purposeless, save that it deepened "the culture of our mental powers to facilitate social communication." The quality that made such subtle communication possible was not cultivated skill so much as sheer genius, "the innate mental predisposition through which nature gives the rule to art." Genius, erupting out of nature, was not something that could be learned; in fact the primary evidence of its presence was originality.[5]

Kant's appeal to genius can easily be dismissed out of hand as hopelessly elitist, though this is now a tired claim. It is more accurate to say that his supersensible genius was not so much elitist as simply rare, the only possible consequence of which was to extract the capacity to create beauty from everyday life.

More troubling still, the supersensible genius required little by way of systematic training in the production of anything at all. Unhinged from the practical and the productive, Kant's ideal could be mangled to justify judgments based not on the intrinsic beauty of a well-made object but on claims to genius or expertise. The standard achieved out of that sort of arrangement could never be genuinely objective, and when one figures in the elements of cultural power— who gets to lay claim to genius and who doesn't—whatever standards are set too easily reflect class-based privilege.

Such was the result when the uniform ugliness of industrial capitalism descended on Western societies in the mid-nineteenth century, and of course it is this part of the story that has been told and retold in recent years. To the extent that they are writing about those bourgeois classes that asserted influence from roughly Arnold's time to World War I, Pierre Bourdieau, Lawrence Levine, Andreas Huyssen, and Paul Gorman, to name just a few of the cultural populists, are quite right to say that standards of taste were imposed in the cause of class privilege. Arnold at once abstracted the idea of refinement and turned subjective standards into what he considered a virtue, and he adopted the word "culture" to encompass both. The curious thing about Arnold's *Culture and Anarchy*, however, is that it was hardly about "culture" at all. When he argued that a "cultured person" sought the "best" in a quest for individual perfection, he was appropriating culture in pursuit of a sort of secularized spiritual cleanliness. *Culture and Anarchy* is a quasi-religious book. Had he bothered to grapple with the similarities between moral judgment and the judgment about what was "best," as both Hume and Kant had done, Arnold might have had something of enduring importance to say about taste and refinement. But he simply avoided such difficult matters.

Still, as a touchstone for understanding how people thought about aesthetic matters, *Culture and Anarchy* remains relevant to the debates a century later. To begin with, it revealed the increasing abstraction of aesthetics. Arnold deployed the term culture as a way of laying judgment against a wide swath of industrialized society. Through culture, people sought "*harmonious* perfection, developing all sides of our humanity," Arnold wrote, "and as a *general* perfection, developing all parts of our society."[6] Culture, at least potentially, was everything. One of Arnold's bugaboos, the newspaper, suddenly became a part of "culture," but it is hard to see how newspapers, which were never meant to do more than polemicize, inform, and entertain, had anything to do, one way or the other, with taste—except that, in Arnold's opinion, people who read the papers instead of literature showed little of it. In seeking perfection in "all parts," Arnold established the unfortunate tendency of cultural critics to pass essentially aesthetic judgments against things that had little aesthetic basis or pretense, and as such he was the predecessor of those twentieth-century nags who scolded people for reading the tabloids, going to the movies, or watching the *Beverly Hillbillies*. Among the effects of this nagging was not only a great deal of wasted time and effort but the ironic dilution of serious aesthetic reflection. If everything was culture, then laying down any clear aesthetic standards was practically impossible. As Arnold's successors increasingly struggled to use "culture" to pass judgment against the enormous outpouring of mere entertainment that twentieth-century consumer capitalism unleashed, it became all the harder for them to establish standards on which to judge serious work.

The overdeployment of culture, accordingly, undermined Kant's hopes for establishing universal standards, and it was this indifference to Kant, rather than Kant himself, that led to the elitist kidnapping of culture. The easiest way to categorize activities that were variously decent and vulgar was to root them in social categories, and it was tempting to define the decent against the vulgar by resorting to the categories of class. That is just what Arnold did. He expected the idea of culture to apply to all three of England's social classes— the barbarians, as he called the aristocracy; the Philistine bourgeoisie; and the "populace"—whose relations had become increasingly tense in the midst of industrialization. He believed that even the Philistine bourgeoisie was capable of developing the spirit of perfection, and certainly the lower classes were, so in a strict sense he cannot be called an elitist.[7] Yet when culture and taste lost their educative and practical functions, they became free-floating concepts, access to which came not from training or skill but from self-proclamation or, as was the case in the late nineteenth century, by following the dictates of social class. A person might simply claim to be "cultured" or might lay claim to delicate sensibilities by adjusting to the transitory standards of a dominant class. Kant's "subjective universality" of taste comes with a vengeance when a population at large confuses universal standards of beauty with the fancies and prejudices of those who control society in general.

In serving this purpose, the Arnoldian conception of culture invited the sham of late-nineteenth-century bourgeois life where taste and culture acquired snob value. In the cause of setting class boundaries, the new bourgeoisie constructed institutions designed to wall off the fine arts from the masses. Whereas early-nineteenth-century museums and orchestral organizations aimed for the widest possible audiences, their late-century counterparts, writes Neil Harris, were "organized more with an eye to protecting the standard of the arts," the purpose of which was the "certification" of a set of guardians of taste.[8] The shift can be seen most clearly in symphonies and museums. Lawrence Levine has shown that the organization of municipal symphonies in the

United States ran hand in hand with increasingly rigid repertories. Early in the century, formal music, often performed by some of Europe's greatest names, regularly indulged their audiences by including popular tunes alongside the classics. By the 1880s, however, self-appointed guardians of taste such as Bostonian John Sullivan Dwight railed against demands that symphonies include vulgar "light" fare and insisted on the performance of classic compositions in what he regarded as pure form. Meanwhile, nineteenth-century museums went from rather casual collections of curiosities, archeological and anthropological items, and artwork to institutions devoted singularly to the fine arts, which permitted museum officials control over what was viewed, how it was viewed, and who viewed it.[9]

Here lay the origins of that unimaginative highbrow/lowbrow gap that continues to energize cultural commentators who want to stick it to the bourgeoisie. But the matter of aesthetic standards has never been so simple as this distinction assumes. Any criticism of late-nineteenth-century guardians of taste, after taking due account of those who were merely snobs—that "ambiguous fauna," Ortega y Gasset once called them[10]—must come to terms with a truth that critics such as Levine, Huyssen, and Gorman pretty much miss: However elitist their attitudes toward and exertions on behalf of the fine arts, their main antagonist was not the seething masses but, more directly, industrialism itself. To Arnold, "faith in machinery" was modernity's "besetting danger," in part because the modern Philistines who held that crimped faith mistook wealth and productivity as ends in themselves. As Raymond Williams noted, Arnold and his Romantic contemporaries, in search of a solution to industrial anguish, had to "stress . . . a mode of human experience and activity which the progress of society seemed increasingly to deny."[11] Even some of the stodgiest, with their exclusive policies and haughty standards, were driven by motives more complex than the assertion of class privilege. The curators of the Boston Museum were entirely justified in scorning the institution's reproductions as "mechanically produced," "mere plaster without a soul," the emptiness of which was apparent when positioned against original work that revealed "the magic of the craftsmen's hands, the beauty of texture and the nobility of form." Levine notes that Henry Lee Higginson, patron of the Boston Symphony, loathed the business world of which he was a part but gives him no credit for appreciating how art can compensate for the deadening life of the stock brokerage.[12] They might have been snobs, but they were also trying to ward off the inroads of industrial forms of production. The beautiful had to be preserved because it was no longer being routinely produced; it had to be quarantined in certain venues because it no longer appeared in daily life.

The problem with the populist interpretation of taste deepens when aimed at the Modernists, who, according to both Andreas Huyssen and Paul Gorman, extended the bourgeois scorn for "popular entertainments," as Gorman puts it, in the frank elitism of the art-for-art's-sake posture. As Gorman sees it, Modernists betrayed their own yearning to overthrow the standards of the World War I–era bourgeoisie because of their contempt for mass tastes, which might well have been harnessed in the cause of cultural revolution precisely because those tastes had been "important as a negative reference in the genteel hierarchy." In other words, because bourgeois snobs ridiculed mass tastes, the Modernists should have found in those same tastes the ingredients for aesthetic revolution; indeed their willingness to do so, Gorman writes, was "a prime test of how revolutionary" Modernism was to be.[13] The first of many difficulties with this expectation is that Modernism was primarily an aesthetic movement, not a political one, regardless of how "radical" so many of its advocates pronounced themselves. The Modernists' two main antagonists were bourgeois hypocrisy and the infusion of commercial calculations of all sorts into art, including the manipulation of aesthetic standards in pursuit of social climbing. Given that the mass production of so much of what Gorman sees as popular entertainment inherently bred commercial motives within mass culture, it is hardly surprising that the Modernists spurned such activities. It made more sense to reclaim aesthetic standards, not only by revolutionizing form and method, as the Modernists indisputably did, but by emphasizing the fundamental importance of artistic skill in the production of worthwhile objects. In so doing, they hit upon the basic truth that the one thing commerce cannot debase is the well-made object.

Cultural populists ignore this fundamental insight. Worse still, they insist that what really matters is not how an object is produced but how it is received. Gorman chastises the Modernists for either ignoring the possibility that the masses were attracted to particular forms for legitimate reasons of their own or for seeing value in the popular arts only for what material those forms might provide for serious art. In both cases, the new aesthetes failed to understand "the circumstances of the public, and, consequently, its real tastes and desires." Invoking the populist theme, Gorman expects the Modernists to have discerned that "one of the most basic human desires is for meaning and order in life and that our popular culture is one source of these." How so? "We create meaning for and give our order to our experiences through our mind's structuring of the world."[14]

In laying out this critique of the Modernists, Huyssen and Gorman believe they have put their fingers on "the great divide," the point at which the intellectuals began to take refuge in "high culture" while becoming increasingly scornful of the "lowbrow." Supposedly the great divide was also the foundation for that last gasp of elitism, the mass-culture critique of mid-century intellectuals such as Dwight Macdonald and Clement Greenberg. The attacks on Macdonald and his colleagues themselves constitute an important stream in recent intellectual history, and they were varied enough that they deserve more than just generalizations. Yet it is fair to say that the populist assaults on mass-culture theory began on the assumption that Macdonald and company were self-appointed guardians of taste who had gone from expecting the masses to accept enlightenment to hating them for not doing so. According to the cultural populists, mass-culture theory portrayed common people as passive stooges, either awaiting the blessings of the highbrows or being force-fed mass-produced entertainment.

A good case can be made, to the contrary, that the mass-culture theorists were not primarily concerned with taste but rather with who produced what and why. Their aesthetic conceptions were part of a broader understanding of modern capitalism, and what they railed against was not mass tastes but the mass production of cultural goods for the sole purpose of profit. Especially in the work of English critics F. W. Leavis, Richard Hoggart, and Herbert Read, and at least in Macdonald's writing in the 1940s and 1950s, the understanding of "culture" that was considered "mass" was more akin to the anthropological tradition than the aesthetic one. But as long as the populists have managed to keep the issue narrowed to the question of taste, they have been able to ridicule mass-culture theory as hopelessly elitist, and because of the inherent subjectivity of this understanding of culture, they have been on safe ground in doing so.

Taste as Choice

By the early 1960s, the first stirrings of cultural populism showed themselves in several lines of sociological thought dedicated to debunking the mass-culture critique. Mass-communications research showed that mass media was not so overwhelmingly effective as its critics—and, for that matter, its advocates—believed. Sociologists such as Edward Shils and Herbert Gans, meanwhile, took to pointing out that the subjective nature of taste made it impossible to prove empirically that the contemporary masses were any more debased than they had been in the past. And Gans took the argument farther when he claimed that ethnic and other distinct sociological groups turned mass media to their own purposes, usually to reinforce group standards and thereby to preserve collective traditions. What all these strains had in common, besides taking the mass-culture critics as antagonists, was that they focused entirely on how mass-produced leisure was received rather than how it was produced. As Gans put it, "the critics of mass culture are creator-oriented; they argue that differences of perspective between creators and users [of culture] should not exist because users must bend to the will of creators, taking what is given them, and treating culture from the creator's perspective." The new line of thought, he claimed, would be "user-oriented" and would acknowledge that the "users" of culture are "more interested in the creator's product than in his or her methods and in the problems associated with being a creator."[15]

More frankly than his successors in contemporary cultural studies want to admit, Gans had his hands here on the real "great divide": It rests not between high and low, but between culture as something to be created or something to be consumed. Gans acknowledged in his *Popular Culture and High Culture* that his conception of culture couldn't stand up to anthropological rigor, but he still insisted that distinct groups of people—"taste publics," he called them—cohered through shared consumer tastes into collectives that could be understood as "taste cultures." He developed this position out of his 1962 sociological ethnography, *The Urban Villagers*, a classic study of Boston's Italian West End. In that justly praised book, Gans observed that the community's solidarity was built around ethnicity, and yet you could hardly call the West Enders happy peasants simply transferred to the city. They were real urbanites who had lost any taste for rural living and who, moreover, were deeply immersed in mainstream American life. They did not reject mass culture outright. Instead they made "highly selective use of the popular culture," according to Gans, usually to reinforce, rather than undermine, their insularity and working-class norms. They were consumers, but hardly typical ones. They gave themselves to nothing more than "careful exuberance"; they held to a downright un-American refusal to buy on credit, and yet, because they saw nothing worth saving for, spent what money they managed to make. Cars, kitchen appliances (to make Italian food), clothes, and televisions constituted their principal investments. They were similarly independent in their approach to mass media. They admired those entertainers who embodied their values—Sinatra, of course—and, as Gans put it, accepted the themes of mass culture without necessarily accepting mass values. A studied distrust of the outside world "allows the West Ender to interpret the media content so as to protect himself from the outset world and to isolate himself from its messages unless he wishes to believe them."[16]

By the time *Popular Culture and High Culture* appeared in 1974, the mass-culture critics largely had been driven on the defensive, if not entirely from the field. Still Gans made several original observations that since have filtered so widely into public consciousness as to appear almost common sense. First, he insisted that "popular culture" was consumer-based, which is to say that it was defined by what sorts of products people chose to buy, and, second, that at least for analytical purposes it was possible to mark off a variety of "taste cultures." In defining taste cultures, the particular "taste public" took a leading role through their choices. His own definition is clear enough:

> I would demarcate taste culture as the culture which results from choice; it has to do with those values and products about which people have some choice. For example, refrigerators are today an accepted product of the larger American culture and it is difficult to live without them. Which of the various kinds and styles of refrigerators to buy is a matter of relatively free choice . . . and that choice involves an application of taste culture.[17]

Dwight Macdonald was being terse when he compared mass culture to mere chewing gum. Herbert Gans was being serious when he suggested that refrigerators reveal the essence of a culture. There, indeed, is a sea change.

For a sociologist such as Gans, it was crucial to see the choice of refrigerators as a function of broader, socially determined settings. He justified the use of the term "culture" here on the grounds that even though his construct was not a culture in the anthropological sense, nonetheless consumer choices were based on collectively shared values and tastes. As he argued in *The Urban Villagers*, the social group to which the individual consumer pledged loyalty largely determined the choices of products. In his view, members of a taste public enjoyed the same sort of television, the same sports, the same music; they esteemed the same heroes, who reflected widely shared values. For Gans, the delineation of taste cultures meant that people were critical consumers who came to any piece of entertainment with previously congealed and internally consistent values against which they judged, by their own group standards, what to consume and what to ignore. They were nobody's dupes. And given the fundamentally subjective nature of taste, no one could ridicule what the members of each "culture" decided was right for them.

In elaborating on the theme, subsequent writers have made use of Gans's strategy to the point that it has settled into a new dogma. It now is widely held that consumers of mass-produced media, information, clothing, and all the rest constantly make informed choices about what products to consume and what to ignore; they make those choices based on both personal aspirations and the values, as the individual understands them, of whatever group they seek to identify with; and because the consumer cornucopia has never been more full, because the information revolution has opened the way for a flood of new forms and vehicles of self-expression, this consumer choice, this "agency," has never been stronger. The mass-culture critique of Dwight Mac-donald and his fellow snobs, as Andrew Ross suggests, has come to be challenged as "a one-sided and inadequate account not only of the contradictory power and significance of popular culture for its users and consumers, but also of the complex process by which popular culture actually creates political and social identities, by rearticulating desires that have deep resonance in people's daily lives."[18] Ross's language is revealing enough: "popular culture" apparently has little to do with creation; it is to be "used and consumed." If there is creative energy to be found, it goes not toward painstaking craftsmanship but in choosing which of the presumably various "identities" resonates most deeply with the consumers' "desires." Invariably cast as a radical critique—though exactly what it threatens has never been very clear—this conception of choice as culture seeks, again as Ross says, to draw "upon forms of popular and minority/marginal culture in ways that explode the 'objective' canons of aesthetic taste. . . . It involves cutting across the pathological spectrum of socially coded tastes and desires, rather than merely arguing that there is more room in the boat for newly legitimate ones."[19] The strategy seems to be to overcome the highbrow-lowbrow divide by giving preference to the subjective whims of the consumer, though how that departs from a conception of taste that has always recognized the faculty's subjectivity is not readily apparent because it is never recognized.

This is not an argument to be taken lightly. We are, needless to say, embedded in a consumer society, and the act of consumption must inherently assume an important function in the expression of values, the regulation of status and rank, and the assertion of identity. In this sense, the consumer conception of culture has a solid anthropology behind it. As the wise scholar Mary Douglas maintained in her 1979 critique of economic theories of consumption, *The World of Goods*, consumption should be understood as "a use of material possessions that is beyond commerce and free within law." Understood this broadly, "consumption decisions become the vital source of the culture of the moment. People who are reared in a particular culture see it change in their lifetime. . . . It evolves and they play a part in the change. Consumption is the very arena in which culture is fought over and licked into shape."[20] Once one eliminates from the act of consumption the grubby element of mere buying and selling, then the choice and possession of one good over another serves to make "visible and stable the categories of culture." The sensible individual tries to make sense out of the world through the possession of goods, which not only reflect already held values but reinforce such values by their simple presence. In this sense, Douglas maintains, consumer choices reflect shared agreement among self-defining groups of people and, arguably, among people who aspire to membership in certain groups; conversely, avoiding one good or another stands as a repudiation of one or more self-defining groups, a certain defiance of categories. If all this is so, then a work of art is no more meaningful than "goods that minister to physical needs—food or drink." It means as well that those theories that "assume a puppet consumer, prey to the advertiser's wiles, . . . are frivolous, even dangerous. . . . Ultimately, consumption is about power."[21]

Douglas rightly insisted that contemporary people are hardly the first to consume goods. In any society above subsistence, access to goods is regulated by social conventions, which typically are used to define class standing and, hence, "power." As Arjun Appadurai has pointed out, for example, sumptuary laws have historically been used to deprive people of access to luxury goods and to define status according to who is permitted to consume a given commodity. If the act of consumption is rich in social meaning and a symbol of power, then any struggle over power will ultimately be reflected in patterns of consumption, if not in specific individual acts. "Value and exchange in the social life of commodities," Appadurai writes, is basically political. For even "ordinary dealings would not be possible were it not for a broad set of agreements concerning what is desirable . . . and who is permitted to exercise what kind of effective demand in what circumstances." The politics of consumption, he continues, rests in "the constant tension between the existing frameworks . . . and the tendency of commodities to breach these frameworks."[22]

If this is true then two important implications follow: first, that the commodity in question is not a thing in itself but the sum of the multiple meanings invested in it, and, second, that the production of the commodity is not primary to those meanings. With these implications, the sensible effort to gather consumption within anthropology as an important part of culture reflects the tendency both to politicize culture and to marginalize production. The effort reflects the broader expansion of the culture concept, however much sense it makes in straightforward anthropological thinking.

Very much part of contemporary intellectual tendencies, the anthropology of consumption lends conceptual weight to cultural populism, but only theoretically or as background. Appadurai's conception of social commodities offers far too little help in understanding the nature of contemporary consumption and its impact on culture. Mass consumption replaced sumptuary laws with their opposite, ever-changing fashion that regulates consumption patterns by offering an illusion of consumer choice. At the very least, whereas Douglas praised consumption as a means of securing a place in a sta-ble social setting, the rule of fashion forces consumers to chase after ever-shifting standards. It hardly does to say that consumption contributes to shifting of values and reflects, therefore, the tension between regulation and subversion, much less that culture in the broader sense is in constant flux and power up for grabs, because the contemporary economic apparatus is con-structed on the management, manipulation, and mastery of that flux. That tension remains where consumerism is being introduced to non-Western so-cieties, but in the United States especially, whatever "flux" exists does so be-cause it too is mass manufactured. To his credit, Appadurai has recognized that who controls the production of commodities is more important than ever in a globalizing economy; the consumer, he concedes, is not the "real so-cial agent" today. Power, maybe more than ever, is in the hands of the "pro-ducer and the many forces that constitute production."[23]

Indeed, the more closely one looks at the anthropological theory of con-sumer culture, the less support it lends to the populist case. While the opti-mist can say that it is possible for people to buy their way across social lines and engage, in so doing, in a sort of social subversion, the chances for signif-icant subversion through consumption actually diminish in a society given to constantly shifting fashions, because as soon as the social climbers or aspir-ing classes begin to acquire goods associated with the elite, the elite change their own objects of desire.

Compare, for instance, a historic instance of subversion through con-sumption with our present condition. In the late eighteenth century, the mu-latto classes in Haiti, then French San Domingo, posed serious social, and then political, challenges to the creole planter class through their acquisition of landed wealth and slaves; as the momentous Age of Revolution neared, mulattos had the audacity to send their sons for Parisian educations, take the long metropolitan holidays that their white counterparts had always used as status symbols, and even set up lobbying bodies to represent their interests within the imperial structure. Haiti's creole planters, victims largely of their own dissipation, deeply resented mulatto pretensions, and as the French Rev-olution quickened, the two classes came to blows in both Paris and in those island provinces where the threat of slave insurrection was not yet keen enough to force them into uneasy alliance. No such thing is possible in America today. A Latino kid with a high school education can make $16 million a year hitting .300 and playing a decent shortstop, or an inner-city son of a single mother can make a fortune doing rap, but neither their ascent nor their acquisition of all the trappings of wealth threaten the power struc-ture in any way whatsoever. Meanwhile, the wealthiest take a fancy to SUVs, the middle classes slavishly follow, and the rich buy bigger SUVs. The middle classes go into hock leasing those monstrosities, and the wealthy move up to Humvees. The elite invent suburbs, and the middle classes follow; the elite move to exurbs, and the middle classes go into hock to follow them there. The elite either go farther out, or execute a U-turn and embrace the "new urbanism" by moving into upscale "renewed" city neighborhoods.

It is a bit mysterious why Andrew Ross and his populist peers choose to ignore the ceaseless status-chasing among American consumers. They want to emphasize the "subversive" quality of individual choices, but doing so obliges them to suspend the commonsense observation that many, and in all honesty probably most, acts of consumption reinforce standards of class status precisely because people engage in them in pursuit of externally created standards. Status-seeking through consumption is the farthest thing imaginable from a subversive act. And it is impossible to see how those dry, old-fashioned things such as aesthetic standards are somehow more reflective of class domination than standards of consumption, constantly reinforced through advertising and mass media, that drive people to imitate their economic betters.

Because anthropology ultimately lends such brittle support to their cause, cultural populists wind up with a shallow conception of culture that amounts to little more than a faith that the consumer "rearticulates desires," as Ross would have it. Oddly enough, commodities, which ought to occupy a place of some importance in any understanding of the culture of consumer society, lend no weight to the populist view. What matters for them is what resides in the consumer's imagination, and it is difficult to conceive of a wispier sort of culture.

Let us take John Fiske as a suitable representative of this common drift of mind. He has all the credentials: He thinks Madonna's naval is a "text," he is a dedicated opponent of "patriarchy," he is all for "pleasure." He knows that culture "can be developed only from within, it cannot be imposed from without or above." Popular culture, in his view, "is made by the people, not produced by the culture industry." Yet, at the same time, popular culture is made "at the interface between everyday life and the consumption of the products of the cultural industries."[24]

What matters for Fiske is what is allegedly in the head of the consumer at the moment of consumption. Who controls the production of a good or why the good is produced in the first place are inconsequential. When any good is produced, it carries with it a meaning, an ideological purpose, an agenda, all set to serve the interests, presumably, of the dominant patriarchal capitalists. No matter: Because "popular culture is the culture of the subordinate who resent their subordination," they simply attach different and "subversive" meanings to the "texts" that the goods they purchase represent.

Fiske wants to pose as a radical and so must acknowledge the presence of a dominant capitalist will in the production of culture. Popular culture, he says, is always the creation of a struggle between the subordinate and the dominant, and for that reason it "is determined by the forces of domination." While it usually subverts the dominant messages, popular culture rarely achieves any more than tactical victories. Popular culture is "resistive," "subversive," evasive—all a bit less than revolutionary. In the "commodity culture," teenage girls who dress like Madonna are actually repudiating the demands of their fathers, women assert their subversive identities by putting bumper stickers about shopping malls on their cars, and surfers snub their noses at respectability by "reading the beach" differently from the patriarchal families who gather there.[25]

Given the extraordinary output of the "culture producers," and given that Fiske sees every commodity as a battleground for the making of popular culture, it becomes a bit difficult to see just who is subordinate and who is dominant. The mystical patriarchal capitalist looms somewhere in the background. But since entertainment is consumed across races, classes, and genders, we are left to presume that subversion is going on all over the place. It is hard to know why a fourteen-year-old suburbanite drooling over Madonna is somehow "resistive" but the six-pack Joe watching professional wrestling somehow is not. My guess is that Fiske would gladly include the wrestling fan in his list of cultural subversives. Maybe he is actually renouncing the "dominant" standards of bourgeois gentility; no doubt he is resisting bourgeois tastes. Indeed, even an obvious member of the "dominant culture" can be subversive. "The businessman entertaining his colleagues in a private box at a football game is not participating in popular culture," Fiske insists. "The same man, however, devoid of his business suit and sporting the favors of his local teams as he cheers them on from the bleachers, can be."[26]

Leaving aside the patently obvious truth that the entertainment industries have established themselves by encouraging and marketing to these "subversions," we have to ask ourselves why it is that all this subversive activity adds up to naught. The political and economic structures of mass production, of which the entertainment industries are an essential part, have only gotten stronger and have established themselves on a global footing. Consumers can imagine anything they please when they visit Disneyland, but they are still putting cash in the pocket of the world's leading media megacorporation. Those people running Disney have names and faces, and their hard-and-fast power interests are perfectly harmonious with these "subversive" fantasies.

Fiske and his fellow cultural populists are free to ignore the concrete truth because they have convinced themselves that, in fact, the subversives win out all the time. Unwilling to follow the money trail, Fiske turns the equation on its head in what has to be reckoned a sheer perversion of reality: "If money is power in capitalism, then buying, particularly if the act is voluntary, is an empowering moment for those whom the economic system otherwise subordinates." If control of production doesn't matter, if the direction of the money flow is irrelevant, then victory in the cultural struggle—Fiske's hedging to the contrary notwithstanding—turns on the simple exercise of choice. It hardly matters that corporations have attempted to assert their dominance "by turning leisure into an industry, and by producing and promoting a range of products that, while preserving the illusion of the self-generation of choice, actually ensure that choice is exercised within a paradigm that is consonant with their own interests." What matters, he insists, is that "the sense of self-interested choice remains" for the consumer.[27]

It is tempting to dismiss Fiske as a symptom of that urge to assume the radical pose. But he is more a symptom of the tendency to want things both ways. He wants to "oppose" capitalism, but he likes the things that capitalism sells us. Reducing culture to consumer choice is the gimmick that permits the comforting illusion of political struggle in the service of being comfortable. In reducing culture to consumer choice, Fiske and his peers ignore not only the importance of refinement to taste but refuse to consider that the other transcendent purpose of culture is to help fix individuals into a stable, comprehensible social setting; the most that can be said about his consumers is that they chase the dictates of fashion laid down, supposedly, by their friends. There is and can be nothing durable in these acts of consumption: no deeper meanings are sought and the goods themselves are unimportant. There is nothing to hand down to one's progeny—but then the very idea of families and children and generations embedded in a sensible world of meaning is "patriarchal." There is precious little meaningful skill involved in buying goods, not in a world of ready-to-hand homogenized commodities. Such a thing as aesthetic judgment, of which working-class people are fully capable, Fiske glibly dismisses with the predictable claim that it is simple domination. It is the choice that matters, and there is nothing more flimsy and transitory than fashionable choice.

It is striking that the age-old conflation of culture with taste has been revived in defense of consumerism. The close logical link between consumption and taste is too intriguing to ignore. What links them together is the connection that both harbor to the life-sustaining process of eating. Yet in that connection both are temporary activities that must be conducted over and over again in order to serve their fundamental purposes. By definition, there can be no permanence in either, and the best that can be said about the processes of which they are a part is to say that they get recycled through the biological rhythm of consumption, waste, and replenishment.

That taste is a subjective quality is as true today as it was in Kant's time. But we ought to consider the consequences of accepting the conflation of culture with taste. It may well make us less snobbish. Once we do so, however, we accept as well the impermanence of things. We renounce our willingness to abide by the past, to acknowledge our humility before what others have learned about the world, and we surrender our capacity to pass on much of anything to the future—and all of these things are the essentials of culture properly understood. If the fundamental purpose of that uniquely human thing we call culture is to cheat death, then conceiving of culture as a collection of consumer choices is to cheat ourselves.

The Abstractions of Our Way of Life

It is one of the most pronounced, and yet unspoken, characteristics of the present turn of mind that culture is understood more as an ideal than a concrete reality. Culture has become immaterial. There is a self-contradictory quality about this immateriality, since it puts thinkers who are products of an age of anti-Enlightenment uncomfortably close to Kant. Fiske's notion that "self-interested choice" dictates culture or Ross's conviction that the users of mass-produced goods "rearticulate desires" are both every bit as fuzzy as Kant's "supersensible" ideal of taste judgments. They are just a lot less rigorously conceived.

The immateriality of contemporary cultural thought forces analysts to search for anchors to their conceptions. In the last twenty years, the preferred manner of adding weight to any particular understanding of this or that culture has taken one of two paths, which, it should be said at the outset, intersect so frequently they might as well be one and the same. First, there is the assertion, clear enough in both Fiske and Ross, that each consumer choice constitutes a political act. In the second method, cultural analysts consistently conflate race and ethnicity—or, indeed, any number of other voluntary or involuntary affiliations—with culture itself. Multiculturalism, as it is conventionally understood, is the intersection of these two tendencies.

In this form, multiculturalism owes a good deal of its persuasive intellectual strength to the inherently abstract nature of the culture concept. If the first flaw of aesthetics was subjectivity, the first flaw of anthropology was abstraction. If

culture was "a way of life," then in effect it subsumed everything. But not everything is cultural. A stone does not take on the qualities of culture until a mason
lays hands on it; a corpse is not in itself a cultural object, though the reverence
with which it is treated most certainly is an element of culture. The inherent
slipperiness of the concept posed real obstacles to analytical precision from the
start for anthropology, not least because the fuzzier the concept the more difficult it was to know exactly how to distinguish one group of people from another
or to understand how cultures were preserved or changed.

One of the immediate problems with the term as anthropologists wanted to
use it was that there were always very closely aligned words that could serve just
as well. In the nineteenth century, the word "civilization" was often used syn-
onymously with "culture." This was certainly one of the tendencies in Johann
Herder, who is usually credited with being the first to abstract the concept of refinement and taste and apply it to whole peoples. Herder believed his *Outlines
of a Philosophy of the History of Man* (1800) was a history of "cultivation," but to
our tastes it was more a gross generalization about how race supposedly dictated
the level of collective achievement. In practice, conceiving "cultivation" as a
collective attribute lent itself predictably to a racialist hierarchy that threw Europe into a favored light. "Asiatics," by Herder's measures, were uniformly "un-
cultivated." "The Chinese, who bear the mungal stamp," were people of "false
tastes" as "a consequence of ill-constructed organs"; the Japanese "are almost
universally ill-made. . . . Their form of government and philosophy abound with
violent restrictions, suited only to their own country."[28] Three-quarters of a century later, Edward Tylor, the father of modern anthropology, similarly conflated
civilization and culture. "Culture or Civilization," he wrote in what became a
boilerplate definition, "taken in its wide ethnographic sense, is that complex
whole which includes knowledge, belief, art, morals, law, custom, and any other
capabilities and habits acquired by man as a member of society."[29] When Freud
used the terms interchangeably in *Civilization and Its Discontents*, a work that
demonstrated how deeply he understood the wellsprings of culture, he was only
extending a long Anglo-Saxon tendency.

Society, like civilization, also has often stood in for culture, and vice versa.
Partly, their mutual use revolved around their snob value in the late nineteenth century. One became cultured so one could join society, but it wasn't
a large jump to conflate the two more or less casually. Logically, the two are
very close, speaking as they do of large groups of presumably distinct people
interacting in systematic ways, and their kinship in this regard bound anthropology and sociology very closely through the twentieth century.

In a very real sense, both of these partner terms, civilization and society,
were associated with the Social Darwinist mentality of the turn-of-the-

century bourgeoisie. The guiding supposition in the use of all these terms was that humanity progressed out of the primitive and toward the light of civilized society, which in practice meant Caucasian society. In its initial form, running from Herder through Tylor, the anthropological conception of culture, like the other natural sciences, was easily put to the service of imperialism. While it probably should be said that Herder's *History* could only lend itself toward such ends through a substantial distortion of his meaning, his work was nonetheless there to be expropriated in the late-century wave of rampant nationalism. There is no question that the willingness to conflate civilization, society, race, and culture hardened amid the rise of European imperialism and the accompanying development of racist ideologies. At the end of the nineteenth century, the German usage of *Kultur* became all-but-official dogma asserting the superiority of German civilization, but the Germans differed from their imperial competitors only by degree. The French had their chauvinistic "*civilization*," the dubious blessings of which they imposed on their colonial subjects; the British developed the same justifications for their dominance in India in particular. In the United States, which was less caught up in the imperial game, the conflation of culture and civilization was turned more toward the internal imperialism of white supremacy (though, to be sure, American foreign policy was shot through with the same bitter logic). Both the eugenics movement and the scientific racism of such writers as Madison Grant based their claims to Anglo-European superiority on cheap evolutionary models of heredity but extended their biological claims to culture as well. To many eugenicists, heredity and refinement blurred in the ascendancy of superior character. To be "well born" was not only to be a man of proper heritage but one of superior learning, carriage, and status. Breeding was both a genetic fate and a social quality. Moreover, because culture was understood as a function of biology, a possession of heredity, it was treated as a rigid, impermeable element. "Moral, intellectual, and spiritual attributes are as persistent as physical characters," Madison Grant claimed, "and are transmitted unchanged from generation to generation."[30]

It cannot be a coincidence that scientific racism and cultural chauvinism were adopted as the ideological bulwarks of imperialism at the very same time as the late-nineteenth-century bourgeoisie steadily expropriated the aesthetic tradition in the cause of domestic class rule. Culture in both senses of the term served dominant interests.

At the same moment when the Modernists launched their movement to save aesthetic judgment from bourgeois corruption, Franz Boas and his colleagues, the pioneers of cultural anthropology, set out to break this synonymous use of culture and civilization. It cannot be stressed enough that from its birth, modern cultural anthropology—specifically, the school of thought that grew out of Boas's program at Columbia in the opening decades of the twentieth century—was staunchly anti-Darwinist and anti-racist. Because the founding of a distinct discipline required a decisive break with the natural sciences, the pioneer generation had to steal the concept of culture and turn it into something distinct and analyzable on its own; they had to extract biological considerations from culture. Two clear convictions followed for them: first, that race and culture were very different things, and, second, that the quality of "civilization," which was conventionally measured by technological sophistication and military-industrial might, did not dictate the quality of culture. Culture, in the hands of these early practitioners, was an inherently radical concept.

The Boasians have never gotten the credit they deserve for their efforts to undermine Darwinism and counter racism. They were arguably the first group of Caucasian intellectuals to repudiate racism systematically; their record on this score is far above their Progressive Era contemporaries then defending immigrants against Anglo xenophobia. Boas's own experience primed him to lead an anti-racist effort. He immigrated to the States in the 1880s apparently expecting to escape the anti-Semitism that had frustrated him in Europe, but instead he was forced to endure a series of humble appointments before taking a position at Columbia University in 1896. By all accounts, his early difficulties made him determined to attack doctrines of racial superiority, a determination that included the desire to use his studies as a means for improving conditions for African Americans. Indeed he hoped to force a modification in racial attitudes in America by demonstrating what "the negro has done and accomplished in his own native country," as he explained to Felix Adler in 1906, "because the evidence of political and industrial achievement that we find practically everywhere [in Africa] . . . is such that we must class the negro among the most highly endowed human races."[31] Though he continued to practice anthropometrics and to take racial classification seriously, Boas took on scientific racism at every important turn. He taught that no group had a monopoly on genius, that the application of Darwinism to human populations was a crock because of consistent intermixing, and that, as we would say today, racial identity was socially constructed. He could hardly have stated his position on African Americans more plainly than when he wrote in 1911 that "we must not forget that the old race feeling of the inferiority of the colored race is as potent as ever, and is a formidable obstacle to its advance and progress." Rather than assuming black inferiority, "we might rather wonder how much has been accomplished in a short period [since emancipation] against heavy odds."[32]

Separating culture from race theoretically gave Boas the capacity to appreciate African achievements and the ammunition to advance the obvious truth that the "lack of attainment" among African Americans was a consequence of oppression, not genetics. And if "the lack of attainment" could not be blamed on heredity, neither could "attainment." Separating race from culture led logically, therefore, to the distinction between civilization and culture. Boas and his students had to concede that Euro-Americans had "attained" a sophisticated civilization; the West was technologically, economically, and militarily dominant. But that did not mean that the West was culturally so. Thus, much as the cultural critics pronounced on the aesthetic vices of industrial society, Boas attacked industrial society for allowing its technological ability to outpace its moral and ethical capacities. Whereas the imperialist presumed that technical sophistication was the best measure of cultural advance, Boas argued that when complexity turned into degradation, as in industrial labor, then that society became culturally impoverished. Presaging Hannah Arendt's important observation that work had been turned to the processes of consumption, Boas insisted that the true mark of cultural achievement lay in how much the store of knowledge in a given society was directed toward activities beyond the survival struggle. "We value a culture the higher," he wrote, "the less the effort required for obtaining the necessities of life and the greater the technical achievements that do not serve the indispensable daily needs."[33] Industrial society had created a "spurious culture," claimed Boas's student Edward Sapir in 1924, in which the cult of progress substituted for humane values. Anticipating the mass-culture critiques of later decades, Sapir suggested that mass production threw American culture out of kilter by bankrupting work. "Our spiritual selves go hungry," Sapir wearily concluded, "for the most part, pretty much all the time." Not only did the distinction between civilization and culture permit critiques of industrialism, but Boas and his colleagues could claim to have established, as Boas put it, "an objective measure of the advance of culture" of the sort that always eluded the aesthetes.[34]

The persuasive power of the Boasian critiques of racism and industrial society lay in their reconceptualization of culture as a thing in itself. To them, culture was the opposite of nature, at least as an adaptive, dynamic element. If there was such a thing as cultural evolution, it arose from the ingenuity of individuals acting collectively, from the deliberate effort to work from inherited material—understood as traditions and customs rather than genetic material—toward some advance in the material itself. If only humans could have culture, then it was something of great importance that "can be explained only in terms of itself," as Robert Lowie wrote. So vital was it to the

Boasians that culture be distinguished from natural processes that they were determined to limit even environmental contributions. As Lowie put it, nature prescribes nothing; it only permits "adjustments."[35] In pursuit of a similarly independent definition, A. L. Kroeber, the most prolific of the many prolific Boas students, took issue with those sociologists who too readily spoke of culture as an "organic" element of life. In an influential 1917 essay, the first purpose of which was to break anthropology's ties to Darwinism, Kroeber argued that the difference between natural adaptation to the environment and the creation of culture was as vast as the difference between the bird and its wings and the human piloting a plane or between the whale and the ship. These human adaptations obviously were not results of natural adaptation; they were the achievements of the exercise of humanity's mental capacity against nature.[36]

But if culture was not natural, how was it to be distinguished from other human creations, say, the political order? This was a difficulty of the first order, because if culture was the sum of a people's way of life, then there really was no way to distinguish it from "civilization" or "society." In the long run, it seems that the harder the Boasians tried to define the term rigorously, the more elusive the thing became. Boas certainly tried to be admirably rigorous in defining terms: Culture was, he wrote, "the totality of the mental and physical reactions and activities that characterize the behavior of the individuals composing a social group collectively and individually in relation to their natural environment, to other groups, to members of the group itself and of each individual to himself. . . . The mere enumeration of these various aspects of life, however, does not constitute culture . . . for its elements are not independent, they have a structure."[37] Individuals in social groups relating to one another and to other groups: the term "society" would have worked here as well. Thirty years after Boas laid down this apparently tight definition, Kroeber stumbled over himself trying to distinguish the social from the cultural. Society was "the organization of individuals into a group and their resulting relations," while culture "is always first of all the *product* of men in groups: a set of ideas, attitudes, and habits—'rules' if one will— evolved by men to help them in their conduct of life."[38] Kroeber's favorite way of illustrating this distinction was by pointing out that bees and ants were social creatures that had organized themselves into systematic relations but were incapable of culture, because they were incapable of handing down learning from one generation to the next or of innovating and elaborating on the environment beyond innate relations. But even with this he admitted that "we seem not yet to have attained a concise, unambiguous, inclusive, and exclusive definition of culture."[39]

Perhaps the wisest way of defining the discipline's focus was to let it define itself through method. By doing field study and attending to the details of various aspects of the daily lives of their subjects, cultural anthropologists in effect did define what they meant by culture in a way that was at once acceptably clear, reasonably limited, and potentially comprehensive. As Boas gradually honed his idea of fieldwork, for example, he settled on a formula for explaining the structure of culture. It was composed of four parts: material culture, which included both the constellation of activities devoted to producing necessities and technical and practical knowledge; social relations, which included economic relations, law, diplomacy, and gender and sexual traditions; art, understood broadly to include myth, song, and other forms of expression; and religion, which contained the beliefs in the sacred as well as ethics. In some form, all people had culture, even the most primitive.[40]

Here was the stuff of culture, the material that gave shape to the discipline as surely as unearthed ruins defined archeology or the fossil record paleontology. Not the least virtue of defining culture in this way was the concrete realism that came with it. By including material culture in this structure, Boas was insisting on the importance of making things and, by extension, the importance of traditions of skill and artistry. Language mattered too, as the glue that bound people together. Art, myth, song, religion, and ethics were in the realm of a people's mental existence, to be sure, but what mattered for the anthropologist was how such elements were enacted in everyday ritual and practice.

The key to Boas's working definition of culture was that all of these elements had to be tied together as elements in a structure. This is a crucial point. It wasn't enough to look at this piece of pottery or that ritual and pronounce on them. These discrete elements assumed importance only when they were understood as parts of a larger and coherent whole. This insistence on finding the structure or system of any given culture was a means of intellectual discipline, a way of reigning in a slippery concept and assuring its substance.

But it is this discipline that has been lost in the diffusion of the culture concept, and a good part of the blame rests on the Boasians themselves. In the United States, the discipline hit the height of its influence in the 1930s and 1940s. Anthropology sat at the center of intellectual gravity during the New Deal, when both officially and unofficially Americans devoted themselves to rediscovering the grassroots. Among many indications of its influence was the widespread popularity of Margaret Mead's work and Ruth Benedict's *Patterns of Culture* (1934), and it ought to be remembered, additionally, that Zora Neale Hurston did her folklore studies in that era. After the New

Deal, the wartime commitment to "one world," as the historian David Hollinger has observed, more than complemented anthropology's longtime claims to universalism and helped sustain the discipline's momentum.[41]

Public influence appears to have had a strange effect on American cultural anthropology. On the one hand, it encouraged a more pronounced universalism embodied not only in the frequent resort to terms such as "mankind" and "the human race" but in the adoption of definitions of culture so simplified that they could fit anything. Perhaps emboldened by the healthy state of the profession, many American anthropologists dispensed with efforts to maintain closely defined parameters of study in exchange for definitions of culture that broadened and simplified. Melville Herskovits, the most important of Boas's later students, was content to define culture as the "man-made part of the environment." Culture was, Carleton Coon wrote, simply the "sum total of how people live" as a "result of having been so taught." It was here, in the midst of searching for humanity's universal traits, that modern anthropology came to define culture as a way of life.[42]

Yet at the very same time, Boas's students, working very much in their mentor's anti-imperialist spirit, became more insistent than ever on the value of cultural relativism. Far from reducing the human story to the "rise of the West," an evolutionary tale ending with the triumph of benevolent and wise white folks, they argued, as Herskovits wrote, that anthropology had moved "from a study of the quaint and unusual in human custom as seen from the point of view of Euroamerican culture."[43] Such a perspective, the rule rather than the exception at mid-century, generated charges for decades that the Boasians were cultural relativists.[44] These charges were more or less accurate. They were also not particularly insightful. Those most closely associated with Boas's legacy—Herskovits, Margaret Mead, and Ruth Benedict—were absolutely without apology in the face of such charges. Benedict closed out *Patterns of Culture* with a defense of relativism as a positive force for social change rather than a doctrine of despair. Were relativism to prevail, she contended, "we should arrive then at a more realistic social faith, accepting as grounds of hope and as new bases for tolerance the coexisting and equally valid patterns of life which mankind has created for itself from the raw materials of existence." As Benedict hinted, relativism was presumed to be the opposite of ethnocentrism, the tendency, as Herskovits defined it, to consider one's own culture superior to all others. Even this simple formulation was tricky. Not all ethnocentrism was bad, he wrote; it was only common sense for people to be committed to the values their world upheld. At the same time, relativism, as he understood it, did not hold that all values were temporary and ultimately unimportant; on the contrary, real relativism appreciated the vital importance of moral and ethical values within any given culture.[45]

Cast in this way, Boasian relativism shared one important feature with universalism. Both perspectives attempted a depiction of culture as a static and insular thing. After all, the view that any given cultural form could not be understood outside the specific context in which it was found might be construed to mean that cultures stubbornly resisted outside pressures for change; meanwhile, drawing universal forms back to primitive man seemed to suggest that culture was at bottom a collection of anciently fixed elements.

Yet as social scientists, they knew—and said often—that culture was a fluid and dynamic thing, which is to say that their work contained an important tension between respecting the integrities of distinct ways of life by granting a certain degree of solidity, not to say permanence, to them, on the one hand, and acknowledging just how permeable culture as a thing is, on the other.

This tension expressed itself at a very specific point: the question of cultural change. Initially, Boas accepted the diffusion theory, which held that most cultures were made up of so many borrowings from cultural predecessors, neighbors, or conquerors. By the end of the 1920s, few professional anthropologists accepted diffusion as decent explanation for cultural change. Indeed, when Boas decided that Margaret Mead's fieldwork should concern child-rearing practices in Somoa, he told Ruth Benedict after the fact that he already had "decided that diffusion was done. It was time to attack another set of problems."[46]

That new "set of problems," to simplify a long and complicated story, was to explain how culture did not change or, to say it more fairly, how people manage to negotiate with outside forces in an ongoing effort to preserve what they can. The theory designed to meet this challenge, acculturation theory, was beautiful in its simplicity and seductively innocent of the dynamics of modernity. It held, simply put, that cultural contact was never a one-way process, that even where people accepted cultural forms from outside, those forms either conformed to already-set traditions or were altered upon acceptance with a studied eye toward such conformity.

Herskovits made the largest contribution to this intellectual finesse and in so doing revealed the long-range implications of post-Boasian thought. In *Man and His Works*, he reviewed the various diffusionist schools and, not surprisingly, judged Boas the most reasonable scholar, given his limited claims and sense of culture as a process of negotiation between peoples. It was probably true, he conceded, that people borrow more than they invent. And yet the very idea of diffusion, with its implication that certain cultural forms overwhelmed others with their power or attracted them with their greater so-phistication, was both too crude an idea of culture and too politically ob-noxious for him to accept. By shifting terms and emphasis from diffusion to acculturation, he sought to put the principal focus on exactly how people in-teracted, what sort of change is negotiated and how, and what sort of mental adjustments were necessary in the whole transaction. Through acculturation, he argued, a people accepted cultural forms from outsiders, but they did so tentatively, cautiously, in limited ways that meshed with their sensibilities and thereafter reshaped them according to their own designs. Herskovits could hardly have been clearer on this point, for it is not too strong to say that it was the central claim of his whole prolific career. His pioneering work on African forms sustained against the deracinating pressures of slavery stands as a social science monument to the conviction that even the lowli-est human being "exerts his influence upon the resultant borrowing" of forms. "Even slaves and prisoners," he wrote in words that clearly presaged our own conceptions, "react to their situations in ways that effectively change them, if only through passive resistance to measures they deem too oppressive."[47]

What Herskovits and his peers were getting at can be put in contempo-rary terms: the borrower was an active agent in cultural change, not a patsy passively accepting cultural impositions. In this regard, it is reasonable to see the mid-century Boasians as important predecessors to the following genera-tion of cultural populists and multiculturalists, who have turned this basic in-sight into hardened dogma. As with all intellectual genealogies, it is impor-tant not to insist on too straight a line of influence here. For whereas the dogma of cultural agency sits at the base of the subjective ideal of culture, the late Boasians deployed acculturation as the best way to tie the particular to the universal. With it, they were able to account for the spread of dynamic forms and acknowledge the readiness with which different peoples embraced especially attractive technological or material change. They were able to sus-tain a concept of culture that caught the ebb and flow of influence and still respected the integrity of distinct people. It allowed them to recognize the universality of idiosyncratic cultural genius.

The great flaw in acculturation theory, however, was that it leaned toward exactly the tendency that one of Boas's greatest critics, Bronislaw Mali-nowski, had always seen in Boas's historical school: an obsession with the "bits and pieces" of culture. In search of those elements that hadn't changed in spite of overwhelming influence, Herskovits and his successors privileged certain rituals or activities over others simply on the basis of the degree to which they reflected distinctiveness or tradition. Such a method implied a certain level of subjective emphasis; far more important, it lost sight of the centrality of structure, the key to Boas's overall definition of culture. Especially after sociologists got hold of acculturation theory and began to employ it as an alternative to the older theory of assimilation, culture came increasingly to be seen as a part of life detached from labor practices, living conditions, language change, and many of the other concrete and material markers that Boas had used to give substance to his concepts. Culture, thus narrowed, became more abstract, not less so. The common use of acculturation theory led to claims that culture changed constantly but never really changed, that distinctions were both in flux and eternal, and that what best revealed this paradox was not the structure of the world people inhabited but rather the ideals people proclaimed. Culture thus once again entered the wispy realm of the imagination. Oddly, cultural anthropology wound up in pretty much the same place Kant had more than a century before: with a conception of culture that was more an ideal than a practical, lived reality.

Is There Culture in Multiculturalism?

In our own time, when universal claims of any sort are treated with scorn, the acculturation theory lends itself to a conception of culture that carries two exceedingly problematic assumptions: first, that people create their own culture, more or less regardless of the power arrangements that prevail around them and, indeed, often as a way of resisting power; and, second, that everyone pretty much enjoys "cultural agency," which gives them the capacity to protect the local and particular and thereby preserve cultural diversity in defiance of the powerful forces at work against it. Today, the idea of cultural autonomy appears in ethnic studies of every sort, in ethnic literature and literary criticism, and in the way mass entertainment is understood. It is not too much to say that multiculturalism would never have arisen had the prior assumption not taken hold that people from different backgrounds could interact on a regular basis without compromising their cultural integrity. Those who speak of multiculturalism actually are intent on bringing marginalized people into the political and economic realms that, together, constitute society as a whole. Their resort to the word "culture" both obscures their intent and permits the delusion that social inclusion can be had without forfeiting cultural distinctiveness. The familiar desire to have it both ways generates the most curious thing of all: that those who see themselves as advocates of multiculturalism rarely take culture very seriously.

At the considerable risk of overgeneralizing, it is fair to say that those who saw themselves as advocates for multiculturalism during the 1990s began with the commonplace observation that, as Bhikhu Parekh flatly asserts, "almost every modern state is characterized by cultural diversity, that is, by the presence of different and sometimes incompatible ways of life that seek in their own different ways to preserve themselves."[48] In an age of widespread immigration, where economic transformation pulls vast numbers of people into urban areas across the world, this claim is indisputable. And no doubt the simple confluence of human differences inspired many writers to see virtue in varied ways of life. To observe this is merely to say, along with Nathan Glazer, among others, that we are all multiculturalists now.[49]

But many multiculturalists, of course, did not stop there. Again, speaking generally, it can fairly be said that they moved on to two further, far more problematic, propositions. First, they assumed that the cultural differences that they were observing would be permanent, and, second, they proceeded to argue that because those differences were virtuous in and of themselves, the role of the state should be to secure, protect, and nurture distinctions. This first presumption, that in some mysterious way, cultural differences would be frozen in time, is aptly enough summed up by Jacob T. Levy (whose *The Multiculturalism of Fear* is not to be mistaken for Barry Glassner's *The Culture of Fear*) when he urges us "to take seriously the enduring power of group loyalty and attachment, and the durability of ethnic and cultural groups. Ethnocultural identities are strongly felt, and experienced by many people at many, perhaps most, times to be permanent and immutable."[50] Given the public presence of "enthnocultural identities," it would seem self-evident that this is so.

But the fundamental flaws here are easy to see. Too many multiculturalists take the present condition of ethnic mixing to be permanent, which flies in the face of the practical ways people live over time. Like it or not, people from different ethnic groups thrown into close proximity will share customs and values. It is a mistake, moreover, to judge "culture" to be a permanent possession of ethnicity and race. And, aside from some of the more extreme ethnic advocates, no one wants to conflate the two absolutely. But that is precisely why multiculturalists are prone to fix on culture. They want to be advocates of minority rights and the incorporation of groups into institutional life, but they don't want to concede the inevitability of intermixing. Culture, that fuzzy and subjective thing, makes it possible to demand inclusion without acknowledging that inclusion will have costs.

Perhaps they implicitly recognize that inevitable mixing when multiculturalists appeal to institutions to protect and recognize group differences. Perhaps the nagging sense that the much-noted differences are in fact not all that sharp and getting less so all the time gives rise to a determination to cast them in stone. Multiculturalism, writes Canadian philosopher Charles Taylor (who is careful enough not to conflate culture and society), is the demand that "Western liberal societies" not only permit different cultures to exist within them "but the further demand . . . that we *recognize* the equal value of different cultures; that we not only let them survive, but acknowledge their worth." "Cultural pluralism," writes Harvard law professor Duncan Kennedy, "means that we should structure the competition of racial and ethnic communities and social classes in markets and bureaucracies, and in the political system, in such a way that no community or class is systematically subordinated."[51]

While there is much to be said for these propositions, rigidifying ethnic groups in formal policy seems unwise on the face of it when one keeps in mind how fluid racial and ethnic categories are. While I give some thought subsequently to what it means to "choose" one's identity in this regard, here I want to keep focus on the central question. Where is the culture in this multiculturalism? When writers talk about "cultural pluralism" and "cultural inclusion," what purchase are they making on culture?

Among the more polemical multiculturalists, there is a pronounced aversion to saying much at all about culture itself. Let me offer the writings of Iris Marion Young as an example. Young's agenda through the 1990s was to promote her "politics of difference," which she conceived as an antidote to the endemic "oppression" of the United States. To create a polity built around the acceptance of group differences, she maintained, would stymie oppression, lead to the representation of once-oppressed groups, and break down the "cultural imperialism" through which the "dominant" ruled the roost. Young routinely throws out a laundry list of "oppressed" groups: "Blacks, Chicanos, Puerto Ricans and other Spanish-speaking Americans, American-Indians, Jews, lesbians, gay men, Arabs, Asians, old people, working-class people, and the physically and mentally disabled." According to Young, members of these groups are victims of "cultural imperialism," the process by which they are made "invisible" and yet "stereotyped" at the same time. "Culturally imperialist groups project their own values, experience, and perspective as normative and universal," Young contends, and in so doing they leave "the members of [oppressed] groups . . . imprisoned in their bodies." Because cultural imperialism rests on standards exerted through the dominant groups' "exclusive or primary access to . . . the means of interpretation and communication," it establishes an oppression that is much broader than the mere processes of capitalism; indeed, in her hands, it is entirely separate from material forms of oppression. Defined as "Other," the oppressed group "*is* culturally different from the dominant group, because the status of Otherness creates specific experiences not shared by the dominant group, and because culturally oppressed groups also are often socially segregated." Brought together as despised and degraded people, members of such groups nonetheless "can affirm and recognize one another as sharing similar experiences and perspectives on social life . . . and can often maintain a sense of positive subjectivity."[52]

Young never bothers to describe exactly what makes up the "cultures" of the oppressed. She has nothing to say about art or literature, music or folklore, and she ignores work. Consequently there is an abstraction to her use of the term that allows her to use culture as a catchall place of refuge. Virtually meaningless, it can be stretched into the great commonality of all these groups, which otherwise share only the equally obtuse condition of having been oppressed. Even here, they don't share a culture; they share the experience of having been victims of cultural imperialism. Culture also serves, in its unfathomable abstraction, as both the source of oppression and the unquenchable fountain of resistance and self-esteem.

She conceives matters this way because she draws her assumptions about culture from the two prevailing uses of the term. Relying on social science claims, she maintains that group loyalties are becoming stronger today. "Despite the modern myth of a decline of parochial attachments and ascribed identities," she writes, "in modern society group differentiation remains endemic. As both markets and social administration increase the web of social interdependency on a world scale, and as more people encounter one another . . . people retain and renew ethnic, locale, age, sex, and occupational group identifications, and form new ones in the processes of encounter."[53] Yet at the very same time, culture is ever shifting and fluid. People often have "multiple" group affiliations, and the great virtue of the politics of difference is that it appreciates that group differences are "ambiguous, relational, shifting, without clear borders that keep people straight—as entailing neither amorphous unity nor pure individuality."[54]

Here is acculturation theory put to polemical purpose: culture as permanent, culture as constantly changing. It is a convenient arrangement, because it permits Young to gloss over substantial difficulties. Young is certainly right to say that marginalized groups can exist so far outside or beneath the social mainstream that they can take on their own peculiar values and customs. Not long ago people in such groups were said to belong to a "subculture," but that word no longer gets much use. To claim that these various groups have their own cultures is to suggest that they rarely interact with the larger society, which is simply not true. The case is difficult enough to make for lesbians and African Americans any longer; to think that the working class and "old people" have cultures of their own today is absurd. Her main theoretical bugaboo is the "assimilationist ideal," which "requires treating everyone according to the same principles, rules, and standards." By contrast, her politics of difference recognizes that, sometimes, achieving equality "requires different treatment for oppressed or disadvantaged groups." To rest with this view, she must assume that cultural differences, whatever they are, will be projected into politics; that cultural assimilation takes place organically and without being compelled by "cultural imperialism" is not a possibility she can entertain, given her need to believe in the permanence of difference. She never dwells on the mutual affection of all these Americans for automobiles over trains, television over reading; she never bothers to account for the breadth of common habits of consumption or the common quest for economic mobility. The overriding element of Christianity among supposedly "oppressive" WASP males and African American women, which speaks to a shared past, is unimportant. At the same time, the countless differences within her groups are ignored. American women have much in common as women, but that is not the same as saying they have a "culture" of their own. Asian Americans hail from a whole range of cultural backgrounds, but the only thing that matters to Young is that they aren't European and therefore are imprisoned in their bodies. She must ignore the ebb and flow of culture and has to assume that culture reduces narrowly to the experience of crudely defined groups. What values and customs supposedly mark these groups as distinct have to be taken for granted or else the entire argument for a politics of difference falls flat. You can't have such a politics without them.

Let us assume for the moment that she is right and that substantial cultural differences continue to animate these various groups. Let us assume further that Young's vision of a politics of difference is achieved. When justice wins out, what happens to those differences, which, after all, she sees as so valuable? If cultural differences are creations largely of oppression, then the removal of oppression ought to result in the erosion of cultural differences. In the end, you'll get assimilation anyway.

That is, you will get assimilation unless state policy is somehow drafted with the intention of maintaining group separation. This is a very dangerous proposition, since the only practical way of maintaining group differences is in the physical and economic separation of groups, which could only have the effect of creating or increasing injustice. Young acknowledges this possibility but waves it off with the extraordinary claim that "group-conscious policies are permitted only when they *promote* inclusiveness—that is, when they enhance oppressed groups' opportunities to participate fully in social and political institutions."[55] Yet again she wants it both ways: Difference now is yoked to another opposite, "inclusion." It might also be noted that this device allows her to claim that opponents of her form of difference are read out of her system, since "only" those who agree with her "are permitted." So much for genuine diversity.[56]

Young avoids the difficult admission that group differences have to be set in some manner of state dependence in order to be preserved. In this regard, Will Kymlicka's similar arguments on behalf of state-sponsored multiculturalism are more rigorous. A Canadian political philosopher whose advocacy of "liberal culturalism" certainly is shaped by his own national experience with Quebec as well as Native societies, Kymlicka has at least taken care to explain what he means by culture. In contrast to Young, he has avoided making cultural claims on behalf of activist groups and works with the far more circumscribed and therefore legitimate understanding of cultural communities as places where members "share a culture, a language and history." All people, he maintains, are members of such communities, and it is in such communities that people come to understand their options in life, including where they stand on moral and political issues. We draw our understandings from the "patterns of activity," the stories and broad expectations, that are given "significance by our *culture*." "We decide how to lead our lives by situating ourselves in these cultural narratives," he writes, "by adopting roles that have struck us as worthwhile ones."[57]

Again in contrast to Young, Kymlicka is careful to disentangle the political community from cultural communities. Political communities are governed by overarching principles that permit people from a variety of backgrounds to claim mutual membership as citizens. To function properly within such political communities, which by definition are liberal democracies, these citizens must be capable of individual moral choices, just as old-fashioned liberal theory has always held. The catch for Kymlicka is that moral choice is never merely individually conceived but rather is conditioned by the "cultural narratives" that surround the individual. In order for liberal democracy to function properly, therefore, in order for it to be confident of its own citizens, it must recognize the importance of their cultural communities. "Liberals should be concerned with the fate of cultural structures, not because they have some moral status of their own, but because it's only through having a rich and secure cultural structure that people can become aware . . . of the options available to them, and intelligently examine their value."[58] Rather than a politics of difference, Kymlicka calls for a "liberal culturalism" in which, among other things, the nation does not "coercively impose a national identity" on its members; that does not restrict citizenship by race, ethnicity, or religion; and that thrives, therefore, with "a much thinner conception of national identity." Liberal nationalism willingly accommodates the coexistence of the state and distinct minority nations within it by recognizing the legitimacy of minority languages, self-government rights, and legal traditions. "Liberal nationalists reject the goal of a world of homogenous nation-states, and accept the necessity and legitimacy of 'multination' states within which two or more self-governing nations are able to co-exist."[59]

Clearly Kymlicka has in mind such minorities as the Quebecois or Catalonians—and even Puerto Ricans—rather than lesbians, old people, and the mentally disabled. As such, his conception of culture as a community with a shared history, language, and value system gives us something a bit more concrete to consider than does Iris Young. It is at least possible to see with him how a state might go about acknowledging and then supporting cultural diversity in this sense—the promotion of distinct languages in schools is but one obvious example. Kymlicka, moreover, obviously has made his peace with the notion of physical separation, which surely would be an essential means for maintaining cultural integrity.

Still he is vulnerable to some of the same criticisms as Young. Why should the state set in stone cultural distinctions that themselves are fluid? Particularly if substantial physical separation between the minority and majority is not maintained, as it is not in the United States, how is it possible to maintain cultural, as opposed to political, distinctiveness? Indeed in the age of global communications, maintaining cultural integrity anywhere is a difficult proposition.

Kymlicka has an answer for this line of criticism. He maintains that his cultural communities are not bound as historical cultures; they do not maintain an absolutist devotion to tradition. It isn't important, he assures us, if cultural communities change, since they inherently do, and do so rapidly these days. What really defines a cultural community, therefore, is less the hold of tradition over its members than the mutual acknowledgment among the members that they share a heritage whether or not they actually live according to the dictates of that heritage. "The cultural community continues to exist," he insists, "even when its members are free to modify the character of the culture, should they find its traditional ways of life no longer worth while." He points again to the Quebecois, who still claim to possess a distinct and shared culture though they have largely jettisoned Catholicism, parochial schools, and traditional family structures. Far from endangering culture, this fluid conception not only dissolves away the dangers of fundamentalism but fits the members of the cultural community well for their roles as citizens in the liberal state. The crucial bond between culture and politics here is that the individual has the right to choose. The cultural community does not dictate individual choices but only sets the environment out of which individual options take on significance. Those changes within Quebec were essentially ones on which community members agreed, Kymlicka says. It is not as though Quebec was an isolated, aboriginal society threatened by bulldozers and MTV. And that is crucial: Change that is a matter of community choice sustains a culture. Thus "the ideal society," he believes, is one "where every individual is free to choose the life she thinks best for her from a rich array of possibilities offered by the cultural structure." The great challenge for liberals rests in "finding a way to liberalize a cultural community without destroying it."[60]

In many ways, this is an edifying political vision. Any community that is so confident in its traditions and values—indeed confident in its very existence—that it can permit its members to pick and choose the options that are best for each of them must be a sturdy community indeed and should hardly need to depend on the liberal state for its continued existence.[61] Clearly, Kymlicka sees this self-confident community as the ideal, which suggests that he harbors serious doubts about the persistence of cultural distinctiveness. Insofar as he is prepared to acknowledge those doubts, he seems to think that the threats to cultural diversity come primarily from the modern state's unwillingness to recognize the value of cultural community. He suffers from the same disciplinary trap as Young; as political philosophers, they naturally put great store in political ideas and ideals. Like Young, he seems to think that maintaining diversity is mostly a matter of getting rid of assimilationist ideas and appreciating the importance of cultural differences. But surely the challenge to cultural differences comes primarily from the deluge of mass-produced, mass-marketed images that pour from the global entertainment industry; certainly the homogenization of the world's labor poses a much graver threat to diversity than Enlightenment liberalism.

To say that change sustains a cultural community when it is a matter of agreed-upon choice is sound as a theoretical matter, but it avoids the practical truth that cultural change is rarely either that simple or, today, that insular. The flagging Catholicism of Quebec reveals the extent to which that "minority nation" is being tossed along with the rest of the West in institutional decay. It is at least possible, moreover, that the recent intensification of Quebec provincialism—along with the similar upsurge in Scotland, Catalonia, the Basque region, and Sardinia, just to name a few places—is at bottom an ambiguous reaction against the effects of those vague cultural forces of postmodernity. Quebecois nationalism is not a sign of community viability at all in this case but rather an indication of cultural defensiveness and a

demonstration that even political and linguistic distinctiveness are inadequate bulwarks against deracination.

It seems that Kymlicka too wants it both ways: enduring cultural communities but communities of choice, where individuals get to make and remake
traditions and values as they go along. He could only come to this point if he
accepted the prevailing conceptions of culture, and I think he does. The very
notion that cultures of choice are good, that choice has anything at all to do
with culture, surely reflects an unacknowledged debt to the popular-culture
sensibility, which is itself very much a creature of a society that hasn't much
regard for cultural durability. He can only take heart that such choices will
not destroy cultural communities if he is convinced that individuals and self-
defined communities have primary "agency" over their cultural fate.

Kymlicka wants the moral structure of "viable" cultural communities, but
he wants individuals to be free to choose from the "rich array of possibilities"
that modernity lays out before them. If communities can command no
greater loyalty than that, it is hard to see how they can claim to be communities at all. As Bhikhu Parekh has written, Kymlicka's concept of autonomy
within culture implicitly rebukes those who remain committed to tradition
for its own sake; many people see themselves permanently bound to traditions that they see as "an ancestral inheritance to be cherished and transmitted, or as a sacred trust to be preserved in a spirit of piety and gratitude."
Any subtle challenges they make to such traditions are advanced, Parekh
goes on, "in a spirit of humility rather than self-creation." Indeed, he says in
another context, culture provides the security of place out of which mature
human beings can deal with the world precisely because "it is not a conscious
human creation" or a mere "voluntary association."[62] If tradition has no
firmer hold over the individual than to offer an array of individual choices,
it is hard to see why any given tradition stands a chance to last much longer
than the average mass-marketed music genre. Tradition reduces to contemporary invention, if not a banal matter of fashion. Even as a theoretical matter, a tradition in such dismal shape can hardly give rise to a truly self-
confident cultural community.

Notes

1. Raymond Williams, *Culture and Society* (New York, 1958), 319.

2. David Hume, "Of the Standard of Taste," in *The Philosophy of David Hume*, ed.
V. C. Chappell (New York, 1963), 481–83, 484.

3. Immanuel Kant, *Critique of Judgment*, trans. Werner S. Pluhar (Indianapolis,
1987), 145–46, 213–14.

4. Ibid., 79, 156, 160–62.

5. Ibid., 170–72, 174, 176.

6. Matthew Arnold, *Culture and Anarchy*, ed. J. Dover Wilson (Cambridge, England, 1954), 11.

7. Ibid., 106.

8. Neal Harris, "Four Stages of Cultural Growth: The American City," in Arthur Mann, Neil Harris, and Sam Bass Warner, Jr., *History and the Role of the City in American Life* (Indianapolis, 1972), reprinted in Harris, *Cultural Excursions* (Chicago, 1990), 19–23.

9. Lawrence Levine, *Highbrow/Lowbrow: The Emergence of Cultural Hierarchy in America* (Cambridge, 1988), 120–23, 151–55.

10. Jose Ortega y Gasset, *The Dehumanization of Art and Other Essays on Art, Culture, and Literature* (Princeton, 1968), 5.

11. Arnold, *Culture and Anarchy*, 49–50, 6. Raymond Williams, "The Idea of Culture," in *Essays in Criticism* (1953), reprinted in *Literary Taste, Culture, and Mass Communication*, ed. Peter Davison, Rolf Meyersohn, and Edward Shils (Teaneck, N.J., 1978), I: 32–33.

12. Levine, *Highbrow/Lowbrow*, 154, 123.

13. Paul Gorman, *Left Intellectuals and Popular Culture in Twentieth Century America* (Chapel Hill, N.C., 1996), 54–55; also Andreas Huyssen, *After the Great Divide: Modernism, Mass Culture, Postmodernism* (Bloomington, Ind., 1986).

14. Gorman, *Left Intellectuals*, 11, 76.

15. Herbert J. Gans, *Popular Culture and High Culture: An Analysis and Evaluation of Taste* (New York, 1974), 25, 76.

16. Herbert J. Gans, *The Urban Villagers: Group and Class in the Life of Italian-Americans* (New York, 1962), 195.

17. Gans, *Popular Culture and High Culture*, 12.

18. Andrew Ross, *No Respect: Intellectuals and Popular Culture* (New York, 1989), 52.

19. Ibid., 211–12.

20. Mary Douglas and Baron Isherwood, *The World of Goods* (New York, 1979), 57.

21. Ibid., 59, 64–66, 75, 72, 89.

22. Arjun Appadurai, "Commodities and the Politics of Value," in *The Social Life of Things: Commodities in Cultural Perspective* (Cambridge, 1986), 17, 57.

23. Arjun Appadurai, "Disjuncture and Difference in the Global Cultural Economy," in *The Globalization Reader*, ed. Frank J. Lechner and John Boli (Malden, Mass., 2000), 330.

24. John Fiske, *Understanding Popular Culture* (Boston, 1989), 23–25; and John Fiske, *Reading the Popular* (Boston, 1989), 6.

25. Fiske, *Understanding Popular Culture*, 45; Fiske, *Reading the Popular*, 7–8, 11.

26. Fiske, *Understanding Popular Culture*, 43.

27. Fiske, *Reading the Popular*, 26, 83.

28. Johann Gottfried Herder, *Outlines of a Philosophy of the History of Man*, trans. T. Churchill (London, 1800; reprint, New York, 1966), 139–53.

29. Edward B. Tylor, *Primitive Culture: Researches into the Development of Mythology, Philosophy, Religion, Language, Art and Custom*, 2nd ed. (New York, 1889), I: 1. While Tylor is routinely considered the "father of cultural anthropology" on the basis of his *Primitive Culture*, George Stocking, Jr. has shown how indebted he was to the "humanist tradition" of culture and how similar his fundamental scheme, with its hierarchical notion of the improving arts and its strong religious sensibility, was to Arnold's. See "Matthew Arnold, E. B. Tylor, and the Uses of Invention," in Stocking, *Race, Culture, and Evolution: Essays in the History of Anthropology* (New York, 1968), 69–90.

30. Michael F. Guyer, *Being Well-Born: An Introduction to Eugenics* (1916; reprint, Indianapolis, 1920); Madison Grant, *The Passing of the Great Race* (New York, 1916), 197.

31. Boas to Adler, 1906, Correspondence of Franz Boas, Box 1, Franz Boas Papers, American Philosophical Society, Philadelphia, Pa.

32. Franz Boas, *The Mind of Primitive Man* (New York, 1911), 15. See also the essays collected in Franz Boas, *Race and Democratic Society* (New York, 1945).

33. Franz Boas, *The Mind of Primitive Man*, rev. ed. (New York, 1938), 200.

34. Ibid.; Edward Sapir, "Culture, Genuine and Spurious," *American Journal of Sociology* 29 (1924), reprinted in Edward Sapir, *Culture, Language, and Personality*, ed. David G. Mandelbaum (Berkeley, Calif., 1966), 93–95, 101–102.

35. Robert F. Lowie, *Are We Civilized? Human Culture in Perspective* (New York, 1929), 21.

36. A. L. Kroeber, "The Superorganic," *American Anthropologist* (1917), reprinted in Kroeber, *The Nature of Culture* (Chicago, 1952), 23–51.

37. Boas, *Mind of Primitive Man*, rev. ed., 159.

38. A. L. Kroeber, *Anthropology: Race, Language, Culture, Psychology, Prehistory* (New York, 1948), 10.

39. Kroeber, "The Superorganic," 23.

40. Boas, *Mind of Primitive Man*, rev. ed., 159–68.

41. David Hollinger, *Postethnic America: Beyond Multiculturalism* (New York, 1995), 52–55.

42. Melville Herskovits, *Man and His Works: The Science of Cultural Anthropology* (New York, 1948), 17; and Carleton Coon, *The Story of Man: From the First Human to Primitive Culture and Beyond* (New York, 1954), 5.

43. Herskovits, *Man and His Works*, 642.

44. See, for example, J. Tennekes, *Anthropology, Relativism, and Method: An Inquiry Into the Methodological Principles of a Science of Culture* (Assen, Netherlands, 1971).

45. Ruth Benedict, *Patterns of Culture* (Boston, 1934), 278; Melville Herskovits, "On Cultural Values," (1942) and "Cultural Relativism and Cultural Values" (1955), reprinted in *Cultural Relativism: Perspectives in Cultural Pluralism*, ed. Frances Herskovits (New York, 1972), 3–10, 11–34. See also Margaret Mead, "The Comparative Study of Culture and the Purposive Cultivation of Democratic Values," in Mead, *Anthropology: A Human Science, Selected Papers, 1939–1960* (Princeton, N.J., 1964), 93–94.

46. Boas quoted in Margaret Mead, *An Anthropologist at Work: Writings of Ruth Benedict* (Boston, 1959), 14.

47. Herskovits, *Man and His Works*, 528–29. See as well the body of his great work on the African diaspora, which stands as the foundation for the best cultural history of Africans in America: *The American Negro: A Study in Racial Crossing* (New York, 1928); *Dahomey: An Ancient African Kingdom* (New York, 1938); and *The Myth of the Negro Past* (New York, 1941).

48. Bhikhu Parekh, "Cultural Diversity and Liberal Democracy," in *Democracy, Difference, and Social Justice*, ed. Gurpreet Mahajan (Oxford, 1998), 203.

49. Nathan Glazer, *We Are All Multiculturalists Now* (Cambridge, 1997). I would also put in this vein David Hollinger, *Postethnic America* (New York, 1995); and Henry Louis Gates, Jr., *Loose Canons: Notes on the Culture Wars* (New York, 1992).

50. Jacob T. Levy, *The Multiculturalism of Fear* (Oxford, 2000), 5.

51. Charles Taylor, "The Politics of Recognition," in *Multiculturalism: Examining the Politics of Recognition*, ed. Amy Gutmann (Princeton, 1994), 64; Duncan Kennedy, *Sexy Dressing* (Cambridge, Mass., 1993), 41.

52. Iris Marion Young, *Justice and the Politics of Difference* (Princeton, 1990), 40, 123, 58–60. The emphasis is hers.

53. Ibid., 47, 163.

54. Ibid., 48, 171.

55. Cheryl Zarlenga Kerchis and Iris Marion Young, "Social Movements and the Politics of Difference," in *Multiculturalism from the Margins: Non-Dominant Voices on Difference and Diversity*, ed. Dean A. Harris (Westport, Conn., 1995), 19.

56. Brian Barry notes rather more bluntly that Young's recipe for a "cultural revolution," designed to intrude into every nook and cranny of life, into everything from political institutions to the individual imagination, "is chillingly reminiscent of *Nineteen Eighty Four*." *Culture and Equality: An Egalitarian Critique of Multiculturalism* (Cambridge, Mass., 2001), 15.

57. Will Kymlicka, *Liberalism, Community, and Culture* (Oxford, 1989), 135, 165.

58. Ibid., 165.

59. Will Kymlicka, *Politics in the Vernacular: Nationalism, Multiculturalism, and Citizenship* (New York, 2001), 39–41.

60. Kymlicka, *Liberalism, Community, and Culture*, 166–67, 170–71.

61. To a certain extent, I share John Gray's conviction that healthy minority cultures do not need paternalistic support. See Gray, "The Politics of Cultural Diversity," in Mahajan, ed., *Democracy, Difference, and Social Justice*, 168–69.

62. Bhikhu Parekh, *Rethinking Multiculturalism: Cultural Diversity and Political Theory* (Cambridge, Mass., 2000), 107, 161–62.

CHAPTER THREE

~

Work and Culture

Conceiving of culture as either the endlessly flexible exercise of choice or the everlasting qualities of once-distinct people, contemporary intellectuals have managed to extend the worst aspects of our two traditions of thought. The aesthetic tradition has been reduced from a defense of cultivated taste to the advocacy of consumer fashion; the anthropological tradition that once tried to define culture as a way of life bound in a discernible structure has become a blanket description for any group of people who want to claim some sort of distinctiveness.

Beyond a similar connection to the past, these two recent versions of the culture concept share an indifference to the material world. To see cultural meaning in consumer choices ignores the fundamentally homogenized products from which most people now choose. To see cultural distinctiveness in the various identity groups of public life is to ignore how people actually go about their daily lives. The versions share an immateriality, which turns the concept of culture into something like Kant's "supersensible" ideal. Their indifference to the material world ignores the importance of work, of how culture is constituted and bounded by its environment, and it fosters the illusion of diversity in a world of deepening homogenization. It ignores the pervasive bureaucratization of contemporary society, which homogenizes the structures of daily life for Americans through the imposition of rules and regulations. It is as though the concept of culture makes it possible to ignore practical reality, and that willful indifference to the two main pillars of contemporary life, mass-produced homogenization and bureaucratization, becomes complicit in the ongoing development of consumer capitalism.

Reflections on Work and the Homogenization of the Material World

Americans have become largely indifferent to the central elements of culture. Many of those who invoke the term care little about the effects of geography and environment and assume that people can imagine whatever culture they please, regardless of the material conditions surrounding them. In practice, however, we lead imitative lives amid increasingly regulated and homogenized surroundings. Consider the physical world Americans created during the 1990s. The housing boom and suburban sprawl laid down hundreds of thousands of mostly indistinguishable new homes. It didn't matter whether the new house was on the fringe of Seattle or Raleigh, nor did it matter whether the builder was a local or a regional contractor. The same construction techniques were used nationwide because of their cost effectiveness, and, indeed, in many cases, builders used the same architectural schemes. Regardless of where it is, the house is likely to have an attached garage that makes an observer wonder whether it was built for people or automobiles; it probably has several bedrooms and baths, apparently because children—those few we have anymore—must all have their own bedrooms. The kitchen almost surely is connected to the family room in an open floor plan, because so few of us do formal entertaining any longer. Its walls are no longer plaster but drywall manufactured in one of the very few plants in the nation that make the stuff. The doors, the sinks, the distance from bath to water heater, the length and make of wood trim, the electric switch boxes are all standardized.

Home builders' demand for standardized construction material, meanwhile, gave rise to those palaces of home-improvement consumption, Home Depot and Lowe's. These stores stock an incredible array of products for every taste and pocketbook—so long as your tastes aren't too quirky or your wallet too skinny—but it is an array of standardized products. If the patio door you want is thirty-two or thirty-six inches wide, they can sell you anything to suit your fancy. Ask them for one that is twenty-nine and seven-eighths, give or take a quarter-inch, and they are likely to treat you as though you have fallen from the moon. As a practical matter, you have to conform to their standards: no matter that you might be remodeling a 200-year-old home built according to the whimsy of a self-taught carpenter. Not only has the material world been steadily homogenized over the last two decades, but the rise of the mega–home stores came at the expense of the small, independent hardware store with sawdust on the floor and nails sold by the pound and not by the box, the sort where the owner, a jack-of-all-trades, mixed paint by himself according to his memory of just what tint the customer had used before; he had no need of the standardized formulae that the corporate operations use to create the thousand or so "designer colors" of their national lines.

The same concentration of power took place across the economy. Restaurants commonly became incorporated, and corporate offices dictated menus and preparation methods. Décor, aimed invariably at the funky but typically just tacky, strained to make an appearance of local control; pictures of the local college or pro sports teams or perhaps copies of local historical photographs were intended to give a homey touch. Independent hotels and motels have been virtually wiped out, as have independent bookstores. When I was a child—not all that long ago—my mother bought meat at a mom-and-pop grocery store on the next block. The butcher was our neighbor, a man named Cecil whose cancerous tongue had been amputated and whose dirty jokes were decipherable only by those who had learned to understand his mumblings. The ma-and-pa grocery with its own butcher is nearly extinct in much of the United States today, even though it remains common in other nations. Here the grocery business, and along with it the food we ingest, is dominated by massive regional chains; with Wal-Mart's entry into the grocery business, it might be just a matter of time before the regionals get buried by national and multinational chains. Because the chains like to buy in bulk, the concentration of power in the grocery business has gone a long way toward encouraging the rapid growth of megafarms, particularly in the South and the Midwest.[1]

The spread of the chains in everyday forms of retail generates still more material standardization. A Wal-Mart is a Wal-Mart whether it is in Maine or Mississippi. They are all the same, immediately recognizable and equally hideous. They are built according to the precise dictates of the central office, which is renowned for its meticulous attention to the details of efficiency. Absolutely no thought is given to architectural beauty, none at all to the possibility that buildings are important public monuments. No thought is given to the future; within a generation, these awful structures will probably be rusting dirty shells that can't be refitted for any other sort of enterprise. And yet there are some who point to Wal-Mart as a splendid example of the flexibility of the new order of business, which, according to Alvin and Heidi Toffler, "promotes diversity and consumer choice to the point that a Wal-Mart store can offer the buyer nearly 100,000 products in various types, sizes, models and colors to choose from."[2]

Because of the domination of large-scale organizations, much of what people commonly throw into "culture"—television, movies, music—takes on the standardization of the labor that produces it. American music producers create the spectrum of niche tastes, but everything that hits commercial radio conforms to a preset formula. A song cannot be much more than three minutes long, and it has to have a catchy "hook" to it because, like an effective ad, a tune is supposed to bounce around in the listeners' heads long enough for them to buy the CD. These music niches, meanwhile, are increasingly being set by national radio marketers such as Clear Channel Communications, which quickly came to dominate the music retail industry after the 1996 Telecommunications Act cleared the way for oligopoly. The diverse tastes of the listener in Orlando are flattered in the exact same way, with the exact same song, at the exact same time as her fellow niche-lover in Oregon. Yet we are led to believe that such people constitute a community of listeners whose shared tastes constitute a distinct culture and contribute to diversity.

The indifference to a homogenized material reality has its direct companion in the indifference to bureaucratic regulation. Just as megaretailers drown us in goods, so the large-scale enterprises that shape our material circumstances—corporations, government entities, public school systems, and universities—assure us that diversity is among their most coveted goals. To the extent that diversity is their antidote to discrimination, the rhetoric is all to the good. But the assurances of bureaucratic diversity turn our attention away from the basic nature of all such organizations: that they impose standardized regulation on all those who work within them and alienate their employees by regimenting work. Here is where the rhetoric of cultural diversity is simply pernicious, for it distracts people from appreciating just how little control they ultimately have over their work and helps make possible the constant standardization of labor that remains the best indication of the condition of a culture.

Moreover, our present indifference to the centrality of work relinquishes the best tool we have for mitigating the inherent sloppiness of the culture concept. Kant's idealist solution to the subjectivity of taste, as I have argued, was pleasing as a form of moral argument but less than satisfactory as a way of thinking about culture, precisely because he ignored the material quality of work. He would have been better off understanding basic craft skills as akin to fine artistry beneath the mantle of well-done work. Standards of creative work, in contrast to aesthetic ideals, carry the weight of the practical and measurable. There is no accounting for taste, but there is always a right way and a wrong way to go about making something, and the standards of work are typically embedded in the hard-won experience of those trained in the given craft.

The commitment to making things well can also carry the broader educative function that both Kant and Hume understood to be vitally important to the general capacity of taste. And for my own tastes, Hume was better than Kant on this issue. One way of approaching the problem of taste was to develop standards of beauty based on experience and the acknowledged requirements of skill. Hume hinted at such standards by shifting attention from the observer, whose passive relationship to the object at hand was the predecessor to the consumer, to the producer. It was possible to assemble guidelines for aesthetic judgment out of the accumulated knowledge of a craft, whether that was literature or furniture-making. Those rules could be cloudy at times, and they changed with time. "We must not imagine," he admitted, "that, on every occasion, the feelings of men will be conformable to these rules." Nonetheless, "amidst all the variety and caprice of taste there are certain general principles of approbation or blame, whose influence a careful eye may trace in all operations of the mind."[3]

That "careful eye" had two crucial functions. First, it helped guide the adjustment of new dispositions to the "general rules of art." Adjustment and change were inevitable, after all, and it was necessary to make "allowance for the continual revolutions of manners and customs." Any such adjustments, however, could not reduce art to only that which "was suitable to the prevailing fashion."[4] The careful eye was a hedge against the transitory and the merely fashionable, an antidote to artistic quackery and bad-faith claims for recognition. It also had an educative function. The careful eye and the delicacy of taste were not instincts. They were the products of training. Just as the trained palate detects tiny and subtle flavors, so "a quick and acute perception of beauty and deformity must be the perfection of our mental taste."[5] And that perfection, in turn, required practice. Experience in a particular art honed the senses to where they could discern the subtle deformities or beauties in a given work. In the eye not of the beholder but rather of the trained observer, "the mist dissipates" and the true nature of the object reveals itself.[6]

I'd like to suggest that this is about as healthy a notion of culture as can be found. Well into the nineteenth century, when the industrial bourgeoisie was turning culture to the cause of snobbery, a great many sensible people continued to extend this conception. The producer ideal saw its fulfillment in William Morris's enormously powerful condemnation of industrial capitalism, and it had its analogue in the aesthetic sensibilities of Third Republic French radicals, as Miriam Levin has shown. Late-nineteenth-century labor radicals understood that the degradation of labor brought with it an accompanying degradation of the craftsmen's sensibilities and produced a world that was, quite frankly, steeped in abiding ugliness, incapable of creating any beauty at all, much less incorporating beauty into everyday life. Lucy Crane, a Morris devotee, appropriated Hume's logic in defense of the domestic tasks of women when she argued that even the most humble of practical arts—sewing, cooking, gardening—helped cultivate a sense for beauty. "Practice in these things," she wrote in echoes of Hume, "helps educate the eye and hand, and gives competence of judging as to the fitness for practical purposes of tools and material, and of the quality of workmanship." Daily experience with well-made things, she hoped, would cultivate the capacities to judge between "good and bad, between beauty and ugliness, in all the furniture and appliances of life, as in other things."[7]

If skilled work can be understood as a reasonable means for cultivating a proper taste for beauty, it also embodies the anthropological qualities of culture. Skilled work is among the most decisive markers of culture because it is rooted in a community's engagement with the natural world at the same time that it marks the will to refine nature. For this reason, particular craft skills embody nothing less than the history of a community as traditions of work are passed down from generation to generation. The best way of preserving genuine cultural diversity, aside from maintaining strict physical isolation and maintaining language, is to preserve craft traditions.

Yet these are the cultural markers that industrialization always has relentlessly destroyed. There is no better example of this than Jane Addams's immigrant neighbors in turn-of-the-century Chicago. Observing the impoverished human beings around her Hull House settlement taught Addams that the "instinct of workmanship," even if it was exhibited in a common craft, inherently included a dignified taste for beauty and defined the older identities that her neighbors sought to preserve. She recalled an Italian who carved beautiful patterns, which he had used at a Neapolitan church, in the doorposts of his tenement, only to be evicted for destroying property. He was less disturbed by being put out, Addams writes, than "that his work was disregarded; and he said that when people traveled to Italy they liked to look at wood carvings but that in America 'they only made money out of you.'" Likewise, there was the Bohemian family bedeviled by the father's drunken tantrums and eventual suicide. Addams discovered that the man had been a goldsmith reduced, through a "stupid maladjustment," to shoveling coal in a factory and that his wife had learned to avert his drinking if only she could put a piece of metal in front of him to work. "We had forgotten," she ruminated with her usual humane grasp, "that a long-established occupation may form the very foundations of the moral life, that the art with which a man has solaced his toil may be the salvation of his uncertain temperament."[8] She could easily have said, using the language of our time, that the "long-established occupation" was central to his "cultural identity."

The Market, Technology, and the Homogenization of Labor

What faced Addams's neighbors in the last decade of the nineteenth century faces much of the world today. The internationalization of capital has imposed a more or less uniform system of labor on the world, one made all the more dominant after the fall of the Soviet Bloc. But well before then and with the full complicity of the communist nations, industrial labor destroyed local traditions of craft work wherever it was imposed. In the last twenty years, that imposition has taken place across the developing world, so that factory work in China resembles the sweatshops of early-twentieth-century New York—as, for that matter, do the sweatshops that have reappeared in New York. It is probably true that the harsh conditions of factory labor often represent a material improvement over the great toil of rural existence. But even the best of contemporary labor, work at its most remunerative and sophisticated, based as it is universally on computers, rewards only one general set of skills, which cannot give voice to the varied expressions of different people any more than it can give rise to qualitatively different products. If everyone in the world were to achieve the rank of skilled laborer as that is now defined, cultural diversity would be impossible. We might see a billion Web sites dedicated to the expression of announced differences, but in the end we will still have nothing but a billion Web sites.

It is important to understand that cultural destruction comes through the manipulation and displacement of work rather than, say, the spread of that nebulous giant we call "the market." The merchant was never so destructive as the industrialist. The marketplace, in the mere sense of buying and selling, generally has not been destructive of culture—far from it. Commerce between people on the whole has had a salubrious, broadening effect. By building contacts between people, merchants historically were agents of cosmopolitanism. The intersections of trade routes, which of course included ports, provided the ground upon which great commercial cities—Timbuktu, Naples, Constantinople—were built, and cities, we would do well to remember, are essential to culture in the best sense of that word. The very history of culture is, in many ways, a history of commercial exchange.

Obviously, even where it created interconnections between people, encouraging as it did cultural borrowing and, as Herskovits would have it, acculturation, merchant trade did not destroy varied cultures. It is true enough that where people came into regular contact, where they gathered in common environments such as cities, they synthesized their ways of life into some new form. It is probably more accurate to say, however, that there were always mediators, mostly merchants, who negotiated between their own society and others. For this reason, commerce meant buying and selling across societies rather than substantial mixing. Mere commerce, on the whole, rarely had an inherently disruptive effect on cultures. The capacity of a people to produce for a market beyond subsistence is itself a cumulative result of social maturation; the rise of commerce out of any given society, a slow, gradual process, must have been fairly natural and innocuous to most social conventions, at least initially. What new cultural forms returned with traders were likely ones that were either quickly deemed useful or somehow in accord with the community's set values, since no premodern trader could afford to experiment with his main customers or run afoul of his sovereigns. In some cases, where seagoing commerce permitted large transactions and thus great merchant profits, merchants themselves became near-sovereigns, as in the great trading families of Genoa, Naples, and Barcelona. Whether obedient to or part of the nobility, merchants tended to be conservative. Limited to transactions between peoples, the old world of commerce was never deeply intrusive and therefore lacked the power to generate deep and abrupt cultural transformation within societies.

Those examples of commerce that radically changed ways of life tended to be exceptions that prove the rule. Such was the case, for instance, among Native American peoples who entered the seventeenth- and eighteenth-century fur trade and in so doing incorporated European technologies and commodities that profoundly reordered their internal relationships. The fur trade had tragic consequences for North American Indians because it caused important internal changes of the sort that did not regularly transpire in commerce between equals on a fairly level playing field. Those changes proved a general rule: Commercial interaction had fundamental cultural effects only when they initiated deep changes in the primary ways a society goes about its daily economic activities. The problem with the fur trade was that it imposed a sort of monocultural economy on the groups that engaged in it so that the internal patterns of work had to be adjusted to the production of the principal commodity.

Otherwise, commerce alone has been typically unobtrusive. But capitalism has been a different thing. Capitalism, by any definition that makes historical sense, is the reorganization of work conducted with the intention of undermining the worker's control of the labor process. The lynchpin of pre-capitalist systems of production is always knowledge that is accumulated through local traditions and that rests in the hands of those who make goods. In this sense, the knowledge of production is every bit as much a cultural matter as an economic one. Any threat to the specific work patterns is a cultural threat; it is an attack on traditional forms of knowledge around which people have constructed their way of life and can only have the effect of reducing some of the most unique qualities of a specific people. The single greatest threat to local patterns of work is the spread of capitalist forms of production. Time and again, wherever the factory sets down, local production is destroyed, and that destruction is invariably felt as a tension between traditions and new ways of life.

It is a staple of social and labor history that the culture of the preindustrial craftsman was destroyed in the process of capitalist reorganization. But the point here is that it amounted to an enormous step toward cultural homogenization within Western society. The artisanal system was built on apprenticeship training that handed skill down through the ranks from master to journeyman to apprentice, which set hierarchical ranks within crafts but also distinguished a given craft from all others; the system was built on distinctions of skill and mastery. Personal identity was typically fixed, as was social status, according to the particular craft a man had entered. In the preindustrial period, craftsmen did not speak of themselves as part of "a working class." They used the plural: They were part of the "laboring classes," the "mechanic classes," or the "artisan classes."

The destruction of the craft system of work, by undermining craft-based skill, destroyed the basis on which artisans had distinguished themselves. The movement of people into the working class, which by the late nineteenth century at the latest constituted a singular collection of wage laborers, marked a crucial step in human homogenization. This in itself was of extraordinary historic importance, since the development of the modern class system was one of the main currents of the nineteenth and twentieth centuries. But what is most important here is that the modern working class was the result of the breakdown of human variety protected by traditional forms of knowledge and skills. The modern working class was a cauldron into which anyone's fate might be tossed, and it reduced workers to the "masses" in the original sense of that word.

It is striking that this economic and cultural history can be regularly ignored in an age when it is so plainly repeating itself. While Jane Addams's neighbors migrated into the maw of industrialization, industrialization now migrates to the workers. The movement of production out of the United States and Western Europe has had the clear effect of undermining local patterns of work throughout Asia and Latin America, and clear historical parallels are emerging. In Malaysia, for instance, many Western-owned plants employ rural women whose impoverished families badly need their wages. Economic necessity crashes against family tradition. Parental control of daughters, an essential ingredient to the control of marriage and therefore of kinship and property, becomes strained in the bargain. As Aihwa Ong shows in one of the finest studies of the wider effects of factory work in the global economy, these young women find themselves in precisely the same situation as the New England mill girls who were coaxed into the textile factories in Massachusetts in the early nineteenth century. The work affords them a bit of new freedom, their wages some independence. But they want to use that independence to reshape traditional values in ways that afford them more dignity and respect. To that extent, economic opportunities provided by Western investment have a positive effect. The problem, of course, is that there is no way to prevent the thoroughgoing unraveling of traditions. The result is not liberation so much as alienation.[9]

The same, generally, can be said about the economic upheavals now dragging migrants from rural to urban areas across the world. A good many of the migrants into the *maquiladoras* in northern Mexico are from rural communities and are being sucked into a world of factory labor, slum living, and ill health; in China, migration from the vast rural hinterland to the coastal cities is one of the basic facts of economic development. Frequently, the vast majority of these workers are women, who must bear the brunt of conditions that can range from awful to downright brutal.[10]

People uprooted from their homes cannot but face a struggle to preserve distinct ways of life that are also products of time and place. Sustaining old ways in new environments inevitably changes both. At the same time, the breadth of the system brings common conditions to tens of millions of otherwise very different people. Sweatshops are not just found in Asia and Mexico; the multinational apparel corporations routinely contract production out to underground assemblers who exploit immigrant labor in Los Angeles, New York, Philadelphia, and other U.S. cities. Even in high-tech centers such as Silicon Valley, workers labor in electronic-assembly plants that, as the *Nation* reported in 1993, resemble assembly lines in Thailand and Tijuana. "Occupying the lowest rung in the [high-tech] structure," the journal concluded, electronics assemblers, 60 percent of whom were women and 70 percent Asian or Latino, "lack even the basic benefits and protections" usually provided to other assembly workers.[11] When they enter the industrial workforce, these global migrants face a dilemma that is a variation on the central cultural dilemma that those in developed societies confront. Joining the workforce, especially when it means leaving one's home, initiates the process of disrupting cultural identity.

If the potent yearning for material improvement naturally drives people to migrate, there is nothing natural about the process in which they take part. The wave of globalization that convulsed the 1990s was the product of standard business decisions and conscious policy at the national and international levels. The doctrine of free trade won the day in Washington, the World Bank, and the International Monetary Fund, and it is revealing that this happened among Democrats, who never tired of pronouncing their commitment to diversity in all things. It is important to remember that political decisions shaped economic developments, if for no other reason than to keep in mind that other political decisions might alter the nature of these economic processes.

Something as simple and old-fashioned as protectionism can frustrate the leveling effects of globalization. Take the case of Japan, the most ingenuous protectionist nation in the world. The Japanese built their advanced economy on the backs of common workers and farmers, both through harsh taxation and by extolling sacrifice as a preeminent virtue; those sacrifices provided the foundation on which the ruling class of bureaucrats and corporate business leaders was able to consolidate itself after World War II. To ensure the continued functioning of this arrangement, Japanese elites understood that they had to offer something back to common folk. They did this by constructing an impressive social welfare state and by inventing and advancing economic policies designed to ensure full employment. These two strategies were part of a bundle that constituted the modern social contract.

This arrangement created a society that is the most economically egalitarian in the industrialized world, one with a notable absence of systemic poverty or ostentatious personal wealth. Japan has managed to remain a middle-class society because the postwar social contract has kept the nation largely a producer's society—to the surprise of many who know the Japanese only from their consumer fads. Japanese traditions are rooted in many things, but the craftsman ideal of good work well done is the most pronounced ingredient, evident in the fine arts, in cooking, in everyday work, and in the widespread devotion to precision. Surely this ideal is sustained by the countless small producers who actually fill the Japanese economy beneath the corporate behemoths. A walk through any Japanese neighborhood takes one past collections of small soba shops, tiny markets, tatami makers, small machine shops, and furniture stores, among countless others.

To a skeptical observer, these small businesses represent anything but diversity, because they are as relentlessly uniform as is much of the rest of Japanese society. What one finds in one household grocery is pretty much the same thing that one finds in the next neighborhood liquor store—the same candies, the same beers, the same boxed lunches. The skeptic should keep in mind that the alternative, which now chokes the United States, is large chain operations that undoubtedly would deliver a greater variety of goods at lower prices. But it is precisely the large chain that Japanese protectionism is aimed at resisting, and thus protectionism is a marvelously democratic mechanism that protects small producers and probably constitutes the foremost structural buffer between Japanese producer culture and the consumerism to which the Japanese are so lamentably prone. When it is rescinded, as it has partly been already, there will be little to protect the Japanese sense of delicacy and beauty from a flood of mass-produced, mass-marketed goods. In short order, those countless small businesses, in many ways the daily symbols of what is best about Japan, will be buried without some sort of government subsidy program, such as is regularly provided to rice farmers.

The difficulty that the Japanese face here is inherent in capitalism. In the face of aggressive globalization, there are no two ways to go about business: The American market model wins out. The various economic models of the mid-twentieth century, whether they were socialist, "corporatist," or the welfare state, have been washed away. Much of the writing on the "Asian miracle" in the late 1980s and early 1990s assumed that the bubble economies proved that Asia had discovered a new brand of capitalism that was both stable and dynamic, and this was clearly wrong. When the bubble popped, it became immediately clear that the "Asian model" was too rigid to compete in the open market. If cultural diversity is important, then bureaucratic rigidity, even corruption, is better than the free market. It is hard to have much sympathy with Japan's bureaucratic elite, but the tragedy is that as their power crumbles, so too will the social contract that has protected the small producer.

The same holds for labor everywhere. Craftsmen who have managed to hold on to special protections, as they have in parts of Western Europe, particularly in Germany, will see their hold slip. Since 1992, when the European Union's "internal market" was created, the most skilled German workers have resisted market pressures even when they stood to benefit from reduced trade barriers. Some labor leaders derided the internal market on the grounds that Germany would flex its export strength at the expense of less-protected workers throughout Europe and the Third World. There have been consistent and legitimate concerns that the leveling of trade barriers also means the leveling of labor itself. Beyond these immediate concerns, many German craftsmen and shopkeepers are protected by guild regulations that date back to the medieval period, which they stand to lose in the course of European integration. And much of what is unique about Germany, like Japan, will disappear as well.[12]

Unskilled and semiskilled labor across the world is now locked essentially into one system, but there is another way in which the present system of production grounds away diversity. The spread of low-skill, assembly-line production of consumer goods has accompanied the spread of high-skill computer and communications jobs. Particularly in the United States, where demand for programmers and other skilled positions outpaced the native supply during the 1990s, the wave of immigration includes very-well-paid professionals—a largely unprecedented development. No matter how well paid one is in this situation, the skills that are in demand are narrow and uniform. There is no difference between how a Hindi programmer approaches his work and how a Canadian programmer does hers, no matter, really, where they are. The spread of the mass-consumption economy, based on the dominance of technologically advanced patterns of labor, represents, accordingly, a twofold homogenization of how we work and, to that extent, of how we live.

The Anthropology of Work and Organizational Culture

While the muddiness of contemporary usages of the culture concept is broadly responsible for the indifference to material homogenization, the belief that contemporary economic organization is capable of producing cultural diversity is more specifically a result of the long relationship between social science and the corporation. For much of the twentieth century, the social sciences—psychology, sociology, and anthropology—acting under the general heading of organizational and human-relations studies, have conferred a certain empirical, if not ethical, justification on the corporate form of organization, and the concept of culture has been used as a doctrinal lynchpin in that blessing. To organizational scholars, what is culturally important is not whether the average store clerk makes pottery with sacred symbols embossed on it but rather that the clerk's work be understood as evidence of how this particular society goes about organizing its day-to-day existence.

There is certainly a good deal of common sense in the assumption that understanding bureaucracies in a bureaucratized society is of fundamental importance. It is akin to seeing consumption as a central feature of life in a consumer society. But just as this latter observation lost its basis in common sense when it encouraged many to imagine consumption as an act of culture creation, so the reasonable effort to understand bureaucracy's cultural place has devolved into the widely deployed contention that bureaucracies are cultures in themselves. Organizational studies have had an important hand, moreover, in relinquishing the concept of culture to the business class, which since the mid-1980s has used it vigorously both to advocate for so-called cultural diversity and to recommend diversity as a means of managing workers most effectively.

That anthropologists should be complicit in management's hijacking of culture is nothing new. To the extent that anthropologists have taken an interest in modern work, they have tended to put their research to the service of improving management's control over workers. The first dalliance between anthropology and industrial management took place within Elton Mayo's famous Hawthorne studies, a series of observations and experiments carried out in Western Electric's Hawthorne Electric plant in Chicago in the 1930s. Though a sociologist by training, Mayo hired anthropologists for his research team and relied upon the functionalist theories of A. R. Radcliffe-Brown, which insisted on looking at institutions almost as semi-autonomous entities within larger social systems. Mayo's studies supposedly demonstrated that the efficient management of large-scale enterprises required careful attention to human relations, to the basic human needs of workers, not just their physical well-being but their need for self-respect and a say in how work was organized. Indeed, Mayo argued that simply being listened to by a concerned interviewer dramatically improved workers' morale. More than that, such an interview "for many thousand persons, was an experience without precedent in the modern world."[13]

Critical though he was of the efficiency experts and managers mired in the dogmas of competitive capitalism, Mayo's purpose was to improve labor relations by ignoring the conflict over work and instead making workers feel better about life in general. Perhaps the main working presumption in Mayo's human-relations approach was that work, important though it was, was not the principal activity of workers; their psychological makeup included everything from the need for sustenance to their sexual urges, spiritual qualms, and primal fears. Addressing workers' anxieties, therefore, required a broad, holistic approach aimed at easing their minds.

Someone trained in the patient but keen observation of social behavior—in contrast to the discrete psychoanalytic observation of the individual—might be best able to adjust individual temperament to organizational rules, and vice versa. Who better to match observation with institutional understanding than the anthropologist? Organizational scholars have never been exactly forthright in acknowledging that they are working with the interests of corporations in mind, and culture has given them a professional screen in this regard. They aren't helping to manipulate workers, they can easily claim. They are studying culture. Because "social anthropology trains students to look at a village, a factory, a community as a social system of people in constant interaction, fitting into a pattern of relationships," wrote Burleigh B. Gardner in 1977, anthropology majors could go into the business world without shame, knowing that they can "stand aside from [their] own culture and view it more objectively than one not trained to understand cultural differences."[14]

The integrity of the functionalist notion that the village and the factory can be understood in essentially the same way required that the observer remember that any bureaucracy is but part of a larger social system and not a world unto itself. While anthropologists among the organizational theorists still remind themselves that organizations "cannot exist separate from larger national cultures," as one puts it, the overwhelming tendency since the early 1980s has been to claim that organizations all inherently have a cultural integrity of their own, for better or worse.[15]

Thus functionalist anthropology loaned the culture concept to corporate apologists, who took it up in earnest as a way to explain why some firms succeed and some fail. Writers such as Tom Peters, Terrence Deal, Allen Kennedy, and Edgar Schein began to argue in the 1970s that each corporation has its own culture. Each has its own rituals, values, heroes, and myths—all the recognized attributes of a culture. According to Schein, a corporate culture typically flows out of the vision of the company's founder, who from the beginning instills in the organization a distinct vision of purpose that takes on a life of its own over time. That founding vision, in a sense, lends immortality to the corporate culture, since it becomes institutionalized in ritual and practice, embodied in the corporate advertising slogan, and lives beyond the founder. And while, of course, the bottom line is important in any corporation, what really matters is how that corporation goes about its business. "The biggest single influence on a company's culture is the broader social and business environment," wrote Deal and Kennedy. "A corporate culture embodies what it takes to succeed in this environment." Rather coyly borrowing from anthropology, they further maintained that different responses to the market "environment" gave rise to distinct "tribes": Some corporations were hard-sell, "macho" cultures, some were technologically oriented "process" cultures. This subtle but telling conception, closely examined, suggests that the marketplace does not constitute part of a larger social structure; indeed, by equating it with the environment, Deal and Kennedy imply that the marketplace is not even a human invention. If the marketplace is akin to the natural world, than presumably the individual corporation is akin to the village. The tribal chief now dons a suit instead of a headdress and is called the chief operating officer.[16]

The timing of these business writers' infatuation with culture is curious. The early 1980s were the tail end of that infamous period of post-Vietnam, post–oil crisis "malaise," when American business, like Americans more broadly, wrestled with considerable self-doubt. But it was also the moment when Ronald Reagan's reawakened nationalism dovetailed with deindustrialization. Poised between stodgy malaise and buoyant expansion, business writers seized hold of culture as a means for instructing American management in how to make the leap from one to the other. Deal and Kennedy's 1982 work, often cited as a pioneering book, reads as though the authors had stolen a page from Christopher Lasch's *Culture of Narcissism*—or at least from Jimmy Carter. Perfectly befitting their moment in time, they were alternately pessimistic and boosterish. "We think that society today suffers from a pervasive uncertainty about values, a relativism that undermines leadership and commitment alike," they insisted. "We find ourselves without responses" to "this fast-paced world." But in contrast to this philosophical malaise, corporate culture contained focused values intended for specific purposes; people adrift could seize such values because they made plain sense, and consequently corporate culture potentially provided the antidote to the nation's mental and spiritual doldrums. Likewise, the age discouraged heroism, but that was exactly the quality that was most urgently needed to resuscitate American business. "America's boardrooms," they believed, "need heroes more than Hollywood's box offices need them."[17]

In this wider context—a political and economic context, it must be noted, that functionalist anthropology supposedly insisted on recognizing as the broad culture of which individual organizational structures were merely parts—invoking culture became a means for coaxing and applauding the transformation of American management out of its Cold War lassitude and into its post–Cold War global expansion. Indeed it was just this purpose that created the wave of business interest in Japanese management models at the time when the Japanese bubble was growing; Japanese success invariably was linked to Japan's unique culture. Thus Tom Peters and Robert Waterman began *In Search of Excellence*: "We hear stories every other day about the Japanese companies, their unique culture and their proclivity for meeting, singing company songs, and chanting the corporate litany." Their thesis was that such corporate behavior was not unique to Japanese firms. "The more we dug, the more we realized that excellent [American] companies abounded in such stories and imagery." What the Japanese and American corporations had in common were "strong cultures." "The trappings of cultural excellence seemed recognizable, no matter what the industry. Whatever the business . . . companies were doing the same, sometimes cornball, always intense, always repetitive things to make sure all employees were buying into their culture."[18]

The culture concept allowed Peters and fellow organizational theorists to urge a corporate cultural revolution on American business, one that drew from the famous lessons of pioneering heroes, from IBM's Tom Watson to Mary Kay Ash, founder and head cultural guru of Mary Kay Cosmetics. Almost invariably, they envisioned a revolution that was anti-bureaucratic and anti-hierarchical. American business, in their view, had grown too fat and happy, too calcified by organizational complexity and content in its power; like a decadent empire, it was ready to be usurped by nimble competitors. Deal and Kennedy described their corporate heroes as free spirits, the opposite of the number-crunching managerial type: "Managers are routinizers; heroes are experimenters. Managers are disciplined; heroes are playful. . . . Managers will spend hours refining their numbers, while the heroes will plant a garden." Clearly, they conclude, "we are not talking about good 'scientific' managers here," those poor stiffs in gray flannel suits whom Lawrence M. Miller diagnosed as "cultural casualt[ies], conditioned by a system that required managers to be tough and unrelenting." Instead of the "rational manager," Deal and Kennedy announced the arrival of the "symbolic manager," with GE's Jack Welsh as the prototype, who goes beyond the management of "systems" to "do what seems right culturally, regardless of what the system says." Human relations, rather than systems analysis, was the forte of the symbolic managers—shades of Elton Mayo.[19]

The purpose of this cultural revolution was perfectly clear to Reagan-era business writers. It was necessary both for fending off the intensifying competition, mostly from Japan, and for succeeding in the new environment of globalization. As Lawrence Miller forthrightly declared: "The future will be characterized by global competition, and those corporations that will succeed will be the ones that adopt a corporate culture with values that promote the behavior of competitive success." Old Taylorist schemes of floor management and stiff bureaucratic structures were creatures of the industrial era of mass production, so these writers maintained, and the new era required far more flexibility both in production and management. Culture, that "soft" element of business, was the mother of flexibility. Indeed, corporate culture was supposed to take the place of bureaucratic structure. "There is a growing international consensus," one observer maintained, that an "economic renaissance is dependent upon the cultural transformation of large-scale business, and in particular on the extent to which decaying bureaucracies can be replaced with dynamic organic cultures." Peters and Waterman clearly preferred the "lean" and flexible organization to the stiff corporation, and one of the chief virtues of a strong corporate culture was that it provided a consistent vision and value system that didn't need to be written down in a manual and could therefore give consistency and structure in the absence of rigid bureaucratic controls. In order to achieve the flexibility that the wide-open market required, argued Peter Anthony in the same vein, employees had to be permitted a good measure of autonomy, which meant that they "*must* be trusted and they *can* be trusted because they will be brought to share the same values and meanings, the same culture."[20]

Culture became the passkey into the "new management" of the "reinvented corporation" of the 1990s. The job of the manager was to toss out the bad culture and bring on the new. Management and organizational experts exhorted companies to root out maladapted cultures that inhibit smooth human relations and harmonious teamwork. "A culture of closure, commitment, and communication" was the antidote to the "culture of muck" that fosters "discomfort . . . in working relationships." "The culture of faulty rationalizations" maintained by "dysfunctional behaviors" of employees had to yield to the clear-eyed grasp of corporate cultural problems on the part of the top-level managers. Particularly in this day and age, "the success of a new strategic intervention or the adoption of a new technology depends on workplace culture," claimed James R. Fisher, Jr., an author who sees himself as a critic of Mayo and who, in contrast to most of his ilk, understands organizational cultures as creatures of the larger world around them. But even he insisted that if inevitable decline is to be resisted, the "culture of comfort" and the "culture of complacency" had to give way to a "culture of contribution" in which workers approach tasks with intelligence and individual commitment. American corporations, according to still another author, had to rediscover the "core cultures" of customer service, innovation, operational excellence, and spirit. And this fulsome sea change had to be managed, beginning with the understanding "that the existing cultural condition is in some way unsatisfactory, and that the preferred condition, the objective of cultural change, is clearly understood."[21]

Managing Diversity

For all the blood and venom spent both defending and condemning the diversity movement during the 1990s as a product of post-Marxist radicalism,

it is more properly understood as an integral part of this burgeoning conflation of bureaucratic order with culture. No doubt the goals of affirmative action, extending recognition to gays and lesbians, and the like smacked of
"radical change." No doubt many diversity advocates, particularly those in
academia, would like to think of themselves as "radical change agents," and
their conservative critics have been eager to agree. If we look beneath the
high-blown rhetoric, however, the diversity movement was in many ways a
product of the functionalist conception of culture; at its core lay the unexamined conviction that private and public bureaucracies contain particular
sorts of cultures that can be replaced with certain other sorts of cultures. For
all their bluster, diversity advocates not only shared the corporate managerial class's conventional understanding of bureaucratic power but largely justified themselves on the grounds that bureaucracies would collapse into irrelevance in the age of globalization unless they bought into diversity
schemes. Much of the diversity movement rested on an unthinking complacency with rule by bureaucracy, a complacency that resulted from the conviction that corporate rule and human diversity are rightly, even necessarily,
compatible. Far from being radical, the diversity movement within American
institutions carried with it the most conventional values, and that its advocates did so without much hard reflection on those values suggests just how
deeply enmeshed in American culture they were. Looked at in this way, the
manner in which the diversity movement played itself out in public life
vividly demonstrated just how powerful the homogenizing tendencies of bureaucracy are.

It is an easy thing to make sport of the diversity movement, with its inflated rhetoric and puffed-up self-importance. One of the more curious things
about it was the way it managed to attract a bizarre collection of self-help gu-
rus and New Age spiritualists; as Frederick R. Lynch describes the movement
in his comprehensive book, *The Diversity Machine*, there were more psychol-
ogists than economists among diversity's advocates—no wonder the movement was so strong in California. As Lynch describes the early movement,
roughly in the late 1980s and early 1990s, its pioneers were a mix of affirmative action officers, campus multicultural types, local race and ethnic activists, and human-relations managers. Precious few were drawn from trade
unions or left-wing political parties. For that matter, very little concrete politics found its way into either the rhetoric or planning of the "diversity machine." Aside from local activists, the bulk of the participants were people already ensconced in public or private bureaucracies, and to some extent the
new doctrine helped justify their professional positions. Beyond that, diversity gave the excuse for the expansion of programs, which is how bureaucrats

make their living. Corporate commitments to diversity typically meant workshops and new offices, which had to be staffed by diversity specialists. The University of Michigan's commitment to diversity, Lynch points out, gave rise to more than 100 different programs splattered across campus, from student affairs to curricular issues and faculty hiring.[22]

Much of the energy behind the movement emanated from freelance consultants who made a cottage industry of advising corporate clients. The profit motive apparently was one of those old-white-male values that diversity advocates were not particularly keen to abandon. According to Heather MacDonald, consultant fees in the mid-1990s averaged $2,000 a day and ran as high as $10,000 a day. Elsie Cross, founder and head of Elsie Cross Associates consulting group and owner-publisher of *The Diversity Factor*, a quarterly journal devoted to the subject, insisted on five-year contracts at more than $2.5 million. Essentially inventing on the fly which "cultures" harbor inequality and racism, consultants whipped up "cultural audits" at anywhere from $30,000 to $100,000; Lewis Griggs and Lennie Copeland sold their video series, *Valuing Diversity*, at $4,500 apiece. With little or no empirical evidence to support their methods, they nonetheless sold their workshops and long-term oversight on the grounds that they would end corporate injustices. "It's nice work if you can get it," quipped journalist Andrew Ferguson. "And even better: Almost anyone can get it. There is no certification . . . to qualify as diversity trainers—no tests to study for, no oral exams to fidget through, no dissertations to prove your expertise." Consultants were quick to figure out how to lay claim to an inexhaustible demand. Achieving diversity, they maintained, required a long-term commitment "requiring years of conscientious effort," as Taylor Cox, a prominent consultant and a University of Michigan professor of organizational behavior and human-resource management, has written. Perhaps such extended effort is necessary because racism and white male privilege are so deeply embedded, but it's hard to ignore the possibility that "years of conscientious effort" is a convenient way of keeping the corporate spigot flowing.[23]

The larger point in any case is that the movement would never have entered into the bureaucratic setting unless its main message was compatible with longstanding management practice and general sentiments. Coming as they did out of the human-resources tradition, diversity programs harkened back to Hawthorne, not Martin Luther King, Jr. or the 1964 Civil Rights Act. The purpose of workshops was always attitudinal change and the mental manipulation of employees. Role-playing, stereotyping games, and plain browbeating were common parts of diversity programs; many included some manner of insisting that all whites admit that they are inherently racist. Price

Cobbs calls his version of diversity training "ethno-therapy," a term that he believes emphasizes the importance of ethnic differences but that resonates more with the therapeutic nature of organizational theory.[24] No wonder herding people into workshops proved difficult and diversity officers faced a good deal of resistance on the ground. Such resistance was chalked up to the "white backlash"; fifty years ago it would have been praised as workers' resistance to managerial foolishness. Indeed, coming as it did on the heels of the Total Quality Management fad, the first broad movement to "re-invent the corporation," the diversity campaign must have seemed like just more of the same silliness to many employees.

For this reason, many consultants insisted that workshops be mandatory. Patricia Arredondo, a psychologist by training and founder of a consulting firm, Empowerment Workshops, insisted that voluntary attendance at workshops "sends two messages," both presumably bad: that "individuals can determine the importance or nature of the program" and that "leadership is not supporting the training and the overall initiative." Frederick Lynch reports hearing a rather more blunt argument for mandatory workshops: Otherwise, he heard a consultant admit, "no one would come. We wouldn't get any work."[25]

Ground-level resistance hardly deterred management. By the mid-1990s, according to Lynch, 70 percent of Fortune 50 corporations had formal diversity programs in place, and 16 percent were either developing one or had what he calls "more scattered programs." Why shouldn't they? Pitched as they were, diversity programs appealed to top-level management. For one thing, because employee resistance was so palpable, diversity advocates almost to a person insisted that change really had to be forced from the top down; there was no troubling with the notion of workplace democracy. Clearly recalling Edgar Schein, R. Roosevelt Thomas, a onetime Harvard business professor who took charge of Morehouse College's American Institute for Managing Diversity while also running his own consulting firm, insisted that diversity, like basic corporate culture, begins with the CEO. Corporate leaders, after all, are the originators and repositories of "overall direction, vision, and culture." If they become dedicated to the cause in their firm, then "they are the true pioneers of diversity, and by their actions and attitudes they serve all members of the organization as models of diversity effectiveness."[26]

Though such thinking corresponded to a half-century of American management theory, diversity advocates still needed to secure their appeals with claims that their recommendations were necessary to the bottom line. While participants in the movement quarreled over whether the bottom line deserved equal attention to anti-discrimination demands, the movement as a whole laid claim to two basic staples. First, they claimed that minorities would constitute the bulk of the future workforce and, second, they maintained that success in the global economy depended on understanding cultural diversity. In order to recruit and retain the best workers and to court an increasingly diverse customer base, every firm would have to show that it "valued differences." A firm that created a "culture of difference" could expect its workers to feel more satisfied and appreciated—to be simply better workers. The first of these claims gained credence in the late 1980s when the Hudson Institute's *Workforce 2000* report indicated that most new entrants into the labor force would be nonwhites, females, or immigrants. The report became a founding document of the diversity movement. *Workforce 2000* claimed that only 15 percent of new entrants would be white males, and if this were true, then only a hopelessly backward outfit could afford to ignore diversity programs. Multiculturalism was not a program to redress past wrongs: It was the future. "In today's rapidly changing world," declared Frederick A. Miller, "monoculturalism has become obsolete. . . . Today's trends toward microproduction, product customization, and niche marketing *demand* diversity." There it was, Andrew Ferguson pointed out, the "banal" bottom line that diversity equaled success. Diversity would create "a workforce that is a gorgeous mosaic, synergistic, accommodating, supernaturally productive, a rainbow Utopia uniting employees of every imaginable gender, skin color, religious affiliation, and ethnic origin," all aligned "so we can beat the hell out of the Japs."[27]

Unfortunately for the diversity movement, neither of its two bottom-line claims has been verified. As Frederick Lynch makes clear, *Workforce 2000* grossly overstated the decline of white male employees. Through either sloppy editing or poor statistical reporting, the authors failed to make clear that 15 percent of new net entrants would be white male; they weren't counting white male replacements for other white males. The largest single group of employees as far as anyone could see would still be white males. The ethnic diversity that is developing, meanwhile, does not necessarily provide support for the sort of race-based programs that are the foundation of the diversity movement. New immigrants, in contrast to what diversity advocates assume, might well decide that they want to "assimilate" into "white male culture." Just as important, there is no persuasive evidence that diversity programs make a firm more competitive in the global economy. Indeed, it is among the many strange implications of the dogma that, if this claim were true, then firms based in Germany, Japan, Taiwan, South Korea, Venezuela, Malaysia, or any other "homogenous culture" would be getting walloped in the global game.[28]

Because the diversity movement's staying power cannot be explained by its contribution to business success, it is not unreasonable to think that its influence is at least partly owed to its marshalling of conventional conceptions of culture. Advocates made sense because they fit in. Even the standard platitudes revealed prevailing notions. To say that "the world is growing more interdependent and diverse" or that "cultural diversity will help individuals achieve their full self-worth," both self-contradictory, is to invoke the dual assumptions of cultural rigidity and subjectivity.

Indeed neither Afrocentrists nor campus activists held more tightly to the prevailing cultural misconceptions than did corporate diversity advocates. "Research has shown," Taylor Cox intoned, "that differences of social-cultural identity such as gender, national origin, race and work specialization represent real differences in culture."[29] The favored metaphors indicated the assumption that human groups were defined by irreducible differences. Taylor Cox illustrated his conception of the successful multicultural organization by describing a fruit salad, in which the wider the choice of fruits, the more excellent the choices for inclusion. R. Roosevelt Thomas built his most recent book on a homemade fable about a giraffe and an elephant. The giraffe is the elephant's boss and genuinely wants him to succeed, but the giraffe's house and his workshop were built entirely for giraffes. Quaint and simple illustrations, these metaphors imply that cultures are like different species, permanently divided by fundamental differences that could only be "valued," not blended.[30]

In the universe of diversity consultants, corporate culture boils down to whether the firm in question demands that its workers assimilate or whether it "values difference." The whole point of diversity programs was to warn corporations away from demanding the former. Cox refers to pressures toward conformity or assimilation as the demands of a "diversity-toxic culture" that emanated from white male power and bad management strategy. "This dominant group has set up and maintains the system that discriminates and is the gatekeeper of access to power and equal opportunity for people," declaimed Elsie Cross. "Subordinated groups don't want to be invited into or perpetuate the system, they want to change it so they can be equal partners." Thomas claimed that "members of minority groups—be they groups delineated by race, gender, physical abilities, whatever—are increasingly disinclined to embrace assimilation."[31]

Given the assumption of permanent differences, it was a given among diversity consultants that corporate cultures, heretofore creations of white males, would themselves become multicultural through the inclusion of minorities. So thoroughgoing was the assumption that heredity equaled culture that few bothered to think through just what each ethnic culture might or might not contain and contented themselves with broad stereotypes. White males are rational and competitive, the assumption ran; blacks are creative and innovative; women are caring team players; Asians are hardworking and humble—crude stereotypes with perhaps a kernel of truth. But the distinguishing features of these assumptions in the hands of diversity consultants were that the multicultural organization would celebrate these different virtues and that cultural distinctions were as permanent as skin color and gender. A corporation could either learn to "value" the differences or try to compel assimilation, but the differences would remain and the corporation would be successful or dysfunctional depending on its cultural adjustment to the new order of things.

Even as they display the cultural misapprehensions of their day—and, again, in so doing, reveal how typical their thinking is—the diversity consultants are on to something. Why indeed should anyone—minority or majority group member—want to accept corporate conformity? When Roosevelt Thomas reported widespread disappointment among African-American white-collar employees, he pointed to the basic reality of bureaucratic inclusion.[32] Bureaucratic organizations do not "assimilate" new members into a "traditional culture." They impose standardized regulations and procedures to which members all conform, but that, sooner rather than later, leave people feeling adrift and disconnected or, in a word, alienated.

The advocates of bureaucratic diversity seemed to sense this process of conformity and alienation, but because they were fixated on the notion of culture, they fundamentally misunderstood it. The process of conformity and alienation is inherent in all large-scale organizations, for white males as for everyone else. Convinced that every group has its immutable ways, that culture equals power, and that there is a constant struggle between assimilation and "pluralism," diversity advocates misapprehended typical bureaucratic realities as "white male culture." Frederick Lynch made this point well in an exchange with a diversity consultant who instructed participants in a convention session that "white male culture is very organized, rational, and mechanistic." White males, according to this advocate, "favor hierarchy, functional efficiency, and carefully defined roles." Lynch countered that these sounded more like "the traits of capitalism and bureaucracy." "Diversity consultants," Lynch concluded, "constantly confused white male culture with capitalism and bureaucracy and just plain formal organization."[33] Working on the assumption that the bulwarks of Western culture—a belief in equal treatment under universal rule, a love of competition, a devotion to "standards"—were both of and for white men, diversity advocates never bothered to consider that contemporary bureaucracies never have been particularly good environments for any of these. The man in the gray flannel suit or William Whyte's "organization man" were never known for their competitiveness. They sought a middling level of bureaucratic status so that they could avoid sticking their necks out. Corporate rules and regulations were things to hide behind, not vehicles to ride to the top. And public bureaucracies have always been inestimably worse. Who in their right mind could look at the federal government and see it as a bastion of the drive for competitive excellence?

If white males appear to thrive better in such a depressing environment, it is less because the rules were crafted out of "their culture" than because theirs has been a much longer period of corporate indoctrination. White males make up that part of the workforce that has adapted to the homogenized environment and has long ceased to harbor much personal uneasiness over wasting their lives in bureaucratic settings. The complacency with such a worklife portends badly for the diversity advocates. The more the demographics they were so fond of pointing to lead to the inclusion of African Americans, women, and immigrants into the bureaucratic workforce, the more complacent they will all become. Bureaucracy, not diversity, wins out in the end. It always does.

Conglomerated Media and the Fiction of Diversity

One of Elton Mayo's most audacious claims in the 1930s was that workers are burdened with concerns that don't have much to do with the class struggle or control over the means of production. It was this claim that inspired the employee interview and that still rests at the core of human relations. Whereas Mayo's workers were concerned about everyday difficulties of life—the mortgage, the wife's varicose veins—the cultural managers of corporate America today think that the inefficient worker is burdened by racism, sexism, ageism, heterosexism, right-handism, blue-eyeism, and beautyism. It isn't surprising that someone with this weighty list of burdens would be a poor worker.

Yet none of the diversity managers speak much about the actual work performance of these burdened souls. If the human-relations consultants have changed the list of emotional troubles, they still share with Mayo a fundamental assumption that work itself doesn't matter much. None of the theorists seem to care about how work is done or what is produced. Reading through the diversity tracts leads one to wonder how American corporations can make any money at all. None of them make anything. There's no work actually being done. Since they have figured out how to produce nothing and get paid for it, the consultants might be forgiven for thinking that every business runs that way. But at some point, somebody has to create a product.

This removal of work from work fosters the illusion that diversity can be maintained within bureaucratic organizations. With the important ingredient of local skills simply wiped away from considerations of a group's integrity, diversity advocates can make the case that heredity equals culture and that the incorporation of ethnically distinct people into the corporate world does not threaten cultural diversity. Yet African Americans do not carry African craft skills into their work at IBM. East Asians might work diligently for Apple, but the products that arise from that labor have no roots in any Asian traditions. Considering the actual processes of labor would undermine the entire diversity dogma; there is only one way to screw in a lug nut on the assembly line.

What goes for IBM or General Motors goes for the so-called apparatus of cultural production, less theoretically known as the entertainment industries. Even as diversity became all the rage in the 1990s, every part of the apparatus of cultural production witnessed mergers and consolidations. Arguably beginning with Rupert Murdoch's acquisition of Twentieth Century Fox in 1984, large multinationals steadily bought up the culture industries. The following year, General Electric gobbled up NBC television (and began, among other things, to dictate the nature of the network's news reporting); in 1988, Sony matched its electronic competitor first by buying CBS and then Columbia and TriStar Pictures. Time Inc. took control of Ted Turner's empire in 1989 and entered the television, film, and music business in one fell swoop. In part because of the deregulatory craze raging in Washington, the pace of the trend picked up in the mid-1990s, with Disney buying ABC, thereby putting each of the three main television networks in the hands of conglomerates. And the period was capped fittingly by the merger of AOL Time Warner in January 2000, which at $106 billion was the largest merger deal in American history.[34]

Many observers decried these developments, and concerns over media monopolies reanimated the anti-trust division of the Justice Department for a brief time. But by the end of the decade, anti-trust actions failed to stop a single large deal, and only the Microsoft case remained unresolved. Anti-trust prosecution was deflected with the argument that the multinationals buying up media outlets were conglomerates that were only adding media and entertainment to the long list of other products that they made, and in contrast to Microsoft their empires were not contained in a single industry. This situation has been long coming, and it is neither new nor surprising; it is exactly the condition that the mass-culture critics of mid-century predicted. When Dwight MacDonald defined mass culture as that cultural material mass produced as though it were mere chewing gum, surely he had in mind a situation in which practically everything in the realm of arts, ideas, and entertainment was produced within the boundaries of the marketplace with profit the main end. It is simply beyond question that MacDonald was right here. When huge corporations buy up newspapers or book publishers, their aim is to make as much money as possible, not to foster diversity in art or ideas. The famed "marketplace of ideas," an offensive metaphor in any case, ultimately has worked just like any other marketplace: The rich get richer, and power is concentrated in a dwindling number of hands.

Corporate apologists argue that precisely because no single producer can control all of a given industry, diversity and creativity will thrive. In truth, however, the inability to control all of a single industry obscures the spread of conglomerate influence in other areas. Take the movie industry, for example. During the 1990s, Disney and Warner Bros. controlled somewhere between 35 and 40 percent of the market between them, hardly the 90 percent market control that John D. Rockefeller's Standard Oil enjoyed in its heyday. But with far-flung enterprises, they can blend the purposes of various appendages. As Thomas Schatz has observed, conglomerate control of Hollywood created the drive for megahits, which could be turned to numerous spin-off products. "The ideal movie today," he writes, "is not only a box-office smash but a two-hour promotion for a multimedia product line. . . . The New Hollywood has been driven (and shaped) by multipurpose entertainment machines which breed movie sequels and TV series, music videos and sound track albums, video games and theme park rides, graphic novels and comic books, and an endless array of licensed tie-ins and brand-name consumer products."[35] To the extent that they spew their goods outward, the conglomerates actually have a more debilitating effect on culture than even MacDonald envisioned, even though they are not technically monopolies.

Still, there is an important difference between most cultural production and the typical mass-production industry. Individuals cannot make their own steel girders; the start-up costs for steel mills or car factories are prohibitively steep. By contrast, books, music, and, to a lesser degree, films, are generated primarily by individuals who have at least some degree of independence. At a basic level, the necessarily individualistic genesis of cultural work ensures variety. Much great art continues to emerge, but it does so because of the resilience of talent and taste, not by any virtue in the system.

A close look at the two most individualistic activities, writing and music, shows that the conglomerates have asserted control where they can. Dependent on quirky individuals for the original creation of what they produce, conglomerates compensate by controlling all other aspects of the consumption pipeline.

Books, for instance, have become big business. In 1996, reports Mark Crispin Miller in an essay so admirable that it is worth summarizing at length, American booksellers enjoyed a record year with over $20 billion in sales. Clearly the technophiles who announced that print was dead in the early 1990s did not take account of the possibility that the book-publishing industry could make use of the same business tactics that worked everywhere else. During the decade, a wave of mergers and acquisitions ended with eight media conglomerates controlling the lion's share of the book market, among them Time Warner, Murdoch's New Corporation, Viacom, and the German firm Bertelsmann.

Conglomeration thus came to a business that was always better understood as a trade than an industry. At the beginning of the twentieth century, independent publishers flourished, and along with them came a generation and more of interesting fiction and a variety of powerful political ideas. Men such as the crusty Adolph Knopf, Jr., made their own decisions about what to publish, usually on hunches that mixed their tastes with a practical sense of what might sell well enough to do a bit better than break even. The trade was famously populated by men as difficult as the writers who wrote for them, stuffy white males I guess we'd consider them today, but the sort of characters who prized their independence of action more than the elusive bottom line. With the rise of the conglomerates, men such as Knopf are as extinct as dinosaurs. It is impossible to imagine the publishing executive of the 1990s lending money to a hard-drinking author or letting another sleep on the office sofa, as mid-century editors often did for the writers they sought to cultivate. In fact, as Miller deftly shows, they don't much care about books.[36]

Common sense, if not decent taste, would raise the suspicion that the shift from publishers who loved books to those whose first loyalty is to the bottom line would alter what was published, and Miller demonstrates how predictably the lists of once-proud houses degenerated into gossip tales, celebrity worship, cookbooks, and worse. Little, Brown, which began in the antebellum period with Louisa May Alcott and Emily Dickinson, promoted Balzac and Victor Hugo at the turn of the century and Evelyn Waugh and C. S. Forester later; in the 1990s, after Time Warner acquired the firm, the list came to include Joan Lunden's *Healthy Cooking*, biographies of Barbra Streisand and Kurt Cobain, and O. J. Simpson's *I Want to Tell You*. Under founder Ian Ballantine, Bantam published *The Great Gatsby* and *The Grapes of Wrath*; acquired by Bertelsmann, it published *Acupressure for Lovers* and a children's list that included *The Legend of Bigfart* and *Dog Doo Afternoon*.

Random House, whose "accidental father" Horace Liveright handled Faulkner, Hemingway, Dorothy Parker, and Lewis Mumford, and later under Bennett Cerf made the best writing easily available through The Modern Library, came under the control of S. I. Newhouse, the richest man no one knows. Miller observes the painfully predictable: "Where Liveright courted T. S. Eliot to get *The Waste Land* . . . and where Cerf went to Paris to ask James Joyce for *Ulysses*, . . . S. I. Newhouse made his bones as publisher by getting Donald Trump to do *The Art of the Deal*."[37]

Miller acknowledges that there was no golden age of publishing. The old guard was often stingy and concerned with making money. They published their fair share of trash. Moreover, as I've suggested, great writing still manages to find the light of day. But the great difference—the crucial distinction, Miller rightly insists—between the independents of the past and the conglomerates of today is that the old guard "did the high-yield trash in order to be able to afford the gems they loved . . . ; whereas today crap is not a means but . . . the end." To this I might add that the independents, committed at once to both profit and quality, executed strategies to make great work cheap and available. The old publishers proved that the masses weren't stupid by selling important books. As Ándre Schiffrin notes in his heartfelt autobiographical account of the recent industry, Henry George's *Progress and Poverty*, hardly a light read, sold two million copies in the late nineteenth century. The purpose of great lists such as Pocket Books or Penguin was to bring classics into the reach of people of humble means. Even as late as the 1950s and 1960s, Schiffrin insists, he and his peers were "animated by the belief that ordinary people could read challenging, daring work and ought to be able to find it in every drugstore."[38] The conglomerates, by contrast, throw money into promoting trash, and where they stoop to publish serious work, they neither promote it nor keep it in print unless it more than pays its own way. Even an academic book published with a commercial house has to sell several thousand copies a year to stay in print. So perhaps things were far from perfect in the old days. But no reasonable person can dispute, Miller concludes, that "books have gotten worse." "Try to find, in all the major houses' prior lists, any memoir as self-serving as *I Want to Tell You* . . . and try to find, on any [prior] lists, a book, for children, about boogers, farts, or puking."[39]

Just as the independent publisher was becoming an artifact—much as independent groceries and hardware stores were being overrun—so too the survival of the independent bookstore, which might hang by the thread of its owner's peculiar tastes, was threatened with the emergence of Barnes & Noble and Borders. The so-called superstores exploded in mid-decade when the competition between the two large chains began to heat up. The fate of independent stores fell quickly into the balance; membership in the association of independents, the American Booksellers Association, fell from better than 5,000 in 1991 to 4,000 in 1998 and 3,000 in 1999, a sign of the quick decline after mid-decade. Over the same period, market share for independents fell from roughly one-third of all book sales to under 20 percent by 1998. Venerable old local institutions either went out of business or, like the Yale Co-op, were bought up by one of the chains. The situation became grave enough by the late 1990s that members of the ABA sued both the publishers and the chains, charging that the publishers were giving the chains favorable treatment that permitted deep discounts.[40]

The leading lights of the retail "revolution" were not much different from the types who laid siege to publishing. Barnes & Noble's chief, Leonard Riggio, has admitted that books mean very little to him other than as commodities. He happened to land a job at the NYU bookstore when he was a student there in the early 1960s. "If I got a job at a hardware store," Riggio has said, "I would have been Home Depot today." Pulling himself up from a modest clerk, Riggio launched his empire by opening a store to compete with the NYU operation in 1965. Six years later he bought the old downtown Barnes & Noble and lured customers with deep discounts on bestsellers and hardcovers. Then, in 1986, he threw himself into mass marketing with the purchase of B. Dalton, one of the two mall chains. With that chain and another Texas-based chain as his base, he applied to the bookstore the same retail concept that was working in everything else: Build big, build aggressively, bury the competition. By the end of the decade, Riggio had over 1,000 stores that were doing nearly $3 billion in annual sales.[41]

There are two lines of thought that conceivably might justify the superstores. The first might be the John D. Rockefeller argument: Who cares? The market is the market, business is business, and if the little outfit fails, so be it. Social Darwinism being rather out of fashion these days, the defenders of the superstores have found comfortable refuge in cultural dogma. The chains, they say, provide far more choice for the book consumer. If the "cultural elite" that made its living by announcing "doom and gloom" would look fairly, they would see that the supers carry far more titles than almost any independent. Measuring diversity and choice in sheer numbers because "more is, quite simply, better," Brooke Allen reassured the "real reader" that the "typical superstore carries about 150,000 titles . . . whereas the typical independent has room for fewer than 20,000." Barnes & Noble, she claims, orders the vast majority of adult trade titles published in any given year. Nor is this quantity mere fluff. Her neighborhood superstore was running shelving space at "189 feet of biography, 196 feet of philosophy, 92 feet of military history, 168 feet of poetry, and 165 feet of books and materials on foreign-language instruction, in Albanian, Amharic, Bengali, Urdu, Welsh, and Yoruba, among others." Behind these sorts of unimpeachable data, Riggio was presumably justified when he took umbrage at the ABA's charges that the superstores threatened "the marketplace and diversity of ideas." The rhetoric of diversity runs hand in hand with claims that the superstores promote grassroots democracy. Riggio set up his outlets with coffee shops (usually Starbucks, incidentally) and overstuffed chairs to serve as "modern village greens," in the words of Business Week reporter Jeanne Dugan, a pretense that allowed him to boast that "the [old] bookstore business was an elitist, stand-offish institution. . . . [But] I liberated it from that." Popular historian David McCullough chimed in by hailing the superstore as having created "the most democratic forum, the most democratic marketplace of ideas imaginable. . . . No civilization has had anything like what we have now."[42] Thus, against obvious evidence of vulgarity, the "vandals of the trade" raise all the standard objections to snobbery and elitism, objections adopted from the academics whose defense of "popular culture" they hide behind even as they snicker.

It is certainly a strange notion of democracy that equates both cultural health and local control with the opportunity to buy books from an increasingly centralized, anti-democratic system of production. It is obscene to equate "the village green," the essence of which was collective ownership, with conglomerate domination. But so long as choice is abundant, then it is perfectly acceptable to the chains' defenders that the entire process of book-making, from publishing through wholesale to retail, is centralized. Indeed, the superstores use only small staffs of buyers to stock all that shelf space; Barnes & Noble, for instance, has a staff of thirty-five buyers for its entire fleet of stores.[43] It is not self-evident why that arrangement is not "elitist." The answer, presumably, is that these buyers are acutely attentive to consumer whims because those desires and interests are constantly exposed in buying surveys and purchasing trends. If the reading public gets Beavis and Butthead: This Book Sucks, it is only because that is what the public demands. Perhaps we should just learn to think of the book as subversive, because it teaches adolescent boys to cast off repressive patriarchal values of self-control, manners, and obligation.

The current state of recorded music offers another way of helping us keep our eyes on how things are produced and sold so that we might temper the impression of cultural diversity. In many ways, music is the exception that proves the rule. It is inconceivable that the vast world of music would become homogenized into one big "easy-listening genre." Such is the stuff of night-mares, as in Norman Spinrad's novel *Little Heroes*, where the music industry is dominated by the MUZIK corporation. In Spinrad's worst dreams, his music behemoth produces half of the music sold, owns a chain of retail super-stores, runs a collection of music clubs, and operates a 24-hour-a-day TV music station. With such vast operations, MUZIK has to have the most employees in the music business, but none of them are musicians. To gener-ate its product, the corporation uses "a black box full of wizardware." Its stars are "Artificial Personalities," APs in corporate parlance, whose personas are creations of the advertising team. When the heroine levels a sarcastic remark about this phony nonmusic, the CEO responds: "Aw, come on, Glorianna, you *know* that APs have to be the future of the industry. . . . It's too cost-effective not to be inevitable."[44]

Sprinrad's novel is scary because so much of it rings true, but music still has one great protection against thorough corporate capture. It is easy to produce. That is to say, anyone can pick up an instrument and create music. With start-up costs as low as they are, music is one activity that really can be as diverse as the number of people picking up their instruments. And because of this grassroots potential, there will always be genres of music produced close to liv-ing communities, which then can seize and hold against inroads from outside. Corporate producers, always on the prowl for new product, are likely to hijack those forms that develop large followings in native lands—take reggae, for example—and run them dry. Because folk forms tend to be more delicate than refined forms, they don't have much staying power once captured. But be-cause of the grassroots nature of music, there will probably always be new folk forms, some of which manage to resist mass-produced perversion. Those gen-res that encourage the greatest sophistication and refinement, meanwhile, are the most resistant to corruption, for the clear reason that artistic excellence cannot be mass produced. This is the lesson that jazz teaches.

But make no mistake: The music industry has seen a thoroughgoing con-glomeration from top to bottom. By the end of the 1990s, SONY, Time Warner, Bertlesmann, Disney, and Seagram's soaked up independent labels and even corporates in the exact same way they were raiding publishing. Sea-gram's 1995 purchase of Universal brought such labels as Motown, Geffen, and Mercury into its fold, and it moved from there to buy PolyGram and A&M records at the end of the decade. AOL Time Warner responded with the purchase of EMI, giving it an estimated 30 percent of the global record producing industry. Together, these conglomerates—largely the same group, mind you, that controls publishing—came to dominate the vast majority of recorded music throughout the world.[45] As with books, meanwhile, recorded music is increasingly sold through chain retailers. Virgin Records was on its way to becoming to music what Barnes & Noble was to books, but Wal-Mart is actually one of the largest music retailers in the world.

For all its clear similarities with publishing, the music industry carried its own disturbing twist when the majority of radio stations fell into the hands of conglomerates. Radio broadcasting could not have followed the trend toward conglomeration so long as the 1934 Communications Act held, with its limitations on the number of radio stations that any one owner could control and prohibitions against cross-ownerships of radio, cable, and broadcast TV stations. In the face of a strenuous lobbying effort by media industries, those limitations were dropped under the 1996 Telecommunications Act. Much was said about the antiquated quality of the 1934 act, which was passed before anyone had televisions, much less personal computers and cell phones. The crucial argument for the overhaul of broadcasting was that technological advances, especially digital communications, rendered the limitations against cross-ownership irrational; it was now possible, argued lobbyists for change, for companies to provide all manner of communications—television, Internet, telephone—to residential customers over the cable line, if only those obsolete restrictions were lifted. Put another way, the 1934 act effectively barred media conglomeration and had to go.

It seems clear that the freedom of media corporations to extend conglomerate control to broadcasting was the crux of the issue. The 1934 act had been passed in a political climate in which suspicions of big business ran very deep indeed, and the act contained both of the tried-and-true methods by which early-century liberals strained to control capital. On the one hand, the various limitations on ownership were designed to prevent any one corporation or individual from dominating the airwaves; on the other, the act recognized that the broadcast spectrum was a public resource, a real modern village commons, and that while private companies would necessarily use the resource, they had an inherent responsibility to the public good. In light of the millions of dollars media companies spent lobbying for the 1996 bill—more than $2 million to members of Congress in the first half of 1995 alone, according to one estimate—it appears that these old political notions, rather than any antiquated technological sensibility, were the "archaic" elements media boosters wanted to trash. Consequently, the 1996 Telecommunications Act both greatly expanded the number of stations a single owner might obtain and simply gave away the digitizing broadcast spectrum to private companies. It was as if the government decided to let private companies control on-off highway ramps. Conservative columnist William Safire called the act a "ripoff . . . on a scale vaster than dreamed of by yesterday's robber barons. It's as if each American family is to be taxed $1,000 to enrich the stockholders of Disney, GE and Westinghouse."[46] In part, corporate lobbyists executed this massive rip-off by marshalling those two now-dominant dogmas, both of which are written into the letter of the law: that the marketplace produces the widest possible array of consumer choices and that it guarantees the widest possible diversity.[47]

As long as they have access to radio stations that broadcast the ads—otherwise known as songs—for "their" music, Americans show no marked concern that their once-public broadcast spectrum now is no more democratic than that of the People's Republic of China. The new Maoist in the industry is Clear Channel Communications, which was a relatively puny operation as late as 1991 with a mere eighteen radio and six television stations; ten years later, the company boasted an empire of 1,202 radio stations, nineteen television stations, and 135 live-entertainment venues and was generating $3.5 billion in annual revenue.[48] The company had expanded, meanwhile, into international markets, including Europe and Brazil, and branched out into concert promotion, which presumably gives it "synergy" with its radio business. Clearly the dominant player in radio, Clear Channel rode the wave of consolidation that by 2001 left three companies with 60 percent of the stations in the top 100 American markets.[49]

Clear Channel's overnight rise to dominance was equaled only by the speed with which the company proved its obnoxiousness. It was as if its chiefs, particularly CEO Randy Michaels, sought to imitate the worst of the old railroad barons simply because they could. Some of the so-called shock jocks and other "personalities" the company hired came under scrutiny for animal cruelty: One dropped chickens from balconies and another hosted a party in which a wild boar was castrated, killed, and roasted, its testicles served up in an eating contest. Unhappy with how much the ratings company Arbitron charged for its survey data, Clear Channel threatened not only to stop doing business with the company but to finance competitors as well. To elude what few restrictions the 1996 act kept on the number of stations a single entity could own, Clear Channel reportedly began to set up front companies to hide its control, apparently in hopes that the FCC will sooner or later remove even the most modest restrictions.[50]

Uglier than most, Clear Channel nonetheless has behaved as most of the other media conglomerates have. Among the many apparently valuable benefits of consolidation has been the rationalization of labor. Formats were quickly standardized so that disc jockeys play what they are told and only that. The mechanization of radio permitted Clear Channel to run many of its stations by computer at night with only a skeleton staff. According to Eric

Boehlert, Clear Channel has pioneered in "the implementation of centralized, bureaucratic control over stations," in which all programming is done at the regional level and little attention, if any, is conceded to local color, much less to the whimsy of disc jockeys. Boehlert writes: "Clear Channel has eliminated hundreds, if not thousands, of DJ positions . . . by simply having one company jock send out his or her show to dozens of sister stations." Because this rationalization is designed to cut labor costs, it can hardly be surprising that the disc jockeys "often receive little or no extra money for filling on-air vacancies in dozens of extra markets." As usual, the standardization of labor created a standardized product; the company's talk radio stations tended to play Dr. Laura and Rush Limbaugh, with the same dash of allegedly local colorful personalities in the mix. Even the same news jingles and lead-ups to weather and sports could be heard from Miami to Anchorage.[51]

One could still argue, along with the cultural populists, that standardization is superficial and that, in fact, consolidation will create greater diversity in programming. In this case, diversity is invoked as a virtue of centralized programming. Business-oriented supporters of consolidation, for example, have argued that Clear Channel has increased diversity in those markets where it has acquired numerous stations by making more "formats" available. In Little Rock, contends Forbes reporter Dorothy Pomerantz, more formats became available; in Atlantic City, where the twenty-four stations are now held by eight owners instead of fifteen as before the 1996 act, formats have increased from ten to fourteen. In Syracuse, where Clear Channel owns twelve stations, it runs ten formats and even "rescued a black urban station that otherwise would have failed on its own."[52]

Clear Channel's critics don't see things quite in this light. In late May 2003, a coalition of groups, including grassroots musicians' organizations and recording-industry representatives, presented a petition to Congress that included a list of grievances against the consolidation of broadcasting. While Clear Channel was not singled out, it was clearly the object of the petition, which charged that radio broadcasting had grown anti-competitive and anti-consumer. The industry had become indifferent to local diversity and developed harmful vertical integration in which concert promotion and radio had resulted in increased prices and unfair competition. Most important, the old—and outlawed—practice of "payola" was back and thriving. In this practice, record companies pay handsome wages to promoters—known as "indies," because they are technically freelancers, or "independent" promoters—to place their products with radio stations. The indies decide which tunes and performers to push; they then pay radio stations to play the chosen few and in return get paid from the record companies. Like the handful of book buyers for Barnes & Noble, the indies thus become the dictators of public taste, again giving the lie to the notion that the consumer dictates the product. This practice has existed since the advent of rock-and-roll radio, but with the rise of Clear Channel, industry observers say the problem has gotten worse. When Clear Channel inked an agreement with TriState promotions, which gave that company sole promotion rights to its stations, it created powerful clout for TriState to jack up rates to record companies. Record companies thus have found common cause with independently minded musicians with whom they have long wrestled over contracts and control.[53]

It remains an open question what will happen to such agitation. Opponents of broadcasting consolidation have their work cut out for them in persuading the FCC to slow or limit the trend. FCC chairman Michael K. Powell is a devotee of market logic and is most likely to let competition—or the lack of it—set the rules. Powell, an African American, should favor diversity in the broadcasting industries if multiculturalist logic were to prevail, and under his leadership the FCC has indeed been attentive to the cause. The rub, however, is that Powell reportedly has embraced the consumer model of diversity. "The commission used to assume diversity would be served by a greater number of small owners," a Washington lawyer familiar with FCC policy told reporter Dorothy Pomerantz. "Now they suggest the opposite—when you have a lot of small companies competing for a mass audience, everyone runs programming aimed at mass appeal. When you have one party that has lots of stations, it can try niches or more experimental programming."[54] There is a certain common sense to this view. If Clear Channel owned everything, it would only be competing with itself if it played the same song at the same time everywhere.

Yet at the point where this defense of Clear Channel begins to make sense, we ought to acknowledge that something is dreadfully wrong with the whole conception of music, art, and culture at work here and that it is high time for some hard rethinking. In truth, both Clear Channel and its anti-consolidation opponents share the same basic notion of music: that music is a business, that its creation means very little unless it is turned into a commodity for sale, and that it gains legitimacy only by virtue of being sold through the various vehicles of cultural production. It is easy to sympathize with the grassroots musicians waging war with the Sonys and the Clear Channels, but they would only do so if they were seeking a piece of the marketplace pie for themselves. The idea that music, as an expression of community cohesion and, therefore, of enduring life, should be woven organically through daily activities such as work and play, that it is at its most noble when embedded in essential rituals, especially religious ones—the idea, in short, that music is a cultural artifact in contrast to a commodity—finds precious little expression in either the defense of or opposition to radio consolidation. Any distinction between the arguments that consumer choice is better met by more or fewer performers is mere hair-splitting. Once the consumer model of culture comes to prevail, then so does the broader framework of marketplace assumptions, and once music is moved into that arena, any real control over the character of the art form is fatally compromised. Even if Clear Channel were dismantled and the 1934 ownership restrictions reconstituted, we would still be left with the sort of general standardization that has accompanied the creation of the "music industry."

Niche Marketing and the Illusion of Diversity

It is still worth asking how, at the very moment when multinational conglomerates came to dominate cultural production, Americans convinced themselves that they were living amid splendiferous cultural diversity. The most obvious answer is that those cultural conglomerates obscured their accumulated power by catering to every consumer whim—let's not call it taste—that held the potential to constitute a profitable market. They called this niche marketing.

The strategy of niche marketing is perfectly straightforward as a business proposition. It represents the effort of mass producers to turn every living soul into a consumer. Its basic tactic is to advertise products with appeals to very general collective self-images more or less rooted in specific group experiences—images, it should be said, that often barely rise above mere stereotypes. Just as any commodity can be mass produced, so any group can be turned into a niche. As with all elements of culture, when a group's collective self-image becomes the stuff of the advertiser, it no longer has control over that image and in some fundamental sense ceases even to be a group of people defined by a culture, properly understood. Instead, they become a market.

Niche marketing came to inform, if not dictate, almost all retail advertising during the 1990s, but as Joseph Turow has ably demonstrated, it has a long history that correlates directly with the debate over mass culture. Even as radio was creating the first phase of mass culture in the 1930s, Turow points out, mass producers, particularly Alfred P. Sloan of General Motors, were already crafting marketing tactics designed to convince consumers that they were unique individuals who might distinguish themselves from the masses by purchasing, say, a white car over the old dingy black of the Ford Model T. The first real niche market, however, emerged when advertisers came to appreciate just what a huge market the baby boom created; they responded as early as the 1950s and 1960s to pitch products directly to children in disregard of their parents. By the 1980s, American advertisers no longer viewed the family as a unit, Turow argues, and instead aimed at family members as discrete individuals essentially estranged from one another. Once the family was disassembled, it was merely another step to begin drawing distinctions between potential consumers of all sorts. Baby boomers were distinguished by income, occupation, and residential location; those born before 1957 were separated from those born afterward.[55]

Then, beginning in the 1970s, advertisers responded to the upsurge of ethnic and racial claims by leveling aim at all the main identity groups, especially African Americans, Hispanics, and gays. "Ethnically correct" toys appeared, including everything from black action figures to the "differentially-abled Barbie"; "Sensual Classics," recordings of orchestral music aimed at gays; and newspapers published in Spanish were among the innumerable products thus developed. Turow points out that ad agencies sold their services by claiming to have acquired special insights into the collective minds and preferences of these groups, and as they did so, the agencies tended to put themselves in niches. Doing so, Turow writes, allowed the niche agencies to claim "the right to shape the words and pictures that national marketers used to speak to and about their constituencies." That claim, in turn, rested on invoking that hallowed dogma, cultural diversity. "The truth is," insisted a prominent African-American ad executive, "that the black community marches to different drummers. . . . It fundamentally is moving from a position that is different from the white consumer. So, for example—and our clients love this—black people still tend to want to buy the more expensive products. . . . You buy your car not because it may be the best product in the world but it's what your neighbor, your peer, feels about the product. The purchase for us is more important than it is to the general market customer."[56] At issue in the emergence of niche appeals was nothing less than "control over images," and, Turow implies, the ad agencies won.

In a sense, advertisers came to serve the same purpose in general as chain-store book buyers and indie record promoters serve in their respective industries. They are the dictators not so much of choice but of the collective images of a society that is determined to understand itself as rich in human differences, and their practices have been defended on the same grounds that the champions of cultural conglomeration have staked out. Hence Marilyn Halter, in a study that demonstrates how relentlessly advertisers have consciously exploited racial and ethnic differences over the last generation, reckons the drive toward niche appeal as merely a response to consumers who "more and more . . . are expressing culturally distinctive desires, needs, and wants in their shopping habits." As she reads it, advertisers and consumers are working in mutually advantageous harmony; consumers want to express their "culturally distinct desires," and advertisers are happy to oblige. Even as she concedes that "consumer products and services are replacing traditional neighborhood and community affiliations as the connective tissue of post-modern life," she still holds to the dogma that consumers are able to sustain and reclaim ethnic identities through their buying choices. If we could just wean ourselves from that tired old notion that how things are made actually matters, she suggests, we could see that "the market serves to foster greater awareness of ethnic identity, offers immediate possibilities for cultural participation, and can even act as an agent of change in that process. . . . Commercialism may indeed dissipate tradition, community, and meaning, but it can also enhance and reinforce such identification."[57]

Culture thus reduces to the corporate flattery of consumer whims. And even if there is any worthwhile substance at all to this dogma, the best that can be said about niche marketing is that it relegates ethnicity to just another category and belittles once-organic identities to the point where they constitute mostly just more frames of consumer choice. They become nothing more substantive than any of the other "lifestyle groups" that marketers identify; to be African American is no more important than to be a pet owner. Maybe this is a good thing; maybe it is indicative of a genuine declining significance of race. But it is not a sign of cultural diversity. Far from it. If indeed mass consumption "dissipates tradition, community, and meaning," there is very little left of a decent human existence. Niche marketing represents the opposite of an institutionalized respect for human differences. Instead it marks the incorporation of once-marginalized groups into the system of mass consumption. In "dissipating tradition, community, and meaning," it marks the insidious invasion and conquest of cultural refuges, places where it was possible for groups to sustain unique folkways outside the structures of mainstream life.

Notes

1. Wal-Mart adds about 8.5 million square feet of retail space annually, which, according to analysts for independent grocers, will result in an estimated 300 store closings annually. Wal-Mart's entry into the grocery business poses such a threat to already embattled independents that the National Grocers Association, the trade group for independents, commissioned a 2002 study on "Wal-Mart customer loyalty" in order to help its members adopt strategies for fending off the competition. See

Daniel Rogers, "With Wal-Mart, Look, Don't Listen," *Supermarket Business*, January 15, 2001.

2. Alvin and Heidi Toffler, *Creating a New Civilization: The Politics of the Third Wave* (Atlanta, 1995), 43.

3. David Hume, "Of the Standard of Taste," in *The Philosophy of David Hume*, ed. V. C. Chappell (New York, 1963), 485–87.

4. Ibid., 498, 486.

5. Ibid., 487, 489.

6. Ibid., 490.

7. Miriam R. Levin, *Republican Art and Ideology in Late Nineteenth-Century France* (Ann Arbor, 1986). William Morris, *On Art and Socialism: Essays and Lectures*, ed. Holbrook Jackson (London, 1947); Lucy Crane, *Art and the Formation of Taste* (London, 1882), 45, 21, 27, 37.

8. Jane Addams, *Twenty Years at Hull-House* (New York, 1981), 177–78.

9. Aihwa Ong, *Spirits of Resistance and Capitalist Discipline: Factory Women in Malaysia* (Albany, N.Y., 1987).

10. Anita Chan, "Labor Standards and Human Rights: The Case of Chinese Workers Under Market Socialism," *Human Rights Quarterly* 20, no. 4 (1998): 886–904; Michael C. Seeborg, Zhenhu Jin, and Yiping Zhu, "The New Rural-to-Urban Labor Mobility in China," *Journal of Socioeconomics* 29, no. 1 (2000): 39–56.

11. Editorial, "Silicon Valley Sweatshops: High-Tech's Dirty Little Secret," *Nation* 256 (April 19, 1993): 517–18.

12. See Andrei S. Markovits and Alexander Otto, "German Labor and Europe '92," *Comparative Politics* 24, no. 2 (January 1992): 163–80. For a quite different and much more sanguine view, see Alan B. Krueger, "From Bismarck to Maastricht: The March to European Union and the Labor Compact," *Labour Economics* 7, no. 2 (March 2000): 117–34.

13. Elton Mayo, *The Social Problems of an Industrial Civilization* (Boston, 1945), 75.

14. Burleigh B. Gardner, "The Anthropologist in Business and Industry," *Anthropological Quarterly* 50 (July 1977): 172.

15. Michael Maccoby, "The Corporation as Part-Culture," in *Anthropological Perspectives on Organizational Culture*, ed. Tomoko Hamada and Willis E. Sibley (Lanham, Md., 1994), 268.

16. Terrence E. Deal and Allen A. Kennedy, *Corporate Cultures: The Rites and Rituals of Corporate Life* (Reading, Mass., 1982), 107–108; Edgar Schein, *Organizational Culture and Leadership* (San Francisco, 1985); Edgar Schein, "What Is Culture," in Peter J. Frost et al. eds., *Reframing Organizational Culture* (Newbury Park, Calif., 1991), 243–53.

17. Deal and Kennedy, *Corporate Cultures*, 22, 37.

18. Thomas J. Peters and Robert H. Waterman, Jr., *In Search of Excellence: Lessons from America's Best-Run Companies* (New York, 1982), xx, xxi–xxii. In a very interesting study that set out to test the "cultural hypothesis" concerning Japan's alleged superiority in workplace values, James R. Lincoln and Arne L. Kalleberg found that

neither general culture nor workplace values seemed to have much direct effect on corporate performance. What did, they concluded, was the extent of corporate welfare—the commitment of a given company, whether Japanese or American, to the long-term employment and security of its workers. *Culture, Control, and Commitment: A Study of Work Organization and Work Attitudes in the United States and Japan* (New York, 1990).

19. Deal and Kennedy, *Corporate Cultures*, 37, 143; Lawrence M. Miller, *American Spirit: Visions of a New Corporate Culture* (New York, 1984), 25–26.

20. Miller, *American Spirit*, 25–26; Philip Sadler, *Managerial Leadership in the Post-Industrial Society* (Aldershot, England, 1988), 125; Peters and Waterman, *In Search of Excellence*, 271–73, 310–11, 318; Peter Anthony, *Managing Culture* (Buckingham, Eng., 1994), 20. On this issue see also Mats Alvesson and Per Olof Berg, *Corporate Culture and Organizational Symbolism* (Berlin, 1992), 28–30.

21. Arky Ciancutti and Thomas L. Steding, *Built on Trust: Gaining Competitive Advantage in Any Organization* (Chicago, 2001), 65; Thierry C. Pauchant and Ian I. Mitroff, *Transforming the Crisis-Prone Organization: Preventing Individual, Organizational, and Environmental Tragedies* (San Francisco, 1992), 81–82, 171–73; James R. Fisher, Jr., *Six Silent Killers: Management's Greatest Challenge* (Boca Raton, Fla., 1998), 7, 154, 202–10; Jim Harris and Joan Brannick, *Finding and Keeping Great Employees* (New York, 1999); Anthony, *Managing Culture*, 52.

22. Frederick R. Lynch, *The Diversity Machine: The Drive to Change the "White Male Workplace"* (New York, 1997), 283–87.

23. Heather MacDonald, "The Diversity Industry," *New Republic* 209 (July 5, 1993): 23; Lynch, *Diversity Machine*, 51; Andrew Ferguson, "Chasing Rainbows," in Ferguson, *Fool's Names, Fool's Faces* (New York, 1996), 163; and Taylor Cox, *Creating the Multicultural Organization* (San Francisco, 2001), 14–15.

24. Price M. Cobbs, "The Challenge and Opportunities of Diversity," in Elsie Cross et al. eds, *The Promise of Diversity: Over 40 Voices Discuss Strategies for Eliminating Discrimination in Organizations* (Burr Ridge, Ill., 1994), 26.

25. MacDonald, "The Diversity Industry," 24; Patricia Arredondo, *Successful Diversity Management Initiatives: A Blueprint for Planning and Implementation* (Thousand Oaks, Calif., 1996), 139; and Lynch, *Diversity Machine*, 51–58, 74, 78.

26. Lynch, *Diversity Machine*, 7; R. Roosevelt Thomas, *Redefining Diversity* (New York, 1996), 58; R. Roosevelt Thomas, *Building a House for Diversity: How a Fable about a Giraffe and Elephant Offers New Strategies for Today's Workforce* (New York, 1999), 62–63. See also Cox, *Creating the Multicultural Organization*, Chapter 3.

27. Frederick A. Miller, "Forks in the Road: Critical Issues on the Path to Diversity," in Cross et al., eds., *Promise of Diversity*, 39; Ferguson, "Chasing Rainbows," 171.

28. William B. Johnston and Arnold H. Packer et al., *Workforce 2000: Work and Workers for the Twenty-First Century* (Indianapolis, 1987), 85–95; Lynch, *Diversity Machine*, 330–31. On the absence of data confirming diversity claims, see 183–95.

29. Cox, *Creating the Multicultural Organization*, 12.

30. Cox, *Creating the Multicultural Organization*, 12–13, 9; and Thomas, *Building a House for Diversity*, chapter 1.

31. Cox, *Creating the Multicultural Organization*, 12–13, 9; Wendy Conklin, "Clarifying the Work of Integration: An Interview with Elsie Y. Cross," *The Diversity Factor* 9 (Winter 2001): 11; Thomas, *Redefining Diversity*, 23.

32. Thomas, *Building a House for Diversity*, 104–15.

33. Lynch, *Diversity Machine*, 121.

34. For a convenient list of media deals, see Dean Alger, *Megamedia: How Giant Corporations Dominate Mass Media, Distort Competition, and Endanger Democracy* (Lanham, Md., 1998), 6–10.

35. Thomas Schatz, "The Return of the Hollywood Studio System," in *Conglomerates and the Media*, ed. Erik Barnouw (New York, 1997), 73–74.

36. Mark Crispin Miller, "The Publishing Industry," in Barnouw, ed., *Conglomerates and the Media*, 107–109.

37. Ibid., 110–11.

38. Ándre Schiffrin, *The Business of Books: How International Conglomerates Took Over Publishing and Changed the Way We Read* (London, 2000), 7–8, 30.

39. Miller, "Publishing Industry," 117, 114.

40. Jeanne Dugan, "The Baron of Books," *Business Week* (June 29, 1998): 109–15; Doug Desjardins, "Book Dealer's Suit Parallels Video," *Video Store* (February 21–27, 1999): 1, 46; Ivan G. Marcus, "Closing the Book on the Yale Co-op," *Chronicle of Higher Education* (October 20, 2000), B5.

41. Dugan, "The Baron of Books," 111.

42. Brooke Allen, "Two—Make that Three—Cheers for the Chain Bookstores," *Atlantic Monthly* (July/August 2001): 148–49; "A Word from the Wings: Riggio Lashes Out at ABA," *Publishers Weekly* (June 8, 1998): 10; Dugan, "The Baron of Books."

43. Dugan, "The Baron of Books."

44. Norman Spinrad, *Little Heroes* (New York, 1987), 4–6.

45. Ronald Grover, Steven V. Brull, Richard Siklos, and Catherine Yang, "A Little Net Music," *Business Week* (February 7, 2000): 34; Steve Hochman, "Death of a Classic Label," *Rolling Stone* (March 18, 1999): 24–25; and Alger, *Megamedia*, 94–95.

46. Safire quoted in Alger, *Megamedia*, 100; for estimates of lobbying donations, see 98.

47. Alger, *Megamedia*, 102–103.

48. Claire Poole, "The Accidental Broadcaster," *Forbes* 149 (June 8, 1992): 58; Ken Kerschbaumer, "Bigger Than Ever," *Broadcasting and Cable* 131 (September 3, 2001): 37; Stephanie Anderson Forest and Tom Lowry, "Is Clear Channel Hogging the Airwaves?" *Business Week* (October 1, 2001): 68–69.

49. Eric Boehlert, "Pay for Play," *Salon.com*, March 14, 2001, available online at http://salon.com/ent/feature/2001/03/14/payola.

50. Frank Saxe, "Boar-Killing Stunt under Investigation: Animal Rights Activists Charge Cruelty," *Billboard* 113 (March 17, 2001): 88; and "Clear Channel, Arbitron

in a Battle Over Costs of Subscription Surveys," *Billboard* 113 (April 14, 2001): 71; Paige Albiniak, "Clear Channel Challenged," *Broadcasting and Cable* 132 (January 28, 2002): 12; Eric Boehlert, "Radio's Big Bully," *Salon.com*, April 30, 2001, available online at http://dir.salon.com/ent/feature/2001/04/30/clear_channel/index.html.

51. Boehlert, "Radio's Big Bully."

52. Dorothy Pomerantz, "Free the Airwaves," *Forbes* 169 (April 15, 2002): 106–107.

53. For accounts of the new payola situation, see Boehlert, "Pay for Play"; and Boehlert, "Fighting Pay-for-Play," *Salon.com*, April 3, 2001, available online at http://dir.salon.com/ent/music/feature/2001/04/03/payola2/index.html. For an account of the coalition and its petition to Congress, see Rick Karr, "Radio Consolidation," National Public Radio, *Morning Edition*, May 24, 2002. The petition can be found at the Future of Music Coalition's Web site, at http://www.futureofmusic.org/news/radioissuesstatement.cfm.

54. Quoted in Pomerantz, "Free the Airwaves," 107.

55. Joseph Turow, *Breaking Up America: Advertisers and the New Media World* (Chicago, 1997).

56. Ibid., 80; Byron Lewis quoted in ibid., 83.

57. Marilyn Halter, *Shopping for Identity: The Marketing of Ethnicity* (New York, 2000), 13–14, 48.

CHAPTER FOUR

~

Culture and Identity

It is no surprise that the idea that consumerism can dissolve away "tradition, community, and meaning" and still sustain viable identities supposedly rooted in tradition and community has such a wide hold today. What runs beneath this conviction is not only the corruption of the aesthetic tradition of cultural thought, seen in the assumption that consumer choice somehow carries significant meaning, but the corruption of the anthropological tradition as well. Just as the indifference to work destroys the material basis of aesthetics, so the anthropological conception of culture is degraded by conceptions of culture that ignore the importance of structures in daily life. If work is the main material of the aesthetic, then the particular concrete environment, the intermediary institutions built on faiths and family, and the rituals of daily life—those traditions and communities too easily dismissed by cultural populists—are the material of the anthropological. Just as aesthetic standards provide a barrier against the debasement of taste by consumerism, so these concrete elements of collective life buffer individuals from social homogenization, the leveling that accompanies the incorporation of new people into the contemporary economy. And this is why those social buffers, like aesthetic standards, are relentlessly ground down: They are obstacles to the spread of global consumerism.

In the last quarter century as the cultural populists dreamed up arguments that sounded radical but in fact lent support to the status quo, identity activists similarly offered false solutions to the leveling of distinct ways of life, and for much the same reason. Like their anti-aesthetic counterparts, identity activists were inheritors of long traditions of cultural thought that they did

111

not fully understand. They drew from streams of thought that made better history than contemporary analysis. Having inherited conceptions of culture as infinitely malleable and eternal, subjective and abstract, identity activists could afford to ignore the systematic erosion of practical buffers against deracination. They discounted the concrete reality of what sociologists called structural assimilation—that is, the inclusion of once-marginalized people into the economic and social system—and still claimed that their distinct ways of life were intact. The cultural populists reveled in consumer abundance, which they confused as popular choice; the identity activists celebrated racial and ethnic consciousness, which they confused as cultural diversity. The results are the same in both cases: Claims that pose as radical lend support, if only unwittingly, to the larger homogenization of life.

Erik Erikson and the Origins of Identity

Before we consider the paradoxical coexistence of identity claims and social leveling, it is worthwhile to give some thought to where the concept of identity comes from. In fact, from its origins in mid-twentieth-century mass-society theory, identity has been a close companion to culture—so close that in some hands they have been virtually the same concepts. The two have a ready affiliation in one curious sense: Just as the modern culture concept was invented as a balm to the elimination of art from daily life, so identity was invented at the historic moment when postindustrial society swallowed up fixed ways of life and replaced them with nothing solid enough to ground a sense of where one stood in the world. As with culture, the less assured identity becomes, the more aggressively it is touted.

We owe our contemporary understanding of identity mostly to Erik Erikson, the great mid-twentieth-century social critic and psychoanalyst. In almost every sense, Erikson's theories of identity formation and identity crisis were entwined with both his own understanding of culture and with the larger—and clearly related—expansion of both concepts. He began his most systematic treatment of identity by commenting on that expansion: "In the twenty years since the term was first employed . . . its popular usage has become so varied and its conceptual context so expanded that the time may seem to have come for a better and final delimitation of what identity is and what it is not." The term identity and its common companion, "identity crisis," had come to be used in ways that were both "so large and so seemingly self-evident" and yet "so narrow for purposes of measurement that the overall meaning is lost." Erikson's lament over the concept of identity was a perfect evocation of the fate of culture as well.[1]

Erikson made the study of identity his central passion. For that reason alone his thinking bears some consideration, but it is all the more important that he framed his ideas while fully immersed in the mass-society concept. The fundamentals of his identity concept, which were much influenced by Erich Fromm, lay in the anxiety that individuality was endangered in an age of totalitarianism, forced migrations of peoples, the general uprootedness of modernity, and the fabrication of value systems pretending to replace organic ways of life. Erikson came to terms with that crisis-ridden time by reformulating psychoanalytic theory in its light. He was a loyal Freudian, and, as his biographers remind us, a practicing clinician first and foremost. But his own experiences, both personal and professional, led him to expand Freudian theory to take wider account of the social and historical context of behavior. As a practical matter, applying his version of psychoanalysis obliged him to hold a systematic understanding of his own time; otherwise, by his own reckoning, he would never have been able to help his patients.

That historical moment, he was convinced, was marked by eroding institutional structures and general uprootedness. It was an era of alienation in which social standards and expectations had grown obscure and weak; the erosion of "deeply rooted or strongly emerging" value systems in the face of rapid "historical and technological development" invited infantile solutions in the form of totalitarian programs.[2] Following Freud, Erikson believed that the core of the human condition lay in the clash between individual desire and social order, the reconciliation of which was the basis of a reasonable individual existence. The breakdown of social order was bound to make that individual adjustment more difficult, and this gap between the objective necessity of individual adjustment and a shifting social order was the crux of the contemporary crisis.

For Freud, the tension between individual desire and social order created the will to refinement, the essence of culture. Erikson held a broader conception of culture, drawn from a lifelong dabbling in anthropology. Deeply concerned with how societies imparted values and norms and how they created institutional settings into which individuals could mature, he was attentive to the particularities of ethnicity; Erikson developed a long-standing working relationship with Alfred Kroeber, who introduced him to the study of the Yurok and the Sioux. Erikson assumed the anthropologist's sense of relativism, believing, in shades of Edward Sapir's "genuine culture," that healthy societies came in many forms and historical settings and should be judged by their capacity to provide clear roles and settled values to which their members could gravitate. The healthy society made it possible for individual members to identify with the prevailing standards and conform to roles while also developing a sense of distinct individuality. The individual obtained what Erikson often called a sense of "self-sameness and continuity," individuality and collective membership. Through this process, both the individual and society gain confirmation—they were "historically verified," as he put it. The development of self-sameness and continuity was, in essence, the process of identity formation.[3]

In the contemporary world, where technological change combined with "the weakened creeds of the West and the manufactured ideologies of the Communist world," the "intricate process" of identity formation was disrupted.[4] The result was the pervasive pathology popularly known as "identity crisis." Devoted to a precise clinical understanding of how identity formation was disrupted, Erikson resisted the overuse of the term. He was uncomfortable with the term itself, in part because "crisis" was necessary for creative adjustment. Crisis was for Erikson what discontent was for Freud: the point at which individuals are faced with moments of truth and either creatively come to terms with reality or falter and fall into varying degrees of pathology. Erikson was convinced, however, that mass society, in its fluidity and its "weakened creeds," had created generalized difficulties and that the disruption of identity formation had become the defining pathology of the time. Identity crisis was to postwar America what hysteria had been to Freud's Viennese bourgeoisie—evidence, as far as Erikson was concerned, that culture and history really did have varying effects on behavior and were fundamentally important to a workable psychoanalytic theory.

His concept of identity and identity crisis, as well as his lifelong interest in adolescence, brought Erikson fame during the 1960s when his work was popularized in efforts to explain the presumably widespread disaffection of youth. But he always resisted the dilution of his work. If there was a generalized pathology around identity formation, Erikson nonetheless refused to render blanket doomsday pronouncements. To him, the "crisis" was as potentially beneficial as it was potentially dangerous. If the West was losing its capacity to impart values, perhaps that was because the value system that still obtained was illegitimate. For people to develop humanely, they would have to reform, if not repudiate, such systems. The contemporary youth rebellion was a symptom of such seeking. Even more so, the anti-colonial movements in the Third World, including in Vietnam, and the American civil rights movement were collective repudiations of oppressive and illegitimate value systems, and, while obviously born of "crisis," they demonstrated how people could work through maladjusted societies toward new and better systems. Aside from the material or political improvements that such movements would bring to oppressed people, they also promised to erase the imposed images of inferiority that had bred self-hate, or in the case of African Americans, the defensive strategy of invisibility. More loosely, the youth rebellion, which he believed was overrated as a phenomenon unique to the 1960s, was an intensified search for values worthy of commitment as well as an effort at widespread experimentation. At its best, the youth rebellion sought out the "fidelity" of true commitment and the "diversity" of individual expression that promised to renew the proper balance of life.

If the contemporary crisis had generated some signs of hope, it also had generated more than its share of maladjustments. It was the peculiarity of the moment that social movements seemed to imitate adolescent behavior—this, incidentally, was one reason why Erikson was so interested in adolescence. At that moment when adolescents, driven by barely bridled sexual and physical energy, were most in need of moral structure, they tended to throw themselves into mythological or utopian frameworks that promised them both eternal identity and comprehensive explanations. In moments of rapid social change, "youth feels endangered, individually and collectively, whereupon it becomes ready to support doctrines offering a total immersion in a synthetic identity (extreme nationalism, racism, or class consciousness) and a collective condemnation of a totally stereotyped enemy of the new identity."[5] In times of flux, people were prone to accept identities that promised "totality," as distinguished from "wholeness," the former being an immature, even infantile, and certainly evasive nonsolution to the growth process.[6] The number of people, especially young people, prepared to accept "pseudo" identities obviously helped explain the modern phenomenon of totalitarianism, for "the fear of loss of identity which fosters such indoctrination contributes significantly to that mixture of righteousness and criminality which, under totalitarian conditions, becomes available for organized terror and for the establishment of major industries of extermination. Since conditions undermining a sense of identity also fixate older individuals on adolescent alternatives, a great number of adults fall in line or are paralyzed in their resistance."[7]

Because identity disruption was the generalized pathology of contemporary society, the tendency for groups to arrest themselves at an adolescent stage of "totality" was more pronounced than ever. It was natural for young people to yearn for complete immersion in an identity, and it was similarly typical for a group to "invent a historical and moral rationale for its exclusively God-ordained uniqueness." The tendency to accept that "futile cycle of evil" seemed stronger than ever. And one could see in such movements as the Black Muslims the willingness of some oppressed people to throw themselves into the "totalistic orientation" that promised, in the end, no real improvement over the systems that they were in rebellion against.[8]

Erikson's conviction that identity disruption was a historically specific twist on universal problems of human development gave rise to a certain equivocation, a sense that these very real dangers coexisted with reasons to hope. But there was no equivocation on his part about what made for maturity, either in the individual or the group. The individual had to assimilate desire and conformity in increasingly sophisticated ways at each successive stage of life; at each stage, the individual had to master the environment, such as it was, by fulfilling expected roles, while mastery became refined in increasingly creative fulfillment as the stages proceeded. As reasonably healthy people grew, their sense of balance and perspective matured so that they at once recognized the social constructs that gave structure to their lives and made individual contributions to that structure, especially through work and social participation. Fixed in a well-defined world and secure in the knowledge of their individual contributions, mature people could survey the world and prepare for challenges, even for radical change, that potentially would permit them to distance themselves from the fixed world of their identity and absorb some of the larger currents of life. Similarly, the mature society was one that gave proper meaning to each stage of life, which among other things meant that it promoted a realistic adjustment between the values it promoted and material fact.

Here, contemporary society had probably unprecedented promise. The technological realities of postwar society made it possible to conceive of identities that transcended the "pseudo-species" of race and nationality and promoted inclusive self-understandings. Even as science and technology seemed to make such a thing possible, however, they also threw up obstacles. As the Boasians always had taught, Erikson understood that technological proficiency and ethical maturity were not the same things. Technological change added to the flux of the world and gave rise to such a variety of possible identities that settling on proper ones was more difficult rather than less so. New, inclusive identities, he believed, could not be formless, for individuals would have nothing against which to develop. "Wholeness," he wrote, required "defined boundaries. In the present state of our civilization, it is not yet possible to foresee whether or not a more *universal identity* promises to embrace all the diversities and dissonances" necessary for healthy individual development.[9]

While he was not so clear about what he ultimately had in mind as we perhaps might wish, Erikson seems to have been thinking that inclusive identities would parallel what he considered to be mature individuality. It is safe to assume that the mature society was by definition what infantile and adolescent societies were not: They were inclusive rather than exclusive, based on ethics of broad humanity rather than on race or ethnicity, and constructed on creative work rather than on oppressive labor or technological dependence. His most provocative thoughts along these lines concerned individuals and societies at their most mature, that is to say, at "meaningful old age." True maturity rested in wisdom, at which point individual and society alike transcended the need for rigid rules and spent their remaining energy on those activities that would, in the end, allow both to transcend the final and inescapable reality of death. In old age, the matured person, having transcended the need for social acceptance, could develop "that detached yet active concern with life bounded by death, which we call *wisdom*." Ultimately people came to an inclusive knowledge of living traditions and, perhaps above all, became "ethically concerned with the 'maintenance of the world.'" Wise people understand that in the end they amount only to their contributions to an enduring world.[10] Those contributions were rendered in the form of creative work, which might, ultimately, be the "most inclusive and most absorbing" identity. The development of "technical skill" allowed the individual to make unique additions to the world's store of knowledge. Beyond that, however, such individual virtues "as faith, will power, purposefulness, competence, fidelity, love, care, wisdom—all criteria of vital individual strength" would take hold only if they managed to "flow into the life of institutions." Only in this way could "civilization" make a proper account of itself; only then could it give real meaning to "the full cycle of life." Through both creative work and institutional reach, society "cannot fail to reach into the beginnings of the next generation, and thus into the chances of others to meet ultimate questions with some clarity and strength."[11]

At their healthiest and most mature, Erikson seems to have been saying, individuals and the societies of which they are a part develop proper culture, with a devotion to serious work that challenges the yearning for competence and in so doing makes it possible to create material that stretches across the generations, invested in institutions that legitimize themselves by their capacity to absorb the unique energies of people across time and thereby give meaning to the individual life.

Reflections on Assimilation and the Identity Crisis of Our Time

If we accept the possibility that Erikson's concept of identity carries some explanatory power, we have to entertain as well the possibility that we stand in a period of arrested adolescence as he understood it. The obsession with identity, which increased from Erikson's time to our own in direct proportion to the inflation of culture, suggests an ongoing disruption in the process of identity formation. One problem is the difficulty of individual adjustment in a society that fabricates so many different identities at once. Erikson addressed this point directly: "The expansiveness of civilization, together with its stratification and specialization, demanded that children base their ego models on shifting, sectional, and contradictory prototypes."[12] Difficult under the best circumstances, identity formation becomes infinitely more so where identities come into head-to-head competition for the loyalty of potential members. It has become a buyer's market in identities, but sheer abundance does not conduce to mental health.

The quantity of identities from which we now pick and choose is proof that Erikson's concern over the flux of contemporary life was well founded, and yet he was in no position to appreciate how that modern flux would work. His perspective was derived from his experience with mid-century totalitarianism, which not surprisingly gave rise to his supposition that flux would encourage demagoguery and vitriolic nationalism. To some extent, that model applies to the religious fundamentalism of our time and parallels Benjamin Barber's argument in *Jihad vs. McWorld* that globalization has set loose the demons of political reaction.

The real problem in the developed world, however, is less the sheer profusion of identities or the danger from reactionary ones than the flimsiness of those that present themselves. Erikson believed that the absence of a solid society with intact and legitimate values—a genuine culture—would encourage the frantic search for alternatives. That seems true on its face. But the submerged truth lying beneath is that the erosion of a clear value system in the West in recent years has rendered it impossible to create substantive alternatives. In Erikson's scheme, individual maturity was a product of an engagement with a sturdy social system, but we are faced with the ambiguous situation in which there is no cultural system worthy of the name against which a person can match wits. Consumer society dissolves all fixed ties, all value systems, all culture, and because it creates, in essence, no place, it is hard for anyone to find any place. The main value this society promotes is the least-common-denominator exhortation to shop and connect one's public self to the sorts of goods one prefers. (omission

The absence of a sturdy value system indicates, among other things, that there is no cultural ruling class in America today. There is, clearly, a political and economic ruling class, and the new dogma of tax cuts in Washington is indication enough of its will to power. There are also cultural managers, people whose occupation is to manage the apparatus of entertainment and advertising. But they do not constitute a class as such. They are not, as the nineteenth-century bourgeoisie was—as for that matter, practically any other ruling class before the age of consumerism was—concerned about defining proper tastes. Instead they are determined to destroy any aesthetic conceptions as obstacles to sales. They are not concerned about imparting a moral structure that might permit them to claim moral superiority while castigating the lower classes for their moral failures. They are amoral. They are not even given to the relatively benign missionary tendency to educate and uplift, such things being distractions to the job of peddling the next blockbuster or elevating the next star.

Mired simultaneously in a bureaucratic existence that inherently alienates and a consumer system that contains no meaningful values, the inhabitants of the developed world launched themselves on any number of identity quests in the 1990s. But the magnitude of people's efforts should not be mistaken as a sign that the identities they professed were healthy. Mere profession of such an affinity cannot even be taken as proof of the material reality of the identity thus claimed. Those who are sanguine about the consumption of identity in all likelihood are missing an important possibility when they mistake the upsurge of ethnic claims as a political self-assertion of identity and a reaffirmation of roots; they ignore the possibility that the intensification of such claims is a result of the emptiness of that very system of mass consumption they praise. The plain fact of the matter is that "tradition, community, and meaning" have always been the bane of consumerism and have always been under heavy pressure accordingly. Cultural populists hold the optimistic view that the consumption of particular goods can make up for the absence of genuine communities. To call this a vain hope is to understate things dramatically, not least because the underlying "meaning" in the act of consumption is the homogenized value of choice, which reflects no tradition at all. As such, it seems more reasonable to suspect that identity claims are announced with an intensity that runs in inverse proportion to the degree to which the community in question exists in the concrete.

In the rise of identity claims, therefore, we have assertions that appeal primarily to abstractions, not only in the sense that they are increasingly shaped to match advertising images but in the sense that the ethnic and racial identities asserted have less and less real substance to them. No doubt some identity claims suggest a pathological condition in which those who seek out and direct their loyalty to this identity or that are living in a world of unreality. While I believe that those on the extremes of identity politics do dwell in a dream world, it is unfair to take this as a general rule. Instead, what is striking about our present condition is that it permits of no substantive resolution.

With neither a potent nor legitimate value system in place, with no true ruling class dictating norms and mores, there is not any "culture" to fix one's loyalty to or to rebel against. Americans are, literally, neither here nor there.

To fill this vacuum, many people sought to establish attachments that
were somehow outside of or disassociated from material realities, while identity activists, whose self-interest was typically convoluted with gaining ad-
herents in one form or another, courted them with narratives that purported
to explain why they are alienated. In a nutshell, this was what multiculturalists set out to do. The multiculturalist narrative essentially held that preserving one's ancestral culture is an essential human right, indeed a moral obligation; more than that, it taught that non-WASPs in America never really
did assimilate and that the very idea of assimilation was an oppressive concoction of the American power structure. Multiculturalists famously insisted
that the "melting pot" be regarded not only as a misinterpretation of reality
but as an instrument of psychological warfare against nonwhites. "African-
American, Asian-American, Puerto Ricans/Latinos and Native Americans
have all been the victims of an intellectual and educational oppression,"
stated New York's 1989 minorities' task force on the state history curriculum,
"that has characterized the culture and institutions of the United States . . .
for centuries." The assimilation policies in American public education, announced Iris Young and her colleague, Charyl Zarlenga Kerchis, were simply
"oppressive," for they demanded that "people . . . transform their sense of
identity in order to 'make it' in mainstream life."[13] No single word fell quite
so deeply into disrepute during the 1990s than "assimilation," and so general
was its disgrace that, as Nathan Glazer wrote, "only a branch of paleoconser-
vatism can now be mustered in its defense."[14]

And yet the sociological reality is that assimilation "continues to flour-
ish," in Glazer's words. Intermarriage across ethnic and religious lines, for example, long has been a reality, and since 1970 rates of interracial marriage
have accelerated as well. "Structural" or "socioeconomic assimilation," the
process by which immigrants and, since the 1960s, African Americans have
been absorbed into the institutional mainstream of American life is a general
fact of life. So much is this true that the multiculturalist condemnation of assimilation is self refuting. If they had not joined the institutional life of
America, they could scarcely have been involved in rewriting school curricula, publishing their tracts with mainstream academic presses, and holding
forth from lecture podiums in the nation's universities. No one should deny
persisting economic gaps between Hispanics and Anglos or African Americans and Anglos, but the overall picture of America's institutional life and
labor markets suggests a complicated picture in which education, rather than

ethnicity, plays a most important role, one that upholds the old-fashioned expectation that ethnic and racial minorities will indeed assimilate.[15]

In light of that reality, multiculturalist identity claims in the 1990s appear no more substantive than the so-called ethnic revival of the 1970s. That earlier identity quest—which in truth was merely a first phase of a continual struggle of people in an affluent society to find roots in a rootless world—was, as Herbert Gans put it at the time, an artificial "resort to the use of ethnic symbols. . . . Ethnicity may be turning into symbolic ethnicity, an ethnicity of last resort, which could, nevertheless, last for generations." For Gans, symbolic ethnicity was the luxury of the third and fourth generations, following the old demographers' maxim—Hansen's Law—that the grandson recovers what the father wishes to forget. What they recover, however, "are now only ancestral memories, or an exotic tradition to be savored once in a while in a museum or at an ethnic festival." Primary ties to distinctly ethnic patterns of life or religion gave way as the third generation made its way up the corporate and bureaucratic ladders and from the old urban neighborhood into the suburbs.[16] Among the recovering ethnics, according to Gans, "ethnic cultures and organizations" were languishing from indifference while "ethnic identity" seemed oddly to be flourishing. Theoretically, perhaps, identity made no sense when detached from group and culture, but such was the peculiar character of symbolic ethnicity that it "does not require functioning groups or networks" or, for that matter, even "practiced cultures." As family, religious, and work life lost its distinctly ethnic character, the social expectations that came with ethnicity dissolved and the pressure to live up either to negative or positive expectations based on stereotypes disappeared. People could pick and choose "when and how to play ethnic roles." For the most part, they chose to be ethnic as "a leisure-time activity." Acted out rather than genuinely lived, ethnicity rested primarily on symbols and myths, which then became "stand-ins" for the real thing.[17]

Still, it ought to be said that the present reality of structural assimilation does not mean that the multiculturalist critique of American history is wrong or that their cultural claims are obviously so. As long as there was an Anglo ruling class that imposed a cultural will to power to match its political and economic dominance, so long then the melting-pot ideal did represent a repressive, not to say oppressive, mechanism. The multiculturalist narrative has lost its basis in truth today; history's reach doesn't quite cover the present situation. Even now, however, multiculturalists can take refuge in acculturation theory and argue with perfect logic that cultural differences do not pass away simply by working alongside WASPs, living in the suburbs, or attending the local sporting events.

Yet it is not acculturation that ought to be posed as assimilation's opposite but deracination, the opposite of both. Acculturation and assimilation both require that the alienated have a culture of substance against which to adjust, something of substance that can provide deep meaning or, in Erikson's formulation, develop the necessary tension to embrace a new way of life or refashion the old in strengthened form. But consumer society offers nothing of psychological, aesthetic, or moral substance that might either justify a conscious abandonment of one's past or provide an honorable enemy to battle against. A person could take a hundred trips to Disney World and never find such substance, because it doesn't exist. Immersion into consumerism can only bring deracination, which necessarily leaves people neither embedded in a new culture nor comforted by the old.

Deracination: The Case of Language

For a people to sustain their distinctiveness they need structures, buffers if you will, that permit the collective body to isolate, protect, and teach their individual members, especially children. It is just common sense that the stronger the boundaries that isolate a group, the stronger that group's cohesion will be. Yet this common sense was glaringly absent from the culture wars of the 1990s. While one side prattled on about the virtues of Western civilization and the other boasted of the integrity of their particular identity group, evidence mounted across the board that life in the affluent society eroded the boundaries between people and dissolved away the buffers necessary both to values and collective distinctions.

Even the most basic of buffers, geographical isolation, was ignored, thanks to the concept of acculturation. Physical boundaries protect cultural distinctions, and yet the 1990s was a decade in which boundaries of every sort dissolved, where technology created something of a blanket experience across the world. Rather than seeing globalization as a threat to cultural diversity, corporate diversity consultants, college presidents, and the like announced that globalization was the very reason why diversity was the future. Cultural commentators ought to take a lesson from biologists, who know that the diversity of species depends on the physical integrity of diverse biospheres. Biologists point out that distinct environments make possible an extraordinary diversity of species because delicate creatures come to specialize in survival according to local conditions; as environments are overridden by development, the highly specialized species are the first to be destroyed, while those that survive environmental change tend to be the most adaptable or, we might say, the "least diverse."

One of the most important indications that the breakdown of physical isolation threatens cultural integrity is in the steady erosion of linguistic diversity. Language is a very special part of culture. It carries with it much of the history of a people's intellectual refinement and contains the whole collective experience. In ways that cannot really be analyzed, language is institutional memory. It is probably the most organic cultural element, embedded nearly as deeply in a person's upbringing as their genes.

Yet the world is poised, according to some estimates, to lose one living language every day. While Americans go on about cultural diversity, the world faces, Jared Diamond has written, "the possible loss of ninety percent of our creative heritage, linked with the loss of ninety percent of our languages." While there are some 6,000 languages in use today, linguists suspect that thousands have been lost over the past 100 years, and 95 percent of the remaining 6,000 are spoken by only 5 percent of the world's people. Like the concentration of capital, there is a concentration of linguistic power in the hands of the few. Spanish, Mandarin Chinese, Hindi, and that great imperialist, English, command the bulk of the global population.[18]

Language extinction is the canary in the mine of cultural homogenization, as anthropologist Daniel Nettle and linguist Suzanne Romaine have written, because language is uniquely sensitive to economic and technological forces. Language extinction is not linguistic at all; people do not shift from a mother tongue to another language because of the inherent superiority of their adopted language. Like all cultural elements, language constantly changes as people describe new intrusions into their environment or as they come into contact with others. Even among the most isolated peoples, there is always some multilingualism, because there is always some point of contact with other people and hence other languages. Forms ebb and flow across trading routes or in marketplaces, and those individuals who obtain some mastery of their neighbors' language can assume pivotal positions in their own communities. Such language exchange tends to preserve linguistic diversity over the long run because the activity that gives rise to it helps sustain the communities themselves.[19]

The ecology of language is upset in the same way the biological environment is, not by the more or less natural interaction of unique elements but by the radical intrusion of outside forces, which come in two forms: through an abrupt and violent intrusion or a steady and subtle alteration in the "enduring social network." A language can be lost because the people who speak it are destroyed. But that sort of catastrophic change is rare and less important than the more subtle, but equally fatal, adjustments that people make for political and economic reasons. Where physical isolation is broken down and social equilibrium upset, people are both forced and given the incentive to shift from a mother language to a metropolitan one. As they do so, they tend to slide more and more into the technological and social environment to which they are adjusting and slip out of the network that previously had sustained the home language. It has always been thus, Nettle and Romaine argue, because people quite sensibly try to better their material circumstances or adjust to the realities of power. So long as there remained a "home"—that is, a distinct realm into which a people could retreat even as they struggled to adjust to new political and economic surroundings—their vernaculars proved remarkably resilient and a certain language equilibrium remained.

Ours is a whole new era because there is no more retreat. As consumer society encroaches everywhere, it brings the wealth and power of the metropolitan language (usually English) into close and constant propinquity to the vernacular. Armed with the allure of material progress and the power to impose itself, the present system has created an unprecedented situation in which "metropolitan languages are advancing staggeringly fast, at the expense of peripheral ones, almost everywhere in the world. . . . Having shown no signs of happening for the first twenty-three hours of the human day, [the massive language shift] has happened in the last twenty minutes in such a revolutionary and uneven way that the shock waves are now resounding through the world's languages."[20]

Hence English, Mandarin, Spanish, and Hindi have emerged through a sort of linguistic Darwinism. But in the case of language, the "fittest" is not the most sophisticated or refined. Nettle and Romaine make the compelling point that the most expansive languages are relatively simplistic, while the most grammatically complex are the most isolated. They argue that this is another way that language resembles the natural world. The more isolated its environment, the more a species is highly adapted to just that one place and the less able it is either to adjust to radical changes or to spread out. So with language—which makes English the cockroach of the world's tongues. As a language spreads out and has to account for more and more experiences, it has to simplify and, in the process, homogenize experience itself. The forms of knowledge and experience that refer specifically to locale are lost. Consequently, Inuits who adopt English are left with one word for ice when their native tongue might have had a dozen or more. A Palauan fisherman born 100 years ago had more than 300 names for fish; English would leave him with one.[21]

The homogenizing tendencies of English are of a piece with an economic system that is similarly destroying unique local patterns of labor, overriding delicate systems of myth and ritual with mass-produced and inherently leveling entertainment, and otherwise turning the fate of humanity into a uniform series of experiences. What Nettle and Romaine say here of language is of the utmost importance for our understanding the whole construct of the world we are seeing loom up today. It is fast becoming one in which all protective isolation is transgressed, the consequence of which might well be to destroy, among many other things, the capacity of people to understand their lives in unique, locally based ways.

Yet even as the extinction of language indicates a cultural leveling of the deepest sort, many students of language take the sanguine view that the fate of language is in the hands of the user. The focus of much linguistic scholarship has shifted from the study of linguistic forms to linguistic usage, a shift that directly resembles the shift in cultural conceptions away from production to consumption. Language in this formulation becomes a matter of transitory choice and subjective instinct; how it is used and what meanings are derived vary from moment to moment according to the disposition of the individual. "We *exploit* linguistic variation," writes Rosina Lippi-Green, "in order to send a complex series of messages about ourselves and the way we position ourselves in the world we live in." Language becomes, as anthropologist Bonnie Urciuoli writes, "a culture-making process, . . . the locus of the construction, re-creation, and emergence of selves as social actors." If so, then there is no need to worry about endangered languages, because whatever is lost can be "recreated."[22]

Anxious to cast their lot with their peers who believe that culture is the main battleground of power struggles, contemporary linguists argue that any insistence on uniformity issues out of political motives. It has become a generally accepted theoretical point that language standardization had its origins in the early stage of nation-state formation, where it revealed a bourgeois will to power. Much influenced by Benedict Anderson's argument that the creation of national vernaculars was crucial to the birth of modern European states, linguists and anthropologists have taken to speaking of "regimes of language" built on the "ideologies of language." Language is imposed "in the interest of a specific social or cultural group," contends Paul V. Kroskrity, and, as with ethnicity and race, it marks boundaries of inclusion and exclusion. Standard English is nothing more than an abstraction, Rosina Lippi-Green insists, one, moreover, that is the mother tongue only "of primarily white, middle- and upper-middle-class, and midwestern American communities." Any effort to demand linguistic uniformity, to claim that there are absolute rules and conventions the violation of which indicates ignorance and inferiority, issues out of racial and class domination and, Bonnie Urciuoli tells us, really "are about whiteness and middle class-ness."[23]

There is unquestionably a hefty grain of truth in this perspective. Yet the linguists accept the first part of Anderson's view of language shifts—that they reflect systematic power—while rejecting the conclusion that power wins out in a monolithic outcome. Those who graft language study on to the culture-as-consumption model believe that while the dominant class insists on uniformity and disparages those "elements that do not fit its interpretative structure," "eradication of the awkward element" is often incomplete. In practical usage, the subversion by the marginalized and colonized often wins out on the ground.[24]

If this is so, then language shifts are really urgent political struggles, the colonial struggle fought over language rather than land. Linguists insist that the marginalized and colonized have become adept at preserving their cultural vitality not by holding to the traditional tongue but by turning English to their own purposes. And among the important upshots of this assumption is the corollary that neither abrupt upheaval nor gradual change really alters cultural cohesion. For that matter, language loss itself becomes less important than the constant "renegotiations" that run their course between the metropolitan language, which represents the dominant voice, and feisty local communities that refuse to relinquish their native identities.

All of these ideas and claims coalesced in vivid form during the Ebonics controversy, which erupted in December 1996 when the Oakland Board of Education passed a resolution declaring Ebonics the "primary language" of the district's African-American students. Leaving aside the details of the brouhaha,[25] let us note that what professional linguists call African American Vernacular English (AAVE) is a historically conditioned consequence of community cohesion born of physical and cultural isolation. Ebonics advocates, however, have not been content with the knowledge that AAVE is a legitimate English dialect; rather, constructing their positions on appeals to culture, they have argued that it is a means of cultural control in the hands of its users, who, correspondingly, are tied into a vast hereditary linkage of people bound together by their genetic origins in West Africa.

The political necessity to prove a link between black vernacular and West African languages gave rise to foolish efforts to show any connection possible. Hence some have claimed that rap music is the contemporary linguistic form of West African drums and that AAVE is the reincarnation of ancient Egyptian. Ernie Smith, the most flamboyant Ebonics advocate and an active participant in the Oakland debacle, has thrown out wild claims that Ebonics is not related to English at all, that it is a descendant of "Niger-Congo African languages" upon which English words have been grafted. He has resorted to a flurry of jargon to insist that Ebonics is "the reflexified morpho-syntactical continuation of the Niger-Congo African linguistic tradition."[26] Fervently searching for any threads, Ebonics advocates expanded the notion of language itself to include "paralinguistic" elements such as body movement, tone, cadence, and, for that matter, the spiritual importance of language. Geneva Smitherman insisted that "the African American Oral Tradition is rooted in a belief in the power of the Word. The African concept of *Nommo*, the Word, is believed to be the force of life itself. To speak is to make something come into being." Here again is the confusion of the ideal and the material, and the claim itself is so abstract as to be both meaningless and irrefutable. One might point out that the belief in the "power of the Word" might well be a function of Christianity. But who is to say?[27]

Even the most reasonable analyses of AAVE's origins contained stretches of imagination that indicate that language claims are elastic enough to be stretched to suit an author's purposes. Along with John Baugh, Geneva Smitherman pioneered in synthesizing otherwise obscure anthropological studies with Afrocentric advocacy. She codified the most noticeable elements of AAVE in her 1977 book *Talkin and Testifyin*—the marking of tense by context, multiple negatives, simplified consonant clusters, and, above all, the nonstandard use or absence of *to be*—the origins of which she contended were clearly West African. Though the words are English, she has written, "Black English's main structural components are, of course, the adaptations based on African language rules." It therefore marks "the continuity of Africanisms in Black English throughout time and space."[28]

But how can cultural continuities be traced reliably "throughout time and space"? Smitherman more or less expected readers to accept on faith that the continuity is there. The best she could do was to offer a very general overview of the historical circumstances in which African speech patterns might have been preserved. It is not an unfair account: Slaves from different societies were tossed together during the trade, she claimed, and they had to negotiate linguistic differences among themselves while trying to assimilate the European languages of slave traders and masters; the result was a creole, or pidgin, that grafted new words to old forms.[29]

The problem with her account is that it is so overly general that one has to nod agreement while willingly ignoring the enormous complexity of three or four hundred years of history. She and younger colleagues appealed to the Caribbean experience as a base of linguistic continuity back to Africa, but the experience of North America was far different from that of Jamaica, Barbados, or Haiti. Because the slave trade was far more important to the sugar colonies, the sheer weight of Africa was inestimably greater there, the regular replenishment of the labor force so much more important in maintaining direct ties with the motherland, and the contact with white folks far less regular. Under such circumstances, it is not surprising that West African linguistic patterns should have survived there. There were only two places in North America that even approximated the Caribbean, the Carolina-Georgia low country and French Louisiana. In both of those places, a creole did develop, but this was not the general experience of North American slaves. Smitherman cited two important studies to backup her optimistic premises, Lorenzo Dow Turner's classic 1949 study of Gullah, a pathbreaking work deeply influenced by Melville Herskovits, and J. L. Dillard's marvelous *Black English* (1972). Yet Turner made no claim that Black English traces back as Smitherman argued and in fact stood by the much more sensible argument that Gullah was maintained because of the physical isolation of its principal speakers. Nor does Dillard lend substantive support to claims of a direct linkage between AAVE and Africa. Indeed, for him, the instinct to trace it to a "direct influence from the African languages spoken by the slaves . . . proves to be too simple."[30]

The overly general historical accounts of Ebonics advocates also floundered about the question of how slaveholders regarded language itself. It is unlikely that either traders or masters cared as much about language as they are given credit for. No doubt ship captains and their crews worried about interslave communication and the possibility of mutiny. Those concerns, however, were unlikely to trump the need to fill a hold and make passage west as quickly as possible. North American slaveholders gave foremost consideration to labor costs, the technical knowledge that Africans brought with them, and other cut-and-dried business matters. The notion that language, like culture, "was power" was not one that they entertained at great length.

In the closest point-by-point examination of the issue, John McWhorter has shown persuasively that the discernable links to Africa are sparse indeed and that the speech forms that constitute AAVE are much more easily traced to nonstandard English. He concludes: "The purported linkages between Black English and African languages has become a bit of a scam. . . . The truth is that the links between Black English and African languages are very broad and very few. . . . Black English is no more an African language than Irish English is Gaelic." John Baugh, whose recent treatise on the subject is almost plaintive, concludes similarly, and he insists, his earlier hopes to the contrary notwithstanding, that "any suggestion that American slave descendants speak a language other than English is overstated, linguistically uninformed, and—frankly—wrong."[31]

McWhorter and Baugh both suggest that the claims of Ebonics advocates grew from the intersection of nationalist politics and sketchy linguistic science. But Ebonics advocates also have come to their assumptions because of the fluid conceptions of culture that prevail today. The reason why so many of the claims to African linkage can be ventured is because the cultural imagination is itself vague and fluid. One could conceivably respond to McWhorter by saying that because language changes constantly, we cannot say for certain that North American slaves did not incorporate Africanisms. None of us has spoken to an eighteenth-century Bambaran brought to New Orleans. Maybe his language was similar to what is being spoken on the South Side—unlikely, but maybe. Almost anything can be asserted when dealing with these sorts of abstractions, and the most important point is that those who wish to imagine a link to Africa can do so because the prevailing conception of culture rests almost entirely in the imagination.

To appreciate how the whole controversy fits into the larger drift of events, we should disentangle it from American race relations and see it against the backdrop of language extinction. Because AAVE is a legitimate, historically important cultural element, it deserves the same analytical treatment and respect as any other language form; its fate, after all, is bound to run parallel to other endangered languages. Its eventual disappearance ought to occasion regret, for its death would indicate the loss of the human stock of knowledge and tradition. But it is hard to see it surviving as a living, organic dialect—save, perhaps, in the manipulated forms of mass entertainment. As some of the more thoughtful participants in the Ebonics controversy recognize, however inherently valuable AAVE is, African Americans, like it or not, will have to master standard English if they are to complete their structural assimilation. If you want economic progress, you have to accept the gradual withering away of the vernacular. You cannot have it both ways, and to think you can is to ignore how cultural forms come and go, lessons the present-day extinction of living languages clearly teaches.

Defenders of linguistic provincialism, many of whom, in the case of Ebonics, are African American, actually reveal how true this is. John McWhorter insists that Ebonics is another example of black separatism, but their loose conceptions of language testify to how indebted Ebonics advocates are to mainstream conceptions of culture. On the one hand, they insist on the permanence of language patterns by insisting that this or that particular element traces directly to an African analogue; on the other hand, they have abandoned the emphasis on refinement and praise mass-produced entertainment, rap music particularly, for allegedly preserving tradition and revel in the faith that control of culture is thoroughly in the hands of grassroots folks, even as those folks take their cues from the entertainment products of multinational conglomerates. Language, in their hands, is the mirror image of culture, both infinitely elastic and solidly enduring. Far from separatism, such thinking rests firmly in the mainstream.

Deracination: The Erosion of the Intermediary World

To the extent that it insulates a people from the outside world, providing them a source of cohesion in which their unique experiences are both reflected and extended over time, language performs some of the tasks of the intermediary world, that realm of institutions that protects individuals from the remote forces of economics and statecraft and form the parameters, accordingly, in which the healthy process of identity formation can take place. The bulwarks of this realm both buffer the individual from the alienation inherent in the impersonal world of commerce and state and socialize the individual for participation in that formal world. Religious rituals and beliefs, small-scale civic life, and family and kinship structures all serve these dual purposes and constitute the main institutions of the intermediary world.

By definition, deracination is the loss of this realm, and if this is so, then it is our fate, because the intermediary world is eroding. Like other elements of cultural change, it happens so gradually that it can be nearly imperceptible. Because it is a gradual withering away, people have time to adjust with half-measures or to refashion institutions in ways that look progressive at the moment but indicate long-term decline.

Religious practice is a case in point. It might sound counterintuitive to claim that religious commitments are in decline, given that Americans routinely profess to believe in God in much higher percentages than other Westerners, that politicians habitually pander to religious groups, and that freethinkers are sure that we're on the verge of a new Puritanism. But it is easy to exaggerate the depth of religious obligation among Americans—or, better put, it is easy to confuse rhetorical expressions of faith with genuine commitment. However much they say they believe in God, Americans actually have been fleeing regular religious participation for decades. Nearly all Americans claim some religious faith, but only slightly more than 35 percent of them regularly attend church, and their participation in wider church-based activities has dwindled as well. To some, God has become a subjective abstraction that apparently commands little more commitment than a vague acknowledgement that there might be an Almighty or, in the form that television recognized it during the 1990s, a belief in angels.

All the public noise that so-called Christian conservatives made during the last two decades of the twentieth century obscured the most important development in American religious life. The most notable trend among Christians was toward nondenominational churches, most spectacularly seen in the explosion of suburban "megachurches," the religious equivalent of Barnes & Noble and Home Depot. Often aggressively conservative in political posture, the nondenominational congregations are nonetheless based on a lowest-common-denominator theology that supplants the finer points of dogma with appeals to individualism. Members are exhorted to no more rigorous a doctrine than to get right with "Jesus Christ, your personal savior." For all their alleged conservatism, they are a notably nonjudgmental bunch, especially when it comes to such things as divorce, the highest rates of which were reported during the 1990s to be found in the Bible Belt states of the South.[32]

We have long known, meanwhile, that civic life suffers in a mass-consumption society, and all indications suggest that public apathy and selfishness are the defining qualities in this regard. As Robert Putnam rather emphatically demonstrated in the mid-1990s, the erosion of civic life ran much deeper than voter apathy or Americans' distressing tendency to see public life as a trough for self-interested gorging. Americans' historic reputation for voluntary association, which Tocqueville first noted as a peculiarity of a democratic people, has degenerated into professionalized interest-group politics. While there are more registered private associations than ever, Putnam observes, they are overwhelmingly advocacy groups that only claim to speak on behalf of members; membership in most of them amounts to little more than an annual check and obliges almost no face-to-face interaction on the local level. Among the so-called citizens' groups founded after 1965, he writes, a mere 25 percent or so were based on local chapters with members. Rather than a proliferation of voluntary associations, he says, we have a "proliferation of letterheads."[33]

Of all the essential intermediary institutions, family and kin organization are the most important, for obviously it is in the intimate relations of family where socialization takes place, culture is transmitted, and identity is formed. Family was also a hot topic among Americans during the 1990s, as gays and lesbians demanded marriage rights, conservatives bemoaned "fatherless America," and Hillary Clinton invoked quaint proverbs to defend the further bureaucratization of private life.

The United States has never been known for its strong family structure. Its political ideals and patterns of property distribution always conduced to comparatively flimsy families. It hasn't helped that since the Revolutionary period, marriage in America has been founded on the romantic ideal—on the professed love between man and woman. Shorn as it is from broader economic and kin-group considerations, predicated on the atomistic decisions of two people, the romantic ideal is the most rickety foundation on which to base an institution so essential to cultural integrity. The fickleness of romance aside, the ideal is based on self-interested calculation, which carries all the overtones of the marketplace. Bad enough when exposed as an application of self-interest, the ideal becomes even more pernicious when what is being calculated is the extent to which one partner chooses a spouse based on how happy that spouse will make them.

By all appearances, the romantic ideal remains vibrant, in direct contrast to the health of family structures. According to the National Marriage Project's 2001 report, *The State of Our Unions*, young adults want to marry, and 94 percent of those surveyed believed that marriage should be between "soul mates, first and foremost." The vast majority of them believe that there is just such a person out there, that one perfect person with whom a lifetime commitment would surely produce bliss. The first generation to be reared after the establishment of no-fault divorce in America, these young adults are wary of divorce, but rather than fortifying marriage by linking it to larger social obligations, they have only intensified the romantic ideal and raised the likelihood that whatever marriages they eventually make will fail to live up to those exalted standards.

The most startling development is how radically isolated marriage has become. It no longer has any economic purpose, the economic independence of women having dissolved the last institutional tie to the family-as-a-working-unit model. Needless to say, parents and grandparents have no voice in whom one's "soul mate" should be. And, not least important, sex and childbearing are no longer understood as functions of marriage. In what authors David Popenoe and Barbara Dafoe Whitehead call this "emotionally deep but socially shallow" conception, the main purpose of marriage is to produce adult happiness.[34]

The isolation of marriage is so well documented that we hardly need to pile on statistical evidence here. But it is important to be clear about the most important trends. Ever since the compilation of the infamous Moynihan Report on "The Negro Family" in 1965, most attention has focused on the emergence of single-parent families. It is clear now that the single-parent family is not a function of race, ethnicity, or even poverty but rather is so generalized today that it is more or less normal; it is certainly nothing remarkable. Rates of children living in single-parent families in white and Hispanic households have risen steadily; and, according to the 2000 Census, there were many more single-parent households in the suburbs than in central cities. But the single-parent family is not the most important demographic development of our time. Rather the growth of what the census calls non-family households, primarily adults living alone, grew from just over 19 percent of all households in 1970 to over 31 percent in 2000. This growth was matched by an inverse decline of married-couple households with children from more than 40 percent in 1970 to 24 percent in 2000. We are not just bowling alone. We are increasingly living alone.[35]

Nor are familial erosion and the intensification of the romantic ideal simply American phenomena. Rather, the two seem to be associated with technological advance and material progress, as survey research among young adults from "individualistic" wealthy societies attests. In a mid-1990s study of the attitudes of college students in eleven different nations, Robert Levine and his colleagues found that those from Pakistan, India, and Thailand were the least given to the romantic ideal, while Americans, Britons, and Brazilians were most enthralled with it. The authors reasonably conclude that the romantic ideal is a function of individualism borne of capitalism, and they further note that the nations most receptive to the ideal have the highest divorce rates and the lowest fertility rates. "After all," they write, "the primary reason for marriage in traditional collectivist culture is, often, to have children, who will then take part in the larger collective."[36]

For those who hail from rigorously traditional societies, contact with the romantic ideal is likely to create ongoing and occasionally severe tension. There is frequent generational conflict, for example, between Indian and Pakistani immigrants to England or the United States, where parents expect to arrange their children's marriages, usually with the idea of reinforcing ties back home, and their Westernizing children's desires to adopt the values of their new homes. For some young people, the very act of migration is a way to exercise "choice" in the business of marriage. Not only does it allow them to escape the fait accompli of parental decisions, it makes it more likely that they will find a spouse among their fellow émigrés, and, accordingly, a spouse also less beholden to tradition.[37]

Where émigré children agree to arranged marriages, they tend to do so with a heavy dose of romantic rationalization. Women's magazines paid their respects to multiculturalism in the 1990s by running stories about arranged marriages that resulted in true love. Jyothi Sampat writes in a 1999 issue of *Good Housekeeping* that she avoids telling Americans that she has an arranged marriage because they usually express sympathetic bewilderment. She was brought up under such a system, she explains, and naturally accepted her mother's invocation that "love happens after marriage." Not even a

Canadian university degree saved her from her fate, for she dutifully connected with her arranged suitor, moved to Phoenix, and discovered that "it
was as my mother had promised. Love did come after marriage."[38]

Or consider the experience of a more Westernized, less dutiful daughter,
Shoba Narayan, who described herself to readers of *New Woman* magazine as
a "rabble-rousing feminist." After five years of college in the States, she
"didn't just want to get married. I wanted to fall in love." When her parents
sprang demands on her, she compromised by insisting that her suitor be a
Greenpeace activist or a Himalayan mountaineer. They obliged by choosing
an investment manager, whose no-nonsense eye for detail would "rein in"
their daughter's impulsiveness. She married him. But even then she "wasn't
sure if our marriage would work . . . America had inculcated Western values
in me." Taking confidence in the knowledge that her many Indian friends
had successful arranged marriages, she plunged ahead, thinking that "unlike
all my Indian friends . . . I could get a divorce if all else failed." The result: "I
could look at my marriage and honestly say that I was a happy and fulfilled
woman."[39]

Ah! The romantic ideal, nestled in the reassurance that one can have tradition and love too! In any realistic way, it is all but impossible to see the custom of arranged marriage surviving among immigrants or, for that matter,
among those groups in developed and developing nations who are more and
more involved in global commerce. The custom is so at odds with the god of
choice that it has no chance of long-term survival.

Even the emotional debates surrounding same-sex unions reflect the pre-
dominance of the romantic ideal. Like the ideal itself, the battle has been
joined on a transnational level. The American Defense of Marriage Act of
1996 corresponded to Britain's Family Law Act of the same year and the
French opposition to the government's decision to extend marriage benefits
to nonmarried couples. Meanwhile, the arguments on behalf of same-sex
marriage are essentially the same throughout the West, and they boil down
to a politicized version of the romantic ideal. As Representative Patrick
Kennedy asserted in opposing the Defense of Marriage Act, "marriage is a basic right. . . . Love and commitment are essential pillars of marriage."[40] Gays
and lesbians deserve the "right" to be married, presumably, because they are
every bit as capable of "love and commitment" as the family-values set.
Polemicists on both sides of the issues seem to agree that "permanent" or
"lasting" relationships between two "committed" individuals is the ideal to
be chased, and yet this ideal has not exactly distinguished itself by its capacity to promote such relationships. The most telling element of the debate
over the Defense of Marriage Act was that it broke down between advocates

of an undeniably radical expansion of the romantic ideal, on the one hand, and, on the other, a slew of politicians who were themselves vivid testimony to the failure of that ideal. There was no more remarkable—not to say brazenly hypocritical—spectacle than to see Bob Barr, Newt Gingrich, and even the modest Ohioan John Kasich, divorcees all, defending the "sanctity" of marriage. And to have Bill Clinton of all people sign the legislation made the whole business an exercise in sarcasm.

There are tangible material stakes involved in the debate, as advocates of gay unions rightly insist. Inheritance rights, child custody rights, health care benefits, and Social Security pensions are all important parts of the argument for expanding the legal definition of marriage. It is not engaging in a slippery-slope argument, however, to say that marriage as a benefit package is another harbinger of the destruction of the institution. If we look away from the same-sex marriage debate, we can see better what is underneath. Though it is perfectly true that a large majority of adults continue to marry, the countertrends are clear. As more and more adults refuse to marry or have children, they have begun to campaign against the extension of tax breaks and other public benefits, as well as against corporate policies such as flex time, designed to aid parents. The contempt for "breeders" is the predictable result of rights-based conceptions of family and marriage. Hence Elinor Burkett, an advocate for the "child-free," scorns "family-friendly" corporate policies as "affirmative action for mothers" and rails against policies that offer tax breaks to "the six-figure income crowd . . . while the childless poor are losing their public benefits." Such policies, she asserts, are "affirmative action . . . based on reproductive choice." Any alleged benefit offered to one group has to be offered to everyone else, and failing to do so in this case amounts to "marital discrimination" that sustains "bigotry." Indeed marital discrimination, according to the opening statement of the American Association of Single People Web site, presumably constitutes today's sharpest social divide. "The law has created two classes of people," the association declares, "those who are married and those who are not." One wonders what Marx would think.[41]

These claims are easily gathered inside the dogma of diversity. The singles rights movement grafts itself on to other advocacy groups, most explicitly the gay rights movement, beneath the commodious claim that the collapse of family structure represents the "real" diversity of American family life. Family structure, the argument goes, differs according to historic time and place; different ethnic groups organize family and kin groups differently. The "traditional nuclear family" was never a historical norm but a mere aberration created by peculiar economic circumstances among white, middle-class Americans in the 1950s. "One of America's strengths," contends the Alternatives to Marriage

Project in its "Affirmation of Family Diversity," "is its diversity, which includes not only a wide range of races, ethnicities, creeds, abilities, genders, and sexual orientations, but also a range of family forms. . . . The family diversity that exists in America today includes people who have chosen not to marry and those who are prevented from marrying, such as same-sex couples. It includes people who have chosen to live together before marriage (the majority of marriages today are preceded by cohabitation) and those who are single."[42]

It is revealing that singles are included beneath the rubric of "family diversity." It is difficult to know how singles deserve to be thought of as "families," except to think that if family is reduced to the radical application of the romantic ideal then family is whatever anyone chooses it to be. If people choose to be single, then they can also choose to think of themselves as a family of one. Or, to be fairer, they can be families of singles, as Kath Wesson implies in her defense of gay families, *Families We Choose*. Wesson defines "chosen families" in opposition to "blood" or "biological families," and their hallmark is their liberating flexibility. Chosen families, she writes, "might incorporate friends, lovers, or children, in any combination." Reconceived thus, people are "released . . . from the genealogical logic of scarcity" that presumably limits them to rigid family forms.[43]

Clearly, there is ample variety in how adults have gone about setting up their lives in the developed world, and whether that variety is a moral or ethical improvement is certainly open to debate. But this variety has nothing whatever to do with cultural diversity. On the contrary: The family diversity school and the singles rights movement have not thought through how culture is supposed to survive in a world where there is no systematic way of passing on values or structures of life to the next generation. The pervasive reduction of family membership to a matter of mere choice corrupts the most important intermediary institution with the single most important value of consumerism. That the cultural centrality of actually passing something on is now ridiculed as a hassle that qualifies adult autonomy is about as clear an indication as any that those who trumpet the virtues of adult choice care little about culture.

Identity as Choice, or Tom Hayden Becomes Irish

In the absence of strong family and community obligations, media-generated images flood the intimate world of individuals where identity is formed. The distance between the individual and the source of origin of the identities so constructed dissolves the tension that Erikson thought was essential to proper maturity and makes it very hard to comprehend how one might struggle against those sources. One can make an honorable fight against a dominating parent or a repressive religion and come to an intellectual maturity thereby, but it is hard to know how to mount a vigorous struggle against abstract images. Identity formation under such circumstances becomes a bit like punching air.

Though it smacks heavily of that single consumer value, the idea that one can choose an identity emerged in the 1990s as a reasonable antidote to the most dogmatic racial and ethnic claims and constituted by the end of the decade the most promising way of reconciling the sociological realities of assimilation with politically progressive hopes for diversity. What made the talk about the "invention" of identity so hopeful was that much of it came from members of racial and ethnic minority groups who were honestly acknowledging their incorporation into the mainstream and asking not to be condemned to the provinces of rigid group identities. They recognized that contemporary life at its best created the opportunity for complex identities, into which might be poured sometimes overlapping, sometimes competing, sometimes completely distinct loyalties. For some, it became possible to be gay, Catholic, Republican, and a National Rifle Association member all at once. Such multiple allegiances could be put forward in rebellion, as Henry Louis Gates, Jr. wrote, against "the notion . . . that I can't construct identities through elective affinity," that as an African American, "race must be the most important thing about me." For Gates and many others, the great virtue of contemporary life was that it had become possible "to experience a humanity that is neither colorless nor reducible to color," to enjoy both "Bach *and* James Brown[,] sushi *and* fried chicken."[44]

What Gates so nicely calls "elective affinity" appears to have been an increasing tendency during the last twenty years. Mary C. Waters and her colleagues have interpreted recent census data as suggesting a consistent connection between mobility into the suburban middle class and the selective embrace of ethnicity. Not only was ethnicity generally felt as an abstract and fairly haphazard element, but, she noted, many Americans actively chose from a series of ethnic options. Because the sociologists had been right and intermarriage, social mobility, and "structural assimilation" had taken place, most white Americans were able to select any one of several ethnicities.

Waters studied the ethnic choices that people made on the 1980 census, the first census that permitted multiple ancestries. Mostly the choices were idiosyncratic: One woman chose to identify with her maternal Italian background because her mother had always linked her temper to the daughter's Irish blood; other interviewees recalled otherwise long-forgotten bits of French or English blood in the course of speaking with Waters. Like Herbert

Gans, Waters could only conclude that ethnicity "does not effect much in everyday life."[45] What is most interesting about Waters's interviews, however, is how intensely her subjects wanted to have an ethnic identity. It was an embarrassment to be a mutt, a colorless nonentity with a "wishy-washy" background, as one woman described her Scotch-Irish ancestry. It is possible that the census not only made it possible to pick and choose an ancestry but encouraged people to do so—indeed many respondents in mixed marriages chose one side or the other as opposed to "American" when asked to categorize their children.[46]

The phenomenon at hand, Waters decided, was best described as the "costs of a costless community." Aside from the standard sociological explanations—status anxiety, the need for community—this symbolic ethnicity was so widespread because of the element of choice it offered. It allowed people to have it both ways: They could have their ancestral connections without the heavy burdens of tradition, crimping communal obligations, or suffocating religious strictures. Nothing fit better with the American spirit than a strategy of identity that tucked individualism and conformity neatly into one package. Ethnicity conferred a sense of unique individuality and yet, obviously, it embedded the individual in an imagined web of community.[47] It is just this mechanism as well that makes culture so attractive in the chase after painless identity. Like the imagined wisps of ethnicity, culture contains the stuff of myth, but where it exacts little more than occasional rituals and exhortations, it levies very little of the obligation that would impinge on choice.

Waters insisted that what went for white ethnics did not go for racial minorities. The former could choose their ancestry because there was no external pressure defining them one way or another nor any particular social advantage for being one over another. For Native, Asian, African, and Hispanic Americans, the choice was made for them and the "options" were either far narrower than for white ethnics or were nonexistent.[48]

By the 1990 census—and even more the 2000 census—accumulating evidence suggested that race was going the way of ethnicity. Out-of-group marriages for African Americans increased over 300 percent from 1970 to 1990, making mixed-race people the fastest-increasing group in the population (though, to be sure, the percentage increase sounds impressive because of the miniscule rate of interracial marriage before 1970). The 2000 enumeration continued the census bureau's drive to encourage identity choice by including controversial mixed-race categories, which inspired nearly seven million respondents, 2.4 percent of the overall population, to own up to being racial hybrids, a preference apparently at odds with Waters's white interviewees who craved an authentic ancestry and yet fully in line with the exercise of free choice. Whites and blacks remained reticent; it is likely that more than 2.5 percent of white Americans are mixed race, and surely more than the reported 4.8 percent of African Americans are. But the choice is there and is likely to be more attractive as time goes on. It already proved itself so for American Indians, whose population seems to have exploded. Just under two million in 1990, the number of American Indians reporting just one race grew over half a million to 2,475,000 by 2000; another 1,600,000 reported two or more races, bringing the total of respondents identifying themselves as at least partly Indian to over four million.[49] One plausible explanation for this considerable jump is that previously "white" respondents, now offered the opportunity to claim partial heritage, were hoping to cash in on governmental benefits and, perhaps, casino profits by laying claim to Indian ancestry. If this is so, it raises the tantalizing prospect of tens of thousands of "white" respondents admitting to ancestral indiscretions should some form of reparations for slavery ever be established. Imagine the one-drop rule reversed.

If it is too early to claim that race has become a matter of choice, the fact remains that many African Americans, following Henry Louis Gates, Jr., began to writhe under that constricting category. It had been imposed, after all, through that terrible night of white supremacy and upheld thereafter by stubborn white habits and lingering ignorance but also through reflexive and understandably self-defensive efforts to maintain group cohesion among African Americans themselves. The willingness of some black intellectuals to break with racial orthodoxy forced them to battle more against the expectations of other African Americans than against the barriers of race, with which, after all, they long before had learned to deal.

There is much more to be said in this regard, enough to take up our energies in the next chapter, but let us see here that the willingness to recognize that our racial heritage is so much more complex than our conventional categories permit rests, as with the ethnic option, on sociological reality. No one has put it more plainly than writer Itabari Njeri, who has pointed out that where African Americans once "tried to find every drop of non-Black blood as a buffer against our caste status, we now tend to proclaim that all of us are exclusively the descendants of African princes, princesses, kings and queens." The demographic facts belie such a search. "We are generically a creolized population," she notes. "As far as I'm concerned, every Black person with White ancestry should . . . own it."[50]

Aside from genetic and demographic facts, the writers who urged us to think about ethnicity and race as a choice were also bound together by a main source of intellectual inspiration, a commitment to cosmopolitanism based on the widely made arguments during the 1990s that identities of every sort were "socially constructed" or "invented." In contrast to self-professed purists, the cosmopolitans argued that if race and nationality were inventions that created misery, then presumably they could be undone in the cause of human improvement.

Such essentially was historian David Hollinger's argument when he called for a "postethnic America." Perhaps the intellectual historian most attached to and influenced by the ethnic revival in the 1970s, Hollinger argued that American notions of race were the historical products of oppression, not biology, lately reinforced by bureaucratically imposed categories. Hollinger wants us to get to the point where identity is largely an individual choice. In a postethnic America, identity formation would begin with voluntary commitments to a group or a tradition; it might well be a composite of different strands with overlapping and competing loyalties, it would encourage tolerance and inclusiveness, and, by acknowledging the "constructed character of ethno-racial groups," it would willingly accept new groups, new traditions, and new identities. Above all, it would abrogate "the right of one's grandfather or grandmother to determine primary identity" for anyone—unless, of course, that individual chooses to let grandmother dictate from the grave. Ethnic and racial identities should assume the character of religious commitments, he suggests: serious commitments of moral and historical depth capable of shaping and even transforming lives but nonetheless ones in which Americans recognize the "right of exit."[51]

There is no more fully considered defense of the proposition that identity should be chosen than *Postethnic America*. Hollinger's vision is a vast improvement over rigid assertions of race and ethnicity and a note of sanity in the multiculturalism debate, especially when the sociological record so clearly suggests that the near future will bring a consistent mingling across all categories. Facing facts is always a good thing. But I fear that postethnic America is fatally flawed by its association with the cult of choice. What happens when the choices are increasingly shallow and manufactured, particularly the new ones? Hollinger largely avoids the hard question of what happens when the niche marketers gut the ethno-racial options of most of their substance. The material that people have to create identity along the lines he wants is increasingly faulty, increasingly the stuff of advertising and focus groups and gimmicks—to say nothing of the bureaucratic policies that he deplores. To be fair to him, he goes out of his way to insist that the freedom to join or not join cannot be reduced to the mere level of whimsy, that the choices that freedom brings are made in due recognition of a historical depth of meaning and carry obligations outside of transitory individual taste. He would be the first to insist that these choices must carry deep meaning. But if we can face the facts of structural assimilation, we ought to face the fact that all traditions are under systematic assault, that the more seriously the traditions are taken, the more aggressively the niche marketers move to control and exploit them. In our mass-produced world, it is hard to see how Hollinger's counsel that we trust in choice, the fundamental value of that empty world, is likely to restore the substance of genuine tradition against which individuals might well come to the maturity that he, like Erik Erikson, seeks for them.

Even if people seek out identities of genuine depth, increasingly they do so through abstract connections with the historic communities they want to embrace. If they are serious, they recognize how flimsy the cultural goods they are asked to work with are, and as a consequence they are left to reach back into a remote world. Like culture itself, identity is more likely under these circumstances to take on the character of a vague ideal than a lived proposition. It might even be that the more serious the pursuit of an identity with a depth of meaning, the more abstract that identity is likely to become.

Such is the conclusion one is left with after considering the most recent writing of Tom Hayden, who has discovered that he is an Irishman. I won't mince words here: Hayden's *Irish on the Inside* is a wretched book. It is a compilation of self-serving absurdities based on the worst aspects of the provincial turn of mind. Bad enough that it was published on the eve of the New York terrorist attacks, all the worse now that even the IRA has apologized for its assaults against civilians, Hayden's exercise in identity assertion might be dismissed as a victim of bad timing except for the self-righteous seriousness with which he takes himself. It is all the more disheartening—if still very telling—that the author of the Port Huron Statement, the thinker responsible for crafting the argument for participatory democracy as an antidote to modern alienation, would trade his youthful good sense for rank cultural phoniness. Life is supposed to work the other way around: Graying wisdom should follow youthful foolhardiness.

Like other identity activists, Hayden condemns the melting-pot ideal. Unlike most, however, he confesses to having been assimilated, and it is against this fate that he has now embraced ethnotherapy. He was assimilation's victim. It was the cause of all his problems—his ceaseless unease in the world, his parents' divorce, his sexual attitudes, his alcoholism. His youthful torments were all a function of his lack of identity; he knew he was alienated but didn't know why. Following his intellectual mentor, C. Wright Mills, he reasoned that his sense of being lost came from the lack of community in

America, and following his political mentor, Che Guevara, he dedicated his energies to political radicalism as an antidote. Hayden has now decided that Mills misdiagnosed the American malady, which made a politically radical effort to fashion participatory democracy a flawed strategy. Most astonishing, it turns out that Mills and Guevara were both Irishmen who had lost touch with their roots. This was particularly true of Mills. As Hayden sees it, Mills's enormously influential body of work as well as his famously unconventional personal life were the flawed results of a man who resisted his Irish identity, "a deeper understanding [of which] might have been medicine for his rootless, nomadic sense of loneliness." Having denied his own past, Mills denied the importance of ethnic and racial issues and was confined—Hayden might well have said "intellectually colonized"—to the stodgy analysis of class and mass society. That we would be so much the poorer had Mills soothed his alienation by recovering his "Irish soul" does not occur to Hayden, who, rather, insists that "it would have made an enormous difference if he had called for a New Left built not only on class but also on the radical strains in ethnic histories that were repressed by the manipulators of power."[52] Having bequeathed this apparently flawed analysis to the New Left, Mills left his most ardent devotee without the intellectual perspective necessary to reach a deep understanding of alienation or, just as important, to keep up with black nationalists, feminists, and the other identity groups that emerged in the latter 1960s.

Hayden thus found himself confused; everyone else seemed to be getting an identity. As they did so, "the assimilated American identity proudly constructed by my parents was hollowed out and near collapse." The identity claims of his onetime radical colleagues, coupled with the emergence of Bobby Kennedy as "a deeper, more contemplative kind of Irish" in contrast to the Cardinal Spellmans, Joe McCarthys, and Mayor Daleys of Irish America jolted Hayden toward rediscovering his own past.[53] There he found all the answers he had been searching for. His parents, both of Irish ancestry, had committed cultural patricide; they had accepted the superficial blandishments of corporate career and suburban household. What Irish ways they kept—drinking, Catholicism, and sexual repression—were themselves imposed forms designed to repress the pure Irish soul. Once the turmoil of the 1960s finally convinced him to explore his Irish roots, he discovered a forgotten history of victimization, poverty, and radicalism, forgotten because of the brainwashing that accompanied Irish assimilation.

Having rediscovered his roots, Hayden arrogates the privilege of defining what a genuine Irish identity is. Like any run-of-the-mill born-again who assumes that he has found The Way, Hayden claims that "the most independent Irish consciousness is rooted in the North of Ireland (officially known as Northern Ireland), where the ancient and enduring conflict between Irish nationalism and British colonialism is most stark." Because injury makes identity, only the Northerners have a genuine claim to Irish consciousness; the Southerners have disqualified themselves as spokespeople by their vacillation, compromises, and gradual acceptance of the British-imposed split. The South sold out, and because coexistence "required . . . a political and cultural distancing from Northern nationalism," Republicans forsook their Irishness. "The Southern Irish began internalizing the British stereotype of a North populated with primitive tribes, utterly alien from the civilized Dubliners who were busy becoming modern."[54]

It would have been enough for Hayden, the chronic activist, to argue that a political life is ample antidote to modern alienation or, better still, that a well-lived life consists of seeking justice wherever injustice reigns. But such a conviction, which Erik Erikson might have considered the healthy conclusion to a lifelong search for meaning, appears nowhere in Hayden's thinking. Instead he appeals to culture and ancestry. His radicalism, he discovered, was not a function of justice-seeking ethics. It was in his blood. If he has been "drawn to causes where the likelihood of winning is remote," it has been because fighting for lost causes is an Irish thing. It is genetic. In researching his genealogy, he noted a Peter Hayden who was hanged for participating in a 1798 uprising. Thomas Emmet, for whom Hayden was named, had been deported to the States for his role in that same uprising and once here became an ally of Jefferson against the Anglophilic Federalists and, most intriguing, "an intimate ally" of none other than Tom Paine. Here again, it might have been both simpler and more plausible for Hayden to note the tradition of Irish progressivism, but he takes this record as evidence of the mystical influence of the ancients. In what might be the most mind-boggling passage in a book full of unbelievable claims, he writes: "I am a believer in invisible ancestral influences, not simply the immediate parental influences so central to current psychological models. Assessing the impacts of one's ancestors is part of the challenge of recovering repressed cultural memory. Where the trail of evidence disappears, where intellect fails, one must rely on imagination, on possibilities that are technically unprovable."[55]

"Where intellect fails" aptly sums up Hayden's efforts. He appeals to the "unprovable," which is to say that his appeals cannot be disproved. Like the resort to immutable culture in defense of language, Hayden's view gives a cheap and phony refuge against the indisputable reality of cultural change and legitimizes any claim, however abstract or implausible. His imagination allows him to think that individual behavior and larger cultural tendencies alike are matters of unadulterated genetics. It allows him to defy time. True Irish culture becomes not only pre-Famine but "pre-Christian." In that golden age before the English imperialists brought their stifling Church with them, the Irish reveled in libertinism, ran wild and free, "enjoyed sex with-out guilt," and exalted fertility goddesses; the "wild Irish" has never quite been bred away, not even through "ten centuries" of Catholic sexual repres-sion.[56]

Since "ten centuries" neither constituted anything that Hayden cares to imagine as culture nor altered the basic nature of the Irish, it is not a stretch to claim that the Irish are not white after all. He began to suspect as much while traveling with Sinn Fein leader Gerry Adams, who visited America in the mid-1990s as part of the first steps in legitimizing the party. Adams evoked enthusiasm among "young African Americans" in California, who "were excited to meet someone 'from the IRA,'" which Hayden took to mean that Adams was "not 'white.'" A Native-American music group clustered about Adams on a flight into Vancouver "because in their eyes Gerry Adams and Sinn Fein . . . were native people like themselves." Adams's easy move-ment among Mexican Indians convinced Hayden finally that the Irish had a chance "to be aligned with the nonwhite majority." Was this alignment to be based on mutual political interests? Of course not: "It was based not only on a common colonial experience, or a common Catholic experience . . . but in the case of Latinos on a common Iberian heritage." It turns out that "the Celtic tribes that gained ascendancy in Ireland around 350 BC were from the Iberian world. . . . That would make me, and all the black-haired Irish, dis-tant blood relations of the Spanish and their descendants in Mexico and Latin America."[57]

There is no need to belabor the obvious, that these sorts of loony claims to blood have given rise to all sorts of frightful atrocities. If Hayden uses them in the cause of Third World liberation, most fundamentalists, including those in the IRA, tend to use them to excuse the dehumanization of enemies and to justify murder.

What strikes me as most bizarre about Hayden's descent into primitivism, however, is what it says about how contemporary notions of culture have al-tered the way we think about the deeply human problem of alienation. This is a subject that Hayden knows a lot about, one to which he has shown an ex-quisite sensitivity through his life. There are no more eloquent reflections on alienation in a mass-consumption society than those found in the Port Huron Statement. If that famous tract is flawed by naiveté, it still represented a sys-tematic effort to grapple with the problem. In middle age, Hayden cannot be forgiven naiveté. What he and his New Left colleagues intuitively grasped in

1962 was that there were no simple solutions to a psychosocial malaise endemic to life in a depersonalized, bureaucratized society. They had learned well from C. Wright Mills, the un-Irishman. But those polemics became obsolete as the Age of Culture developed. In their place has emerged a view of culture as, among other things, eternal and therefore immune to the impositions and adulterations of economic and technological forces, indeed, impervious to time. Culture in this sense is not even human, the creation of people trying to come to grips with the hard realities of existence imposed by a capricious natural world or the need to reconcile impulse to social order. Alienation, the inevitable by-product of the technological and bureaucratic order we dwell in, is done away with in a flight of superstition.

Perhaps we ought not to take Hayden too seriously—indeed with many of the formulations noted above, he almost relinquishes any claim to our attention—but his thinking is symptomatic of the tendency to advance ethnic and racial claims as the proper antidotes to alienation. That tendency, which has been at the heart of multiculturalism, does deserve our attention. We have to take it seriously because the prevalence of identity claims is ample demonstration that the same alienation that greeted the generation of mostly white men who, after World War II, entered the ranks of corporations and public bureaucracies continues to burden bureaucracy's new captives. The outpouring of identity claims stands as a commentary on the emptiness of our present way of life, and their irrefutable power, vested in the attraction they obviously held to millions of Americans, revealed a vitality that aesthetic claims or radical politics just as obviously lacked.

But because they misunderstood the enemy as "assimilation" and wrongly judged contemporary culture as a creature of white male supremacy, identity activists held out a most inadequate cure for alienation, that long-standing malady of the industrial age. Their misdiagnoses led bureaucracy's new captives to believe that a mere shift of consciousness, even a change in favored metaphors, would soothe alienation. So they urged us to give up the melting pot and think of America as a "mosaic," a quilt, or a taco salad. Yet these new metaphors were mostly the products of professionals of various sorts, public schoolteachers, university people, governmental bureaucrats, and the like, who themselves were absorbed into the institutional life of American society. Claiming cultural difference thus became the preferred manner of soothing alienation not because it worked but because it was largely painless. Because the concept of culture at work here assumed that differences could be "imagined" and freely chosen regardless of material circumstances, it was possible to cloak oneself in ancestral identities without either opting out of the bureaucratic-technological order of things or, for that matter, embracing the rigid orthodoxies and self-denying obligations that every ancestral culture contained. Many Americans want a heritage, but very few of them actually want to return to worlds of patriarchal domination, oppressive religion, or material scarcity. This means, in turn, that the recovery and practice of mere vestiges does not in itself constitute cultural recovery or re-creation, and the sum of all these attempts does not represent cultural diversity. If anything the superficiality of such practices creates a new sort of alienation. Rather than the sense of loss and loneliness of C. Wright Mills's white-collar clerk, those who assimilate in practice but insist on keeping their distinct identities have to assert their sense of difference all the more vociferously in order to give meaning to those vestiges of the past that they try to hold on to. Rather than emptiness, today's alienated citizen senses mostly frustration, an indication itself, perhaps, of a nagging awareness that their strategy is all for naught.

Notes

1. Erik Erikson, *Identity, Youth, and Crisis* (New York, 1968), 9–11.

2. Lawrence J. Friedman, *Identity's Architect: A Biography of Erik Erikson* (Cambridge, Mass., 1999), 89.

3. Erik Erikson, "Identity and Uprootedness in Our Time," in *Bulletin of the World Federation for Mental Health* (1959), reprinted in Erikson, *Insight and Responsibility: Lectures on the Ethical Implications of Psychoanalytic Insight* (New York, 1964), 90–91.

4. Ibid., 91.

5. Ibid., 93.

6. Erikson, *Identity, Youth, and Crisis*, 80–81.

7. Erikson, "Identity and Uprootedness in Our Time," 93.

8. Erikson, *Identity, Youth, and Crisis*, 241.

9. Ibid., 299, 90.

10. Ibid., 140–41.

11. Ibid., 140–41, 316–17.

12. Ibid., 49.

13. Quoted in Arthur M. Schlesinger, Jr., *The Disuniting of America* (New York: 1992), 66–67; Charyl Zarlenga Kerchis and Iris Young, "Social Movements and the Politics of Difference," in *Multiculturalism from the Margins: Non-Dominant Voices on Difference and Diversity*, ed. Dean A. Harris (Westport, Conn.: 1995), 21.

14. Nathan Glazer, "Is Assimilation Dead?" *Annals of the American Academy of Political and Social Science* 530 (November 1993), reprinted in *Multiculturalism and American Democracy*, ed. Arthur M. Melzer, Jerry Weinberger, and M. Richard Zinman (Lawrence, Kans., 1998), 16.

15. See Herbert J. Gans, "Toward a Reconciliation of 'Assimilation' and 'Pluralism': The Interplay of Acculturation and Ethnic Retention," in *The Handbook of Interna-*

tional Migration: The American Experience, ed. Charles Hirschman, Philip Kasinitz, and Josh DeWind (New York, 1999), 161–71; and Richard Alba and Victor Nee, "Rethinking Assimilation Theory for a New Era of Immigration," in ibid., 139–60.

16. Herbert Gans, "Symbolic Ethnicity: The Future of Ethnic Groups in America," in *On the Making of Americans: Essays in Honor of David Riesman*, ed. Herbert J. Gans et al. (Philadelphia, 1979), 193, 201.

17. Ibid., 209, 202–204.

18. See the editorial "English Kills," *The Economist* 347 (June 6, 1998): 83–84; Jared Diamond, "Losing Languages: Speaking with a Single Tongue," *Conformity and Change* (1994): 97; Robert M. W. Dixon, *The Rise and Fall of Languages* (New York, 1997); Lenore A. Grenoble and Lindsay J. Whaley, eds., *Endangered Languages: Language Loss and Community Response* (New York, 1998); and Daniel Nettle and Suzanne Romaine, *Vanishing Voices: The Extinction of the World's Languages* (New York, 2000).

19. Nettle and Romaine, *Vanishing Voices*, 10–18; Dixon, *Rise and Fall of Languages*, chapter 3.

20. Nettle and Romaine, *Vanishing Voices*, 130–31.

21. Ibid., 11–12, 16.

22. Rosina Lippi-Green, *English with an Accent: Language, Ideology, and Discrimination in the United States* (New York, 1997), 30; Bonnie Urciuoli, "The Complex Diversity of Language in the United States," in *Cultural Diversity in the United States*, ed. Ida Susser and Thomas C. Patterson (Malden, Mass., 2001), 191–92.

23. Benedict Anderson, *Imagined Communities: Reflections on the Origin and Spread of Nationalism* (New York, 1983); Paul V. Kroskrity, ed., *Regimes of Language: Ideologies, Polities, and Identities* (Santa Fe, N.M., 2000), 8; Lippi-Green, *English with an Accent*, 56, 62; Urciuoli, "The Complex Diversity of Language in the United States," 201.

24. Judith T. Irvine and Susan Gal, "Language Ideology and Linguistic Differentiation," in Kroskrity, ed., *Regimes of Language*, 38.

25. For an overview of the controversy, see Robin R. Means-Coleman and Jack L. Daniel, "Mediating Ebonics," *Journal of Black Studies* 31 (September 2000): 74–95.

26. John McWhorter, *Losing the Race: Self-Sabotage in Black America* (New York, 2000), 206; Marcyliena Morgan, "Shout-Outs to the Ancestors: 'Here Come the Drum,'" *Black Scholar* 30 (Fall 2000): 44–50; Charles Green and Ian Isidore Smart, "Ebonics as Cultural Resistance," *Peace Review* 9 (December 1997): 521–26; Smith quoted in John McWhorter, *The Word on the Street: Fact and Fable About American English* (New York, 1998), 157.

27. Geneva Smitherman, *Black Talk: Words and Phrases from the Hood to the Amen Corner* (Boston, 1994), 7.

28. Geneva Smitherman, *Talkin and Testifyin: The Language of Black America* (Detroit, 1977), 9.

29. Ibid., 11–15.

30. Lorenzo D. Turner, *Africanisms in the Gullah Dialect* (Chicago, 1949); J. L. Dillard, *Black English: Its History and Usage in the United States* (New York, 1972), 9, 73.

31. McWhorter, *Word on the Street*, 157–58, 175; John Baugh, *Beyond Ebonics: Linguistic Pride and Racial Prejudice* (New York, 2000), 41.

32. See Robert Putnam, *Bowling Alone: The Collapse and Renewal of American Community* (New York, 2000), 73–75; Suzi Parker, "Staying Hitched Ozark Style," *Christian Science Monitor* (February 9, 1998), 1; Chris Reinolds, "High Divorce Rate in County Is Called a Cost of Hectic Life," *Atlanta Journal and Constitution*, November 18, 1999, J:4.

33. Putnam, *Bowling Alone*, 49–51.

34. David Popenoe and Barbara Dafoe Whitehead, *The State of Our Unions 2001: The Social Health of Marital Health & Wellbeing*, available online at http://marriage.rutgers.edu/Publications/SOOU/NMPAR2001.pdf. For Whitehead's report on cohabitation, see Popenoe and Whitehead, "Should We Live Together? What Young Adults Need to Know about Cohabitation Before Marriage," available online at www.smartmarriages.com/cohabit.html.

35. See the census statistics in "One-Parent Family Groups with Own Children Under 18, by Labor Force Status, and Race and Hispanic Origin/1 of the Reference Person: March 2000," http://www.census.gov/population/socdemo/hh-fam/p20-537/2000/tabFG5.pdf; and Jason Fields and Lynne M Casper, "America's Families and Living Arrangements: Population Characteristics," (June 2001), at www.census.gov/prod/2001pubs/p20-537.pdf

36. Robert Levine, Suguru Sato, Tsukasa Hashimoto, and Jyoti Vermo, "Love and Marriage in Eleven Cultures," *Journal of Cross-Cultural Psychology* 26 (September 1995): 554–71.

37. John Lievens, "Family-Forming Migration from Turkey to Morocco to Belgium: The Demand for Marriage Partners from the Countries of Origin," *International Migration Review* (1999): 716–44.

38. Jyothi Sampat, "My Problem and How I Solved It: My Marriage Was Arranged," *Good Housekeeping* 228 (February 1999): 76–78.

39. Shoba Narayan, "Lessons from an Arranged Marriage," *New Woman* 28 (January 1998): 78–81; also in this vein, Claudia Ford, "Autobiography of an Arranged Marriage," *Essence* 28 (April 1998): 83–84.

40. Quoted in Alec Walden, "The Defense of Marriage Act and Authoritarian Morality," *Dissent* 44 (Summer 1997): 85. See also Andrew Sullivan, "State of the Union: Why 'Civil Union' Isn't Marriage," *New Republic* 222 (8 May 2000): 18–23; John Lloyd, "A Culture War Rages in Scotland," *New Statesman* (March 27, 2000), 11–12; and Frederic Martel, "Gay Rights and Civil Unions: The French Debate," *Dissent* 47 (Fall 2000): 20–23.

41. Elinor Burkett, *The Baby Boon: How Family-Friendly America Cheats the Childless* (New York, 2000), 12, 21; The American Association of Single People Web site's address is www.singlesrights.com/main.html.

42. Stephanie Coontz, *The Way We Never Were: American Families and the Nostalgia Trap* (New York, 1992); "Historical Perspectives on Family Diversity," in *Handbook of Family Diversity*, ed. David H. Demo, Katherine R. Allen, and Mike Fine

(New York, 2000), 15–31; and Stephanie Coontz, ed., *American Families: A Multicultural Reader* (New York, 1999); Alternatives to Marriage Project, "Affirmation of Family Diversity," available online at http://www.unmarried.org/family.html.

43. Kath Wesson, *Families We Choose: Lesbians, Gays, Kinship* (New York, 1991), 27, 196.

44. Henry Louis Gates, Jr., *Colored People: A Memoir* (New York, 1994), xv.

45. Mary C. Waters, *Ethnic Options: Choosing Identities in America* (Berkeley, Calif., 1990), 25, 147.

46. Ibid., 152, 28–30.

47. Ibid., 150–55.

48. Ibid., 156–58.

49. On interracial marriages, see Hollinger, *Postethnic America: Beyond Multiculturalism* (New York, 1995), 42; and Kerry Ann Rockquemore and David L. Brunsma, *Beyond Black: Biracial Identity in America* (Thousand Oaks, Calif., 2002), 1–2; for 2000 census statistics, see Census 2000 Brief, "Two or More Races Population: 2000" (November 2001), at http://www.census.gov/prod/2001pubs/c2kbr01-6.pdf.

50. Itabari Njeri, "Sushi and Grits: Ethnic Identity and Conflict in a Newly Multicultural America," in *Lure and Loathing: Essays on Race, Identity, and the Ambivalence of Assimilation*, ed. Gerald Early (New York, 1993), 38–39. See also Njeri, *The Last Plantation: Color, Conflict, and Identity: Reflections of a New World Black* (Boston, 1997).

51. Hollinger, *Postethnic America*, 116–17, 120–24.

52. Tom Hayden, *Irish on the Inside: In Search of the Soul of Irish America* (London, 2001), 22–25.

53. Ibid., 4, 92.

54. Ibid., 8, 20.

55. Ibid., 67–71.

56. Ibid., 58–60.

57. Ibid., 175–77.

CHAPTER FIVE

~

Race and Culture

Ideas, like fashions, have a way of recirculating. In the nineteenth century, the concept of culture was routinely linked to biology and genetics to justify Western imperialism and white supremacy. Culture was made captive to race. The nonwhite masses of the world needed Euro-American domination, the argument routinely went, because they were hopelessly primitive. Civilization was obviously a function of heredity, for only that could explain why Caucasians had developed the fine arts, representative government, technology, medicine, architecture, and all the other signs of refinement to their highest expressions while the colored portions of the world lay prone, awaiting cultural salvation, like it or not, from their stern but benevolent Western taskmasters. These same claims plainly undergirded white supremacy in the United States, where racial domination was long justified on the grounds that the "Negro's primitive culture" had to be quarantined. All of the foregoing, moreover, had the sanction of science in the form of evolutionary thought.

It is to modern anthropology's enduring credit—a credit insufficiently extended—that it led the way in debunking these doctrines, which Franz Boas and his followers did by insisting on a complete disengagement of race from culture. The two, the anthropologists insisted, were simply different things.

Nearly a century after the link between race and culture was severed, the rhetoric of diversity remarried them. The reunion, however, has been joined on very different grounds. In the old doctrines of Anglo-Saxon supremacy, race made culture. It was assumed that heredity directly dictated the nature and quality of cultural and technological attainments; blood determined the state of any given civilization or, for that matter, whether a given people had any hope of ever being civilized. Read closely, the apparently racialist doctrines of our time—and I think this can probably be said of casual usage as well—reverse the order: Culture now determines race. Now that genetic science has proved indisputably that Boas's instincts were correct by showing that there is no such thing as race on a genetic level, now that it is widely understood that race is "socially constructed," race becomes as much a matter of how one behaves as of how one looks.

Implicitly, this looser conception of race indicates its declining role in determining a person's individual fate in America. While we can only be grateful that this is so, the slackening of racial orthodoxies has produced an uneasiness among African Americans, the group that stands to benefit most materially from that loosening and yet stands to lose the most in a cultural sense. Because the lot of African Americans in the United States has been uniquely difficult, the structural assimilation that has been realized in most sociological measures in the last generation has carried with it something like a cultural crisis. The first generation to be incorporated into the mainstream of American society had the dubious privilege of being the first generation to discover how empty that life is. The natural and predictable response was to voice alienation, as indeed they have done. Their marginalization had always been keener than other ethnic and racial groups, and their incorporation, which in a sense has forced them to travel farther faster than other groups, was bound to be more painful. When it became clear that the cost of assimilating was the loss of a buffer world, one always more substantial than those that surrounded European immigrants precisely because it had been built as protection against the harshest oppression, there was bound to be a reaction that was expressed mostly in terms of culture.

African Americans before the 1970s were always doubly vexed. Clearly they were marginalized from the nation's institutional life, yet they were always included in the nation's collective life, if for no other reason than that white people fattened on their labors. It might also be conceded that, as the "theorists of whiteness" tell us today, lower-class whites needed "an other" to assuage their own powerlessness. In any case, African Americans were bound to invest enormous psychic resources, to say nothing of their own institutional commitments, in race consciousness as a means of making sense of an absurd situation. That race consciousness was often expressed in cultural terms; because they lacked control over their collective economic and political fate, African Americans had to see in culture the one realm of life through which they might realize a dignified independence. Precisely because culture can be abstracted from those social realms, it could offer an autonomous refuge into which people might escape from economic misery and political oppression. At the same time, the defining characteristic of that culture was indeed race.

But the strong tendency toward cultural autonomy set up, inevitably, tension between that goal and the social goals of institutional integration, the achievement of which was absolutely necessary to the realization of racial justice in America. For plain historical reasons, this tension came to a head in the 1960s, not only because this was the pinnacle of the civil rights movement but because it was the moment when the WASP ideal was disintegrating and the cultural ruling class was giving up. Just at that moment, in the brief heyday of black nationalism, it was plausible to argue that culture trumped economics and politics and that the integrationist ideal was a farce. "As long as the Negro's cultural identity is in question, or open to self-doubt," wrote Harold Cruse in his brilliant 1967 evocation of the tension between cultural and integrationist ends, "then there can be no positive identification with the real demands of his political and economic existence. Further than that, without a cultural identity that adequately defines *himself*, the Negro cannot even identify with the American nation as a whole." Cruse's diagnosis encompassed the whole century, but his mind was very much of the moment. He saw that integrationism had come to fruition at the very time when it was an open question as to whether there was anything worth integrating into. Without confidence in an autonomous cultural identity, Cruse went on, African Americans were "left in the limbo of social marginality, alienated and directionless on the landscape of America, in a variegated nation of whites who have not yet decided on their own identity. The fact of the matter is that American whites, as a whole, are just as much in doubt about their nationality, their cultural identity, as are the Negroes." What was required, Cruse concluded, was not a rush into economic and political integration but rather a clear "cultural analysis."[1]

If the dream of cultural autonomy proved no more achievable in practice for African Americans than it did for Czechs or Italians, the long tradition of seeking that autonomy still remained. The result was the African American commitment to the rhetoric of diversity, which washes away the tension between culture and social structure in the delusion that cultural identity can be preserved in spite of bureaucratic and technological leveling.

On Race and Culture

It hardly seems controversial to say that race and culture are different things, and, on the whole, a few moments' thought would convince most people of the distinction. My sense is that most people who speak about Latino culture or African American culture do not mean to imply that whatever cultural elements they happen to be referring to are created by blood or that people are genetically predisposed to certain cultural forms. Leaving aside for the moment the obvious scientific reasons for distinguishing the two, linking culture and race, even in a good cause, hovers perilously close to the old racism. And yet Americans, after a fashion, routinely do so.

The reasons for this are probably close to hand. Since multiculturalism is really a political construct as opposed to a cultural one, its advocates find it convenient to link culture with broad racial categories for the purposes of defending their institutional self-interest. The racial categories that we tend to work with, what David Hollinger calls the ethnoracial pentagon that demarks the heritages of Europeans, Africans, Hispanics, Indigenous people, and Asian-Pacific Islanders for official purposes, have grown out of movements for racial equality and bureaucratic regulation but today stand as crude barometers of political interests.[2]

If it is not readily apparent why culture should be mobilized in defense of political equality, what is clear is that our understanding of race as a human category is almost as amorphous as our understanding of culture and, if nothing else, the two have that much in common. We know now that there is no such thing as race on the genetic level and that, therefore, race is indeed socially constructed, a human creation, or, more precisely, a function of the consistent tendency among human beings to mark their kind off against all others. Race is fundamentally a political category in the very real sense that those categories that stick do so because one group has accumulated the power to impose categorical demarcations on those they read out of their group while corralling their own constituencies.

This observation can only get us so far, though, because it fails to guide us into a world in which the power of racial classification is unraveling. It is getting harder and harder to know just who is "black"; it makes even less sense to impose crude racial classifications such as "Asian" or "Hispanic." In a world where the ruling class itself has lost its taste for imposing racial domination, to a large extent whatever racial categories people identify with are increasingly self-imposed. Surely this is an indication of a fairer world. But it also gives a clue as to why race and culture have been conflated once again, even if in an anti-racist purpose. As it becomes harder to fix race as a definitive and clear category, those who try to define their group find it convenient to appeal to culture, since culture is so infinitely malleable that it can be used to cover all bases. It is much easier—and more plausible—to lay claim to a group culture than to purity of blood; no one can dispute the former, subjective as such a thing is, but it is hard to make a serious case that those you want to gather into your racial group are pure-blooded. Culture, among other things, allows a new version of the one-drop rule: Pretty much anyone with a hint of the proper heritage can lay claim to cultural purity, regardless of what their genetic mix actually is. Hence we have a doubling of the Native-American population in a mere decade.

Not the least curious element of the renewed connection of race and culture in recent years is that it encourages claims to purity that cannot stand even casual scrutiny. Surely this is so of Hayden. In purely genetic terms, racial purity was lost the moment when people began to talk to each other. This was a point, in fact, that Franz Boas and his students made repeatedly and in several different ways, because they knew that it fundamentally undermined the claims of scientific racism. Boas dispatched almost all of his students to carry out at least some fieldwork among indigenous groups because he understood that unsullied native societies were vanishing quickly, and for the same reason, he encouraged Zora Neale Hurston to study her own native world, the African American world of the rural South.

The essence of Boasian anthropology was that individuals were creatures of their histories far more than of their race, which meant that change, fluidity, and variation ruled. Scientific racism assumed that racial type was permanent, which was then translated into a biological divine right to claim cultural and political supremacy. Boas and his early and influential students, A. L. Kroeber and Robert Lowie, insisted that such a view denied a common human ancestry and ignored the historical reality that all "races" were amalgamations of peoples who came before them. After all, "we are all still savages," Lowie once mused. "But the word loses its sting when we recall what savages achieved."[3] By defining race "as a population derived from a common ancestry and by virtue of its descent endowed with definite biological characteristics," Boas laid down standards so rigorous that only the most isolated peoples could hope to qualify as "pure." In practice Boas found it necessary to entertain a looser notion of race in order to account for those physical attributes that obviously distinguished peoples. Even here, however, the "races" were actually combinations of people and were better thought of as "types," for no "pure" ancestry could reasonably be traced.[4]

In the same spirit with which his Columbia colleague, philosopher John Dewey, had taken issue with a priori reasoning in philosophy, Boas's assault on scientific racism was an assault on dogma and conventional wisdom. Where his fellow anthropologists tended to see progress as the consequence of successive civilizations, which race supremacists took as an endorsement of white superiority, Boas insisted on the "instability of human types." To prove his point, he turned evolutionary theory back on the Darwinists. To see some sort of linear advance from the primitive through to twentieth-century Western Europe was to engage in the crudest sort of Darwinism, for it ignored the problem of natural variations. The racists could never explain how or why their "races" adapted. Evolution does not move in uniform groups but through random variations that take hold for one odd reason or another, and this part of evolutionary theory simply sank race arguments. Boas perceived—correctly, it has turned out—that there was more variation over time within hereditary lines than between contemporary members of different races. And as a consequence, it was perfectly clear that "primitive" and "cultured" types—his words—could coexist not only between racial lines but contemporaneously within races. How else was it possible to have the fine gentlemen of Europe standing beside uneducated peasants?[5]

What was true of physical type was even truer of the other two essential elements in human life, language and culture. All three of these fundamentals were fluid, and what was more, they neither changed in any uniform way nor changed together. Race, language, and culture just did not "have the same fate." A cursory glance across time and distance demonstrated that racially similar people had any number of discordant languages, and, at the same time, different races clearly shared the same language. Language muddied the supremacist picture by suggesting disunity among races and similar aptitudes, to say nothing of shared life, across races. Indeed language blurred the evolutionary model in another way. Darwinist dogma assumed that human society, like biological systems, moved from the simple to the complex. But Boas, understanding that one important measure of human homogenization is the elimination of living languages, noted that there were fewer distinct languages as technological sophistication increased. In this case, the evolutionary model ran backward, where primitive worlds held greater complexity than the modern.[6]

Strange to say, the very fluidity of these concepts has made it possible in recent years to revive a connection between race and culture because it becomes possible to stretch them to meet most any inclination. Critics of multiculturalism who have fixed on this reunion as a main counterpoint have misunderstood just how loose the concepts remain. Linda Chavez, for one, has accused multiculturalists, and Afrocentrists in particular, of reinventing the worst of old racist doctrines when they "insist on treating race and ethnicity as if they were synonymous with culture. They presume that skin color and national origin, which are immutable traits, determine values, mores, language, and other cultural attributes, which are, of course, learned. . . . The multiculturalists seem to believe," Chavez wrote, "that a person's character is *determined* by the color of his skin and by his ancestry."[7]

Chavez fails to see, however, that at least in the case of Molefi Kete Asante, the usual suspect in these accusations, the order of race and culture is reversed. Race in Asante's writings is completely vague; perhaps it is taken for granted. Because he never dwells on the issue of what allows someone to claim African ancestry, we are left to assume that anyone who has any African heritage at all is free to join. Yet Asante also advocates Afrocentricity in order to add to the world's accumulated knowledge, which implies that everyone should benefit from learning African values. If everyone benefits from absorbing the "Afrocentric idea," then perhaps everyone can become African.

Asante might find such a reading preposterous, but the loose way he conceives of culture invites such a conclusion. Ignoring the messy realities of time and distance, he takes as his reference point the "centrality of the ancient Kemet (Egyptian) civilization and the Nile Valley cultural complex" to the "African culture complex."[8] From there, Africa blossomed and, in defiance of the usual forces that thwart the endurance of culture, spread not only across all of Africa but throughout the diaspora of its people. He defines culture as a "spatial" reality, by which he seems to mean that African culture reaches across any sort of boundaries. "African American culture and history," accordingly, "represent developments in African culture and history, inseparable from place and time." If they are "inseparable" in spite of place and time—clearly Asante's meaning here—then of course "Africa is at the heart of *all* African American behavior. Communication styles," in particular, which constitute his principal evidence, "are reflective of the internal mythic clock, the epic memory, the psychic stain of Africa in our spirits."[9] Note that he does not say that call and response or signifying the monkey are products of blood. On the contrary, they are the links to the "ancient Kemetic" tradition, the mysterious stuff of "epic memory" and "psychic stains."

Cast in such an abstraction, Asante's Afrocentrism is completely elastic and capable of ringing in "all African American behavior." Anything an African American does, accordingly, is because that individual must have his "mythic clock" adjusted to his African spirit, not because of his genetic ancestry but because the cultural complex extends so far. Race, in this ideal, has not reconquered culture, as multiculturalism's critics would have us think. Rather, culture has conquered race, turning the historic tables. The result is not a new form of the old racism but rather the possibility that thinkers such as Asante can hold tenure at American universities and still proclaim themselves culturally distinct from the world they choose to inhabit.

Du Bois's Dilemma

In this form, the conflation of race and culture represents a contemporary version of W. E. B. Du Bois's plaintive hope, expressed in *The Souls of Black Folk*, that the "American Negro" could preserve the best of African influences while partaking of the American promise. Du Bois's African American "would not Africanize America, for America has too much to teach the world and Africa. He would not bleach his Negro soul in a flood of white Americanism, for he knows that Negro blood has a message for the world. He simply wishes to make it possible for a man to be both a Negro and an American, without being cursed and spit upon by his fellows, without having the doors of opportunity closed roughly in his face."[10] This rightly famous passage, which concludes Du Bois's pointed description of living with "double-consciousness, this sense of always looking at one's self through the eyes of others," deserves hard reflection in light of contemporary notions of culture and identity, for it anticipates in fundamental ways the situation of African American intellectuals in the 1990s. Indeed Du Bois's reputation has enjoyed a vibrant revival in the last twenty years because a century ago he struggled to think through the intersecting problems of cultural attainment, race consciousness, and justice, essentially the same tangle his successors now confront.

Du Bois is still more intriguing because, particularly in his earlier thinking, the two traditions of cultural analysis were completely entwined, even interdependent. Du Bois was both a race man and an aesthete. Coming of age in the heyday of both scientific racism and snobbery, encouraged to embrace mainstream thought at a point in his life where he believed he had much to prove, Du Bois could hardly help absorbing a bit of both of these distortions of culture. But neither did him much good, in their pure forms, as instruments for advocating racial or human progress, which only made his thought more interesting as he strove to hash out a coherent agenda against hostility from practically every corner.

In his monumental biography of Du Bois, David Levering Lewis makes clear how the young scholar absorbed his convictions on these matters. He seemed a bit too eager to find his place by taking on many of the standard notions of the day, including, to some degree, the rigid notions of racial difference. Du Bois was indoctrinated in the German Historical School while a student in Berlin, and his early work resonates with both Herder and Hegel;

he refracted the German influences through his American experience and the sway of Alexander Crummell, the Episcopal priest who, with Martin Delany and others, constituted a small but vocal group that sustained the back-to-Africa movement through the postbellum period and served as a bridge to Garveyism. Though certainly committed to maintaining racial distinction, Crummell had absorbed a hefty measure of Anglo-Episcopalian stuffiness, and one can see in his insistence on the leadership of the educated and morally upright black elite the origins of Du Bois's faith in the talented tenth.[11]

In one of his first public forays into the subject of race, delivered before the American Negro Academy in 1897, Du Bois put these influences together in an argument at once intended to confront white supremacy and reproach those who would do away with races as a solution to prejudice. His "The Conservation of Races" took Herder as its point of departure and moved directly to a defense of racial distinction. Humanity was made up of "eight distinctly differentiated races," including several strains of Europeans, the Negroes, the "Hindoos," and the Mongolians, Du Bois asserted. It was, therefore, mere wishful thinking to believe that racial differences could be done away with; more to the point, human progress itself depended on maintaining those differences so that each race might make its own special contribution. To date, the "Negro race . . . [has] not as yet given to civilization the full spiritual message" of which it was capable. Raised on the individualistic nostrums of Jefferson and laissez-faire, Americans, including African Americans, often failed to see that progress ran its upward course through collective advance within each race. "The advance guard of the Negro people," Du Bois counseled, "must soon come to realize that if they are to take their just place in the van of Pan-Negroism, then their destiny is *not* absorption by the white Americans." If they were to make their unique contribution, "the 8,000,000 people of Negro blood in the United States" would have to hoist their own banner on "the broad ramparts of civilization."[12]

While Du Bois plainly believed in a connection by blood that crossed the Atlantic, his broader conception of race was not so reductionist. K. Anthony Appiah asserts that Du Bois's racial categories are primarily geographic in origin, solidly in the tradition of Herder. Though clearly his debt to Herder was large, Du Bois added an important, somewhat more elusive (and humanistic) element—history. The movement of blood followed history, which "teach[es] that the grosser physical differences of color, hair and bone go but a short way toward explaining the different roles which groups of men have played." Indeed, later in life he put down "birth, nationality, language, color and race" as but "artificial criteria" separating out human beings. The "subtle, delicate, and elusive" differences that distinguish the races were abstract enough that they "transcend scientific definition" but they made their impact felt through history. In contrast to Herder—and probably more like Hegel—Du Bois linked the development of the distinct civilizations to "spiritual, psychical differences" that collectively obtained over time as "nomadic tribes" settled together in cities and then nations. Important as "common blood" might be, the more definitive bond was forged through "a common history, common laws and religion, similar habits of thought and a conscious striving together for certain ideals of life." Anyone today would simply have summed up this list of common bonds as "culture," which Du Bois was properly distinguishing from physical race.[13]

It is revealing, however, that he does not resort to that word here, for he used it frequently throughout his life. In 1897, Du Bois was writing when Franz Boas was only beginning his prolific career, and he did not have access to the concept of culture as a way of life. But in part because he did often speak about culture, it is not altogether obvious that he would have resorted to it if he had. True, after the turn of the century, he came to know Boas and value the anthropologist's contributions on the role of sub-Saharan Africa to the development of the ancient world.[14] In a 1925 essay, "What Is Civilization—Africa's Answer," for instance, Du Bois employed Boas's conceptions about the African past and the singular origins of human development: "Wherever one sees the first faint steps of human culture, the first successful fight against wild beasts, the striving against weather and disease, there one sees black men." Beyond those first steps, Africans pioneered in two developments utterly essential to culture, village life and the arts. In the African village—in contrast, he wrote, to the alienating and disorienting city—community life was founded, and there the collective commitments seen in religion and government had their start as well.[15] If there was a tinge of romance here, still he was working with both the spirit and the details, such as they were, that Boasian anthropology had established at that point.

Through his long career, Du Bois was prone to exaggerated rhetoric, racial romanticization, and, occasionally, crude generalizations about racial types, all of which were at odds with an otherwise consistent desire to argue from demonstrable fact. The frustrated activist warred often with the careful scholar. He also was prone to a tendency to conflate civilization and culture, which as we have seen was a confusion that the Boasians worked hard to dispel. But most consistently, Du Bois understood culture as human refinement—he generally called it "progress"—and, in contrast to the historic races and their clashing civilizations, culture in his hands was a universal endeavor. Even when he deployed the anthropological understanding of culture to publicize Africa's contributions to "civilization," he understood these three gifts—"beginnings, the village unit, and Art in sculpture and music"—as contributions to the store of human refinement. He knew that the original source of culture was the will to distinguish human existence from nature; his point, of course, was that the urge had its earliest exposition in Africa. He also understood the fundamental importance of social order and the arts to culture. Du Bois, in short, understood culture properly as human refinement in the broadest sense, and it was in that sense that he fixed on it as both a universal good in itself and the hallmark of racial self-development. For an individual to be cultured was to have admittance to the best that was thought and said; for a community, or a race, to develop culture was to act out the essential human endeavor and claim a rightful spot in history.

Du Bois believed in human distinctions, and it is usually this quality that has earned him the reputation as an elitist. In Du Bois's case, the hard question was how to draw distinctions. In a setting in which the main distinctions were created on the "artificial criteria" of race, he strove to assert new sorts of criteria of which African Americans were perfectly capable, criteria, moreover, that could be realized through self-help, self-development, and racial solidarity in general. Obviously such a strategy depended on "the thinking colored people of the United States," on the "Negro leadership," or, if you will, his "talented tenth." But because his conception was generous, culture was by no means limited to elites, particularly if all that elite could envision was a sorry imitation of white snobbery. His criteria of culture permitted both simple acceptance and transcendence of the mean categories imposed by race prejudice. When Du Bois rebuked the unions for barring black workers, it was to the criteria of skill that he appealed. When he waxed over the importance of art, he claimed that beauty might well "set the world right."[16]

Building refinement was at the heart of Du Bois's lifelong passion for education, and understanding his conception of culture is in turn the key to appreciating what he wanted out of education. Committed to an educated life himself, he defended learning for its own sake more vigorously than any peer, and it was the crux of his disagreement with Booker T. Washington that African American children should have access to higher education. By the turn of the century, Du Bois had arrayed against him the entire complex of racial attitudes on this matter. On the one side, he faced white supremacists for whom educating blacks in anything other than menial skills was too much; on the other side, Du Bois squared off against Washington and the powerful white philanthropists who bankrolled the Great Accommodation that kept Tuskegee afloat and Washington at the pinnacle of black leadership.[17]

As is well known, Du Bois's opposition to Washington's program of industrial education did not rest on the issue of school segregation but rather on the quality and character of the learning involved. "A black man born in Boston," he wrote in 1934, "has a duty to insist that the public school attended by all kinds and conditions of people, is the best and only door to true democracy and human understanding. But this black man in Boston has no right . . . to send his own helpless immature child into school where white children kick, cuff or abuse him, or where teachers openly and persistently neglect or hurt or dwarf its soul."[18] The crux of the issue for Du Bois was quality, not integration. "Patience, humility, manners, and taste," he wrote, were all valuable creations of "knowledge and culture, the children of the university."[19] Washington was not above getting a jab in at that small group of black intellectuals among whom Du Bois was gaining in prestige; the arrogant, impractical dreamer was just the sort to applaud when the ignorant field hand demanded his seat at the Opera House, when anyone with common sense knew that he ought to be laboring with his back and hands. For Washington and his allies, writes David Levering Lewis, "cosmopolitans like Du Bois, espousing higher learning for African Americans, embodied all the deracination and uppityness bred by the cities." And while the Wizard of Tuskegee did not have Du Bois personally in mind when he commented about the field hand in the Opera House in his historic "Atlanta Exposition Address," clearly he believed that cultural refinement was an even bigger waste of time than seeking political equality, which is to say that he dismissed it as useless.[20]

Du Bois drew these issues starkly in *The Souls of Black Folk*. It was here that he unleashed his scorching criticism of the Tuskegee Plan, built as it was not only on accommodation with white supremacy but also on the spirit of an industrial age that valued money above all other things. Du Bois had no quarrel with the theory that accumulating wealth in black hands was a prerequisite to racial advance or the idea that hard and honest work was necessary to that accumulation. But economic self-development and the husbanding of property were impossible where due process of law was systematically denied, and due process could not exist among a politically disenfranchised people. In addition to Washington's civil and political failure, however, Du Bois rarely failed to note the importance of higher learning. And while he insisted that the collapse of educational opportunities would have the practical effect of denying even Tuskegee the teachers it needed just to stay open, Du Bois rose to his most indignant at the thought of Washington deprecating learning for its own sake. "So thoroughly did he learn the speech and thought of triumphant commercialism, and the ideals of material prosperity," the scholar wrote of Washington in what for my taste is one of the most stirring images in all of American writing, "that the picture of a lone black boy poring over a French grammar amid the weeds and dirt of a neglected home soon seemed to him the acme of absurdities. One wonders what Socrates and St. Francis of Assisi would say to this."[21]

Such thinking could be construed as elitist only if Du Bois believed that intellectual skills alone were worth having. Rather than posing rarefied learning against industrial learning as the pivot on which culture lived or died, however, Du Bois praised learning of all sorts against the gospel of wealth; he defended beauty and skill against vulgarity. The gospel of wealth, increasingly offered as the solution to the South's numerous ills, was in many ways the opposite of "that fine adjustment between real life and the growing knowledge of life, an adjustment which forms the secret of civilization." That "fine adjustment" required the achievement of balance, an awareness that people were suited to different but not necessarily superior tasks. "Teach workers to work," he counseled, and "teach teachers to think." The end of such an adjustment was cultural advance. "The final product of our training must be neither a psychologist nor a brickmason, but a man. And to make men, we must have ideals, broad, pure, and inspiring ends of living. . . . The worker must work for the glory of his handiwork, not simply for pay; the thinker must think for truth, not for fame."[22]

These "broad ideals" that the educated life could bring—"patience, humility, manners, taste"—were universal in character and transcended race. Yet the particular forms that they conceivably took carried overtones of those historically constructed racial categories. If we consider how he wove poetry and musical scores together throughout *Souls*, for instance, it is clear that he considered black folk culture worthy of equal time with Euro-American symphonic art. Indeed, because Americans typically cared little for beauty while chasing material development, it was left to slaves to invent the "most beautiful expression of human experience born this side the seas," the folk song. "Persistently mistaken and misunderstood," the sorrow song "remains as the singular spiritual heritage of the nation and the greatest gift of the Negro people."[23] This juxtaposition of Europe and Africa stayed with him when the Harlem Renaissance sent him on a defense of "Negro Art" as a pan-African cultural creation. When he thought of beauty, he thought of "the cathedral at Cologne" and then "a village of the Veys in Africa," Venus de Milo, and the melancholy of the spiritual.[24]

All told, Du Bois deployed a concept of culture that drew from Boas and Matthew Arnold, a blended concept serviceable in at least four ways: Culture as learning and cultivation was the avenue for individual improvement; culture as the best that was thought and said provided the objective criteria by which the race should be measured and to which blacks were poised to contribute; culture as universal excellence and true beauty, once apprehended, made African Americans the equal of all peoples; and, finally, culture as a way of life created the glue of collective self-respect and racial solidarity against unyielding racism. When he defined the goal of collective striving—that the American Negro "be a co-worker in the kingdom of culture, to escape both death and isolation, to husband and use his best powers and his latent genius"[25]—he was thinking mostly of cultural contributions under the assumption that refinement broadly speaking would heal wounded souls and substantiate the worthiness of his race. Culture permitted Du Bois to believe that racial solidarity and achievement were to be realized along with civil equality and economic opportunity.

Ultimately, Du Bois's thinking collides in retrospect with the economic and cultural history that developed after his famous plea that economic opportunity and civil equality not bleach his Negro soul. We cannot expect him to have foreseen in 1903, when *Souls* appeared, the two imposing developments, the degradation of culture itself into a money-grubbing enterprise and the gradual assimilation of African Americans into the nation's political and economic mainstream, that have turned the tables on him. Late in life, in the aftermath of the *Brown v Board of Education* decision, he did despair over the prospects for his dream. "The very loosening" of formal segregation, he observed, had not "left Negroes free to become a group cemented into a new cultural unity, capable of absorbing socialism, tolerance, and democracy. . . . Rather, partial emancipation is freeing some of them to ape the worst of American and Anglo-Saxon chauvinism, luxury, showing-off, and 'social climbing.'"[26] His prosecution and exile as a Communist during the McCarthy-era witch hunts, through which the black intelligentsia barely summoned a word of sympathy, bitterly convinced him that the elimination of racial barriers would create a population of African Americans that resembled whites in the most ugly particulars, especially in the class divisions and political obsequiousness of its bourgeoisie.[27] While his reliance upon culture as a practical instrument of emancipation and as an ideal waned as his commitment to Marxism steadily grew after 1930, these late reflections arouse the suspicion that he might have been the first to suggest that an internal contradiction dashed his initial hopes, that when the "doors of opportunity" were finally opened, the price of entry was the bleaching of the Negro soul.

Race and Mass Culture

Du Bois's most mature assessment of Booker T. Washington was that the program of industrial self-help was based on a nineteenth-century understanding of capitalism that the rise of oligopoly and the application of technology to production made obsolete. It was hard to see how Tuskegee's recipe of individual self-help could help much in an economy built on corporate mass production.[28] Something of the same could be said about Du Bois's program of cultural advance and racial solidarity. He never quite appreciated the extent to which those very same bulwarks of capitalism would infest the cultural realm; he never anticipated that culture would become the arena of the profiteer. He never anticipated mass culture.

Even with the benefit of hindsight, coming to terms with the relationship between African Americans and mass culture is tricky business. Mass culture— and what can fairly be called popular culture in regard to the nineteenth century—has been the one realm of American life most receptive to black influence, if not participation. From minstrelsy and nineteenth-century folk music through Bugs Bunny and other trickster figures to rock and roll and now rap, African American influences have shown up frequently and have often predominated. Rather in the same way that professional sports soak up the talent and energies of the most publicly acclaimed black men, popular and mass culture have been the avenues through which many African Americans had their lives funneled. All too often, poor youths still see their futures only as jocks or entertainers. A distinctly mass culture presents yet another dilemma, then. It is an avenue of acceptance and, at least in the most celebrated instances, the road to wealth and fame, but it also exacts at least two heavy costs. First, mass culture sucks away any organic connection of performance to community, whitewashing, in effect, whatever distinctly black character originally existed; and, second, it discourages the sort of commitment to excellence that Du Bois saw as so important to the universal criteria of culture.

In light of the entertainment industry's tendency to expropriate black art forms, it makes sense to say that racial solidarity can best be preserved by remaining aloof to mass culture. But here is the rub: For African Americans, remaining outside the mainstream historically has meant accepting social and political marginalization, accepting, in other words, the unacceptable. In contemporary America, African Americans confront a choice between marginalization and alienation, and it is important to keep this distinction in mind. A marginalized people can maintain cultural integrity because they reside mostly outside institutional structures; only people immersed in mass society can be alienated, because there they lose recourse to the protective buffers of an intact world but are deprived of the necessary materials to rebuild the intermediary world.

One way of appreciating this intractable dilemma is to consider mass media and race. While mass culture had begun to incorporate African Americans in the 1920s and 1930s through the production and distribution of jazz and blues, that inclusion was incomplete through the 1950s. So-called race music was marketed almost entirely to African Americans and could be heard over only a few radio stations nationwide. The early rock DJs, such as Cleveland's Alan Freed, became legendary only because they were willing to tweak the racial barrier by playing some race music under a new name, rock and roll. With African American buying power negligible, advertisers of cars and other mainstream products spent no effort to court their dollars with black images in ads. This indifference to African Americans as consumers helped foster parallel racial universes and create that semi-autonomous world of black life that many contemporary writers now remember with passionate reverence.

Through the 1950s, what images appeared on television were drawn from age-old stereotypes: There was Jack Benny's butler, Rochester, and Amos and Andy. That was the decade in which the television industry exploded, with ownership running from barely a few thousand in 1950 to nearly 90 percent of American households by 1960. Television was part of the world of "colored people," as Henry Louis Gates, Jr. recalls, and brought the outside world to what otherwise was a deeply provincial setting. "Literally overnight," he writes in his recent memoir, television introduced him and his family to a world "light-years away" from what they had known. Having interacted only with whites through that stilted, arm's-length relationship that segregation demanded, Gates "first got to know white people as 'people' through their flickering images on television shows." From them he learned of what appeared to be the interior lives of whites and, most of all, of the material prosperity that whites had evidently come to expect. It never occurred to the young Gates—and why should it have?—that these were artificial images that eluded most whites. The point was that Beaver Cleaver's suburban comfort was something to aspire to, something that was worth going to a recently integrated public school for. Otherwise, there was not much else to see. The only "colored" folks permitted to grace the screen were mostly athletes, such as Joe Louis or Jackie Robinson. "Lord knows, we weren't going to learn how to be colored by watching television," he writes. "Seeing somebody colored on TV was an event." And so when anyone came on, everyone tuned in. The neighbors yelled across porches or huffed over the phone: "Colored, colored on Channel Two." And the one show that featured colored people, Amos 'n Andy, that holdover from the age of minstrelsy, was, by Gates's reckoning, the best show of all. While finer people might scorn it as buffoonery, the residents of Piedmont, West Virginia, saw the show as good comedy that, after all, included colored people as doctors, lawyers, landowners, and the like.

Both their status and silliness set them apart from "the colored people we knew."[29]

Gates's point in this amusing discussion is severalfold. For one thing, he wants to describe just how seldom a nonwhite face came across the screen and how thoroughly white the image of the good life was. But because he, his family, and his community believed that their life was, all things considered, pretty good, they viewed those images with a mix of envy, a craving for justice, and cynicism; at least they were critical viewers who diffracted what they saw through their own sense of the world. But the larger point may be that television was a powerful medium that intruded into a close-knit and cloistered world, suckering people into surrounding themselves with artificial images to which they were more or less forced to respond.

So here is the difficulty: In a society in which television is a central medium, the dominant imparter of information and images alike, basic justice required that African Americans be represented and represented fairly; yet as soon as television gets into the business of projecting images, local communities lose control over self-definition. Say all you want about the critical viewer or the "agency" of the consumer, the fact is that the mass-produced image is still the public image that must be responded to and that goes far to define people in the eyes of others. Surely one of the clear messages from Gates's memoir is that young people growing up in the warmth of a stable home and community have the resources necessary to maintain control over their identities. But he presents a frozen moment in time when television was just beginning its intrusion into provincial lives, and as those communities, made paradoxically strong and stable by the rigidity of segregation, dissolved, so too did the capacity of young people—and adults—to control their public definitions.

On the whole, African Americans have worked two characteristic solutions to this dilemma, neither of which, to my mind, is very fruitful. The first, the answer of the integrationists, is to negotiate with, plead with, or cajole television executives to increase the number of minority roles in their shows, their newsrooms, and their boardrooms and to make sure that the images depicted are positive—call it the *Cosby* solution. Under Kweisi Mfume and behind the jargon of cultural diversity, the NAACP has aggressively pursued this strategy, with decidedly mixed results. The newsrooms of all the networks, and their local affiliates to a great degree, have been integrated for years, and in many cities the African American anchors on local channels are prominent community members and celebrities whose images are invariably positive. Yet the national networks have not responded to pressure with any solid commitment to expanding roles for African American actors.

One wonders where the wisdom is in the NAACP's position. If the organization's goal was simply to increase black employment in the entertainment industry, that is one thing. But the effort is typically discussed as part of the quest for diversity. Yet it is impossible to see how black actors on yet another sitcom, hospital show, or cop show would serve the cause of cultural diversity. Inevitably, the more television complies with NAACP demands, the more television executives influence the image and identities of African Americans, thus depriving people of control over community self-understanding.

The second solution to this dilemma, the nationalist plan, is black ownership of the means of cultural production, the only way for African Americans to move into the commercial heart of the nation and still enjoy the creative control necessary for preserving heritage. This has been the age-old wish dream of cultural nationalists, none of whom have ever been more passionate or persuasive than Harold Cruse, who rested his thesis in *The Crisis of the Negro Intellectual* on just this point. Cruse put the Harlem Renaissance—for that matter Harlem itself—squarely at the heart of black cultural nationalism and argued that the white conquest of the theaters, clubs, and other cultural institutions during the 1930s doomed the movement. Without economic control, black artists had no choice but to seek to integrate into the wider white-dominated cultural scene, which compelled them, Cruse complained, to participate "either on the basis of white middle-class standards, or as stepping stones to middle-class status using Negro art expression." Posing the matter as starkly as anyone could imagine, he wrote: "Harlem, once the artistic and cultural mecca of the Negro world, has been almost completely deracinated culturally; this deracination happens to coincide with the Northern Negroes' highest gains in integration. Integration is thus leading to cultural negation." Every genuine innovation in "the popular arts idiom" came from African Americans and specifically from Harlem, he insisted, but for its generosity, Harlem was repaid with "a cultural scorched earth policy."[30]

Cruse called for community reconquest built solidly on black ownership and entrepreneurship as the means of preserving black culture in both senses—that is, distinctly black art in a coherent black community. It was an edifying vision in that it merged economic structure with community solidarity and cultural production. But during the 1990s, the theory has been put to the test and has not borne the sort of fruit he and many others had hoped for it. The theory is flawed because it assumed that race and culture would remain loyally bound, that the former would inherently follow the latter, and that black control would necessarily sustain black culture. The nationalist argument, which is largely caught up in the contemporary romance with culture, never adequately accounted for the strength of market behavior. If the nature of mass-communications technologies created the dilemma for the integrationists, the unvarying dictates of the market spoil the nationalist dream. To put it simply, where African Americans have controlled cultural production, they have behaved according to the same rules of business that prevail elsewhere. In the cases of television and music, black control has indeed translated into more African American participation and arguably more cultural influence by African Americans. But this is different from saying that it has encouraged an expansion or improved the health of African American culture. It is crucial to see that instead of fostering black creativity or excellence, widened influence extended through the market has only meant the dilution of forms and the triumph of bad black art.

The most obvious example is that of Robert Johnson's Black Entertainment Television, the nation's first black-owned and black-operated television network, the first one geared to an African American audience, and one of the first black-owned enterprises listed on the New York stock exchange. During the 1990s, Johnson made himself an archetype of the new cultural entrepreneur, boldly laying claim to a place at the core of mainstream culture while just as boldly aiming to produce for blacks, about blacks, and with blacks. He took advantage of the opportunities provided by the recent expansion of cable and found his foothold in the niche of music videos; because MTV was originally reluctant to carry "race" music, Johnson was able to get a start by broadcasting rap videos. As cable expanded, so did BET, until it became available to an estimated 90 percent of African American cable subscribers. BET promised not only race-conscious programming but more intelligent programming by securing the talents of talk show hosts such as Tavis Smiley, whose programs were both unabashedly political and consistently provocative.

By the end of the decade, however, Johnson had sold the network to the media giant Viacom. The network lost its most talented people, including Smiley, whose talk show was cancelled after the Viacom buyout, and settled into a routine of programming that was mostly a mix of popular music videos and stand-up comedy. Under Viacom, the network retains the veneer of race consciousness—its nightly news program continues to boast its attention to "our people, our issues, our culture"—but BET's programming clearly has become retrograde, its political content increasingly diluted and its cultural programming dedicated almost entirely to two entertainment genres far too closely associated with a narrow and limited black presence in mainstream life. Meanwhile, Johnson has moved ahead with his plans to widen his reach.

In the late 1990s, he launched a BET Internet business, began building large shopping developments in the Washington area, and proposed the first black-owned and -operated airline, which was to use Washington as its hub. He has made himself wealthy—he is among the wealthiest African Americans—and has quite publicly both promoted black entrepreneurship and cultivated young managerial talent. He has succeeded on the basis of race consciousness and in pursuit of a racially distinct consumer base. It is not at all clear, however, that BET has in any way either sustained a distinctly African American culture or improved the medium of television. If there is a defense for Johnson, it isn't that he has to act like a businessman in order to compete effectively but rather that improving television is a thankless task because the very nature of the medium defies refinement.

A still better example of how the control of production does not translate into either cultural solidarity or artistic excellence is the rise of rap. No other product has been so aggressively promoted as a distinct creation of young urban black males. No other product has been so lauded among the intellectual classes for its gritty authenticity and political confrontationalism. No other product has been so regularly claimed as the most recent expression of enduring African American cultural forms. And no other product has had quite the same combination of commercial success and black entrepreneurial control.

The rise of rap to dominance in mass-produced youth entertainment provided unique opportunities for go-getting, aspiring producers to edge their way into the music industry, in part because the genre emerged from very recent street-level origins and in part because mainstream executives, particularly established African American producers, saw the genre as a flash in the pan hardly worth their time. The most successful—or perhaps notorious is a better word—rap labels were organized and run by young black men who drove their way into the business largely by sheer pluck, not to say intimidation, as is alleged in the case of Suge Knight and Death Row Records. At the same time, hailing as they did from urban areas amid America's inner-city catastrophes during the 1970s and 1980s, they were self-consciously determined to stay true to their roots by promoting acts that for the most part also came out of inner cities.

As a lesson in how to build an industry, the story of Def Jam and other rap labels ought to be included in introductory business classes. Through the energies of young men such as Russell Simmons, Def Jam's founder, rap was taken from an underground piece of cultural ephemera to a commercial phenomenon, and Simmons, for one, is perfectly honest about how and why he did so. He likes money. Rap was mostly a great big business opportunity, and he had the gumption to take advantage of it. Rap was supposed to be the voice of young African Americans for whom the juxtaposition of poverty amid the nation's consumer splendor generated what Cornel West spoke of as "a detachment from others and a self-destructive disposition toward the world."[31] To Simmons, these roots in despair and alienation only made it all the more marketable, since alienation is typically the sentiment that moves all young people. What he perceived, correctly it turned out, was that rap's alienated voice would appeal to young people regardless of race, which he saw as a guaranteed access to a nearly insatiable global market. Alienation was "the creative touchstone for . . . aggressive youth culture around the world," he boasts. "That's why my business is bigger than it's ever been." He also figured that rap was more than just music—I doubt that it rates even as that. "Hip-hop is more expansive," he tells us in his autobiography. "The ideas of hip-hop are spread not just through music, but in fashion, movies, television, advertising, dancing, slang, and attitude." The market for rap is huge, in other words, and from the first Simmons counted on developing his "artists" as movie stars, inaugurating a clothing line, and organizing comedy tours. His model was not Berry Gordy, Jr., the famous founder of Motown Records, the writer Ellis Cashmore has perceptively observed, but Time Warner. Given such a model, it was inevitable that Def Jam would be snapped up in a merger, in this case with CBS. "I knew I couldn't do it on my own," Simmons admitted.[32]

Simmons's autobiography makes for fascinating reading. He is very much a man of his time. Note, for instance, how loosely he uses culture. Hip-hop culture essentially is a disposition toward the world or, he might say, an attitude, and that attitude is a simple one: It is rebellious, but rebellion aimed "to acquire all the things normally denied me." Its "raw" honesty is in its brazen acquisitiveness. At the same time, Simmons places hip-hop culture within African American culture. But he also suggests that hip-hop culture has become "the new American mainstream," which is probably the most accurate description, if indeed the defining value in hip-hop is acquisitiveness.[33]

In describing hip-hop this way, Simmons is far more honest than many of the academics, white and black, who have lauded rap variously—and sometimes simultaneously—as a notable form of "cultural resistance" and the most important recent expression of the Afro-American oral tradition, reaching back at the very least to the game of the dozens, if not back, as some would say, to the grand oral traditions of Africa itself. It is hard to see just what people obsessed with obtaining material goods can be said to be resisting, so that even an author inclined to be sympathetic to rappers might lament, as does

Todd Boyd, that they "accept the violent tropes of political resistance without the informed ideology that separates gangsters from freedom fighters."[34]

It is almost as difficult to stretch rap back to the African American oral tradition. On the face of it, that stretch is not outrageous, but that it makes any sense is another example of how culture is so flexible that it can loop together any two things. Rap probably had its start not in New York but in Jamaica, where disk jockeys first began to speak over recorded music at festivals and parties, but in any event it found a home in New York's black neighborhoods and party clubs in the late 1970s. At a point when the dominant genre was disco, practically anything this side of country-pop sounded good, so when a handful of local DJs began to scratch up records while "rapping" over them, they sounded interesting; when they started putting those to the heavy beats of rhythm machines, they created a stir.

If this constitutes another point in a cultural tradition, then so be it. But it is doubtful that there was much self-conscious knowledge of African American oral traditions among rappers. Rap's claim to fame is that its creators and performers are steeped in that most marginalized of social environments, the inner-city ghetto, an environment otherwise known for its social annihilation, for the absence of institutions across which cultural values and forms are typically passed. Young people reared in the absence of or in utter hostility to civil society are not likely to have very firm grasps of traditions of any sort, and where they do, those traditions come in the form of half-digested bits of partial knowledge diluted by rumor and falsehood.

There is, additionally, a more plausible explanation for the origins of rap: "It was a cheap form of entertainment," Ellis Cashmore wryly observes, "well-suited to the times."[35] Because it required only some sound equipment, the performers did not need big bands, with all their overhead and heavy equipment. Indeed, there was no need for musicians. A rap DJ could play a party or a club and be assured of the whole night's take. No wonder "there was a lot of resentment" from established acts, as Russell Simmons remembers. "Big bands with horn sections and background singers were the norm in black music. Guys were on the road with seven or eight pieces, plus the roadies and a road manager. They'd walk away with $10 per gig." By contrast, "there was no big nightly nut to crack for a rap act. We were revolutionizing the concert business by playing major venues without a band. People acted like we were stealing money, so they treated us like thieves."[36]

Considering how important musicianship has been to African American culture in this century, the casting out of musicians themselves would seem to qualify the claim that rap was rooted in that culture. Here again Simmons helps us see things for what they are. Rappers were not musicians, which freed them up to be artists, so-called. Entertainers would be the fairer word, of course, but the point is that because they had no real craft, they could be lucrative jacks-of-all-trades. They could make CDs, they could make movies, and they had to make videos. There are no Duke Ellingtons among the rappers: They, Simmons gladly admits, are more like WWF wrestlers. Like pro wrestlers, rappers "took basic young male fantasies of power and inflated them into . . . over-the-top cartoons." At the same time, they dispensed with all the fuss of learning an instrument, which made for a quicker and easier path to wealth and fame. "No longer would learning instruments be the only way or even the best way to build a career in music." [37]

Simmons could not have been more blunt. Music without instruments—there is a formula appropriate to a society that no longer cares about skill. Even if we generously grant that rappers are talented people who cultivate the tricky skill of rhyming, it can in no way compare to the arduous task of mastering an instrument, not the least important part of which rests in becoming familiar with the history of what has been accomplished already with that instrument. Simmons is right to see rap as the heir not to jazz, blues, or Motown but to rock, which has gone stale and lost its capacity to represent youthful rebelliousness. This connection is true in another way: One of the hallmarks of rock in its infancy was the simplicity of the music and ease of entry into the "industry"; another was the poverty of its musicianship. If rock was to music what mass production was to work, then rap is to music what computers are to work; the first debased skill, the latter does away with the worker altogether.

Rap is not only anti-culture in its mock nihilism, it is distinctly anti-African American culture. This is why Wynton Marsalis has lately and courageously been attacking rap as a modern form of minstrelsy. "People get confused a lot of times with race," Marsalis explained in a NPR interview. Rap has nothing to do with the black musical tradition, and everything to do with the demeaning activity of caricaturing African Americans, he said. Indeed, rap is "a cousin to rock," not to gospel, blues, or jazz. It plays on the same "I-want-you-to-pay-me-to-insult-you" notes as adolescent pop rebellion.[38]

Marsalis's criticisms have the wisdom of authority and expertise behind them, but even they exhibit an unfortunate tendency, inherent to Du Bois's dilemma, to be obsessed with authenticity. To some extent, the craving for authentic expression is like alienation in that it grips thinking people of all sorts who are rightly dissatisfied with the shallow reproductions of once-genuine folk art. In the same way that the country music purist detests the suburbanized sewage that sells today, where a cowboy hat and jeans allows Garth

Brooks to masquerade as Hank Williams's heir, those genuinely concerned with the preservation of African American music rightly scorn rap. The rap industry itself struggles against this pressure; all of their performers are marketed as real gangstas, even white boys such as Eminem, beneath claims that they are the true voices of the 'hood. That many of them, like Russell Simmons, hail from middle-class backgrounds and stable families only makes the claims to authenticity more urgent. In this sense, the craving for authenticity is closely related to the quest for identity and, indeed, for culture: Authenticity is one of those things that people do not think about until it disappears. And as with identity, mass-marketed claims to it only serve as a final insult to cultural origins, for they turn authenticity itself into a phony facsimile for sale.

The African American quest for authenticity is a reflection of the larger effects of mass society, and while those effects are not unique to them, it seems to me that the sense of dislocation and its accompanying yearning for genuine culture are more intense, given the long and doleful history of race relations in America. Having long found refuge in a largely autonomous cultural realm, the one realm where a people denied economic opportunity or a civic existence might exercise some collective self-control and solidarity, African Americans must necessarily fear the ebbing away of that control as the political and economic realms open up to them. At the very least, Du Bois's dilemma encourages a constant loyalty test, which manifests itself in the sort of pressure against "acting white" that John McWhorter recently bemoaned as one of the forms of "self-sabotage" in his 2000 polemic, *Losing the Race*. Because the loyalty test questions racial solidarity rather than how culture is created, it misses the point entirely. For it both insists on the opportunity to produce and market music or film or what have you and at the same time insists that the material produced reflect a commitment to racial purity. What the cultural loyalty test never confronts, however, is that the very means of cultural production today, whether in music, television, or film, cannot stay "true" to the community; by its technological nature, in contrast to its racial point of origins, it will be inauthentic and, paradoxically, intensify the yearning for authenticity.

The New Crisis of the Black Intellectual

The same dilemma that frustrates cultural nationalists greets black intellectuals as well, who must struggle with the added burdens of being intellectuals in America, which has never particularly liked its thinkers and, more to the point here, has adeptly confined them to the university, where they can be controlled with the blandishments of the bureaucratic order.

If the general preoccupation with identity surges in direct proportion to the extent of structural assimilation, then it stands to reason that African American intellectuals would be the most preoccupied of people. Consider the mind-boggling conundrums they face. Those writers and thinkers who now occupy the upper ranks of the black intellectual elite constitute the first postsegregation generation, and they are old enough to remember well what segregation was like. Largely too young to have confronted the worst of the system, most probably protected by caring, hardworking parents, they are more likely to recall those years with fondness than with bitterness. They remember the local, provincial life among the protective buffers of extended families, thriving churches, black teachers in all-black schools—all told, the cohesive communities that were at once the products of racial injustice and the birthing grounds of civil rights activism. They have benefited enormously from the collapse of segregation, some specifically from affirmative action; the most productive and celebrated have taken positions in elite universities, where they enjoy the privileges of tenured professorships and, in some cases, are among the highest-paid humanists in the history of American academia. By all the measurements that notoriously insecure and status-conscious American academics use to rank themselves, the African American intellectual elite is the cream of the crop—not just of black academics but of all academics. Yet, it is safe to say, many of them secured their reputations by holding to the contemporary version of radicalism, with all its culture-conscious attention to various forms of oppression and minority "empowerment." Having come of age at the moment when the WASP ideal was collapsing in the face of black nationalism and the ethnic revival, they imbibed cultural determinism from their formative mental world, much as Marxism provided the entire framework of thinkers growing up in the 1930s.

As that "crossover" generation of African Americans whom history asked to start the dance with white-dominated institutions, much was being asked of them, both by fellow blacks who wanted them to be "credits to the race" and by university officials who developed a considerable vested interest in their success. Such pressures had to be enormous and were compounded by the discomfort that accompanies all contemporary radicalism in America, which ingeniously rewards its critics with such comfortable positions that their radicalism tends to appear self-contradictory. Much as mass culture rewards the rappers who have made nice livings insulting people, the present black intellectual elite has secured tenure and reputation by scolding the very system whose perks they have accepted. The rappers have one important advantage over the intellectuals: Never shy about laying claim to gold, they can be more honest.

During the 1990s, this situation, as perplexing as it is torturous, predictably encouraged some African American writers to insist on white America's unflagging will to racial dominance. At odds with the facts of black economic and institutional progress, more clearly in contradiction to their own secure positions, writers such as bell hooks, Derrick Bell, Patricia Williams, and Ellis Cose sustained a steady drumbeat of accusation. The gap between reality and rhetoric gave rise, predictably, to exaggeration. Every slight was turned into evidence of unrelenting racism. It goes without saying that small slights are unfortunate, but the very tendency to see them as proof of racial dominance proves just how much has changed. Moreover, the "rage of the privileged class," the "excruciating pain" of the otherwise healthy black middle class, is rarely accounted for as an inevitable result of the alienation that always accompanies the inclusion into the bureaucratic order; instead the easy tendency is to chalk it up to racism.

John McWhorter argues that these exaggerations result from the "cult of victimology," and his explanation for this "disease" is an interesting one. It festers, he says, from two sources. On the one hand, the moral standing of the civil rights movement gave African Americans a pass "to confront whites with their indignation and frustration on a regular basis and be listened to." On the other, the long history of "abasement and marginalization" embedded in the collective psyche an inferiority complex that encourages people to "downplay and detract attention from [their] victories, carefully shielding their children from the good in favor of the bad." This "lethal combination" of an "inherited inferiority complex with the privilege of dressing down the former oppressor" has created a "race driven by self-hate and fear to spend more time inventing reasons to cry 'racism' than working to be the best that it can be."[39]

In my view, the first part of McWhorter's explanation makes sense. Particularly for thinkers weaned on a certain energetic level of racist-baiting and whose present positions to some extent were realized through that activity, conceding racial progress cannot be an easy thing; doing so might wreak havoc on a career, to say nothing of the individual psychological readjustment that it would exact. His second explanation, however, is less convincing. One of the strengths of McWhorter's book is that it is crafted to speak directly to African Americans, in contrast to, say, Shelby Steele's writings, which are not specifically aimed at fellow blacks and, it might be said, were all the more comforting to white readers for that reason. But this strength has a downside: McWhorter himself works on the assumption that there is a coherent, steady "cultural blackness" that dictates public form for African Americans. It is hard for him to see, accordingly, that the cult of victimization is hardly peculiar to African Americans, that in fact it is the standard ticket that all political interest groups punch these days; rather than a sign of or a holdover from the days of marginalization, the cult of victimization places the black intellectual elite solidly in the American mainstream. The only way McWhorter can address African Americans at large is to hold to the impression that there still is a coherent African American culture, but it is that coherence that can no longer be taken for granted, and it is the ero-sion of that culture that is more likely behind the generalized sense of alien-ation that undergirds the intellectuals' unease with their world.

One indication that such is the case is the surprising emergence of racial nostalgia. The most obvious purveyor of that tendency in recent years has been Clifton Taulbert, whose *Once Upon a Time When We Were Colored* used the gentle beams of moonlight and the sweet scent of magnolias, which once graced the white folks' mental picture of the South, to swath the world of African Americans under segregation. Taulbert's work is astonishing, cer-tainly not because of its depth but for its studied elimination of racial injus-tice from a society built on racial injustice. Growing up in a time and place where white thugs could drag Emmett Till out of his grandfather's house, blow his head off, dump his corpse into a river, and be acquitted, Taulbert nonetheless sees little that was unfortunate "once upon a time." The title is indicative: Like most fairy tales, it evokes a sense of unreality from the be-ginning.

Taulbert is not an academic, it is true, and his work was received uneasily in intellectual circles. But the nostalgic tendencies manifested themselves there as well; bell hooks, for one, was perfectly frank about it. "Nostalgia for that time [of segregation] often enters my dreams," she admitted in 1990. She recalled "the world of Southern, rural, black growing up," where the adults, especially the women schoolteachers, "knew your people . . . and shared their insight, keeping us in touch with generations. It was a world where we had a history." That "sacred world" began to crumble, in her mind, when the schools were desegregated, which cast her out of the comfort of segregated life and into a high school where the white students held "mostly contempt for us." What she remembers of the time, mostly, was "a deep sense of loss."[40] Desegregation was a distinctly unpleasant experience because school author-ities expected the black students to do all the hard work of changing. Hooks ends by saying that "we . . . long[ed] for the days when school was a place where we learned to love and celebrate ourselves, a place where we were number one."[41]

Or consider Henry Louis Gates, Jr.'s memoir, *Colored People*. Gates is now the commanding presence among African American academics and, if not the most widely known, at least the most conventionally successful. A graduate of Yale, a Rhodes Scholar with a Cambridge Ph.D., Gates was the architect of Harvard's famed Department of African and African American Studies, the finest collection of black intellectual talent this side of wherever W. E. B. Du Bois happened to be at any given time. Gates made his career as a literary critic, but he spent a good deal of his time during the 1990s either organizing material for or writing about issues of culture and identity, and one senses that these were the concerns that goaded him into writing an autobiography.

Unlike hooks, Gates stops short of admitting to nostalgia, but the memoir is an exercise in it from front to back. And that is a strange thing. People write memoirs for many reasons, after all: some as catharsis, some in self-exculpation, some because they were involved in dramatic events or led high-profile lives, some simply as self-advertisement. None of these apply to Gates. One would think that a Harvard professor, the chair no less of the most eminent department in the field, would not be eager to share his provincial upbringing with the reading public unless it was to illustrate his escape from his country confines, his liberation from the rural folk. His could have been a new version of the country-boy-makes-good-in-the-big-city tale. But it is none of that. *Colored People* is, instead, a wistful, heartfelt remembrance of how good the provincial life was, warts and all. Why admit to harboring loving memories of segregated papermill "pic-a-nics" or boozing at the VFW unless Harvard Square just hadn't been able to replicate the spiritual depth and psychological comfort of smalltown life under segregation? Gates is a radiant example of structural assimilation, and surely the security and comfort from which he writes gives him leave to romanticize about the provinces in ways that would be impossible for someone still striving for achievement. Yet like the assimilated white ethnics who romanticized thirty years ago about grandmother's cooking or grandfather's wine-making, Gates salivates over Uncle Nemo's corn on the cob. Something, evidently, is still missing in Cambridge.

There is some profit to be had in comparing *Colored People* to some of the more widely read African American memoirs, particularly Zora Neale Hurston's *Dust Tracks on a Road*, in part because Gates has written about Hurston and certainly knows the book and because there are reasons to suspect that Hurston crept into his thinking as he wrote, consciously or not. Moreover, Gates positions Hurston in a quite crucial role in his broad study of African American literature, *The Signifying Monkey*, as a pioneer of sorts, one of the first writers willing to put a distinctly powerful black voice, with all the tradition of rhetorical strategies and wordplay behind it, in fiction. In a cer-

tain sense, Hurston marks the moment when black culture-consciousness began to work its way into African American writing and is a bridge, accordingly, to Alice Walker and Toni Morrison.

These two autobiographies are very much alike in at least one crucial respect: Both speak well of growing up in the web of black life within segregation. Hurston's Eatonville, Florida, was not just a black community but a
"Negro town—charter, mayor, council, town marshal and all."[42] Gates's Piedmont, West Virginia, had its white folks, but Gates and his neighbors barely
knew them. "Our neighborhoods were clearly demarcated, as if by ropes or
turnstiles. Welcome to the Colored Zone, a large stretched banner could
have said. And it felt good in there, like walking around your house in bare
feet and underwear . . . swaddled by the comforts of home, the warmth of
those you love."[43]

Beyond that, though, Hurston's autobiography smacks heavily of the pick-
yourself-up-by your-bootstraps story, beginning with the fond descriptions of
her father as a hardworking family provider and her account of how a love of
learning carried her through Morgan to Howard to Barnard. Gates's account,
as I've hinted, is more an anti–upwardly mobile story. While Hurston likes to
drop names as road markers—in Baltimore she rubbed shoulders with the
children of the town's "best Negro families," for instance—Gates writes with
a measure of hesitation of his father's family. In contrast to his mother's family, the Colemans, his father's folks hailed mostly from that distant metropo-
lis, Cumberland, Maryland; they were light skinned, many of them; and they
were professionals whose credentials included Howard and Harvard. Though
it is obviously this side of the family whose path he followed in life, Gates
writes with a tinge of sarcasm of their obsession with education, telling them
at his grandfather's funeral that he intended to be a doctor too: "Maybe a
brain surgeon. I'd seen that on *Ben Casey*."[44]

Hardly a note of disrespect, Gates's quip about that old show is nonetheless indicative of a very different disposition toward learning, education, and
refinement when compared to Hurston's account. Education was absolutely
central to Hurston's life; she sought self-conscious refinement through the
acquisition of the classics and came to identify with "the immortal brains of
Coleridge." Her love of reading is a constant thread, and even where she
sheepishly admits to having cut her teeth on a good deal of "trash," she accounts her dalliance with pulp fiction as "a help, because acquiring the reading habit early is the important thing. Taste and natural development will
take care of the rest later on." No doubt, in her mind, taste and natural development came her way. It is curious, by contrast, that Gates, the very
model of the present-day scholar, has almost nothing to say about those

things that excited his intellectual passions as a boy. The literary critic never seems to have read a book, much less Coleridge; he acknowledges nothing more than a love of "globes and maps and geography."[45] Television and recorded music, the sort of material Hurston at least admitted was trashy, figure far more prominently in Gates's coming of age. It is hard to believe that his disciplinarian parents let him stew in front of the television as much as he suggests; elsewhere, in fact, he writes that they repeatedly insisted that "education is the one thing nobody can take from you."[46] So it is strange that he doesn't want to own up to reading books as a kid. And given the immensely learned quality of his mature work, one can only conclude that he neglects the subject because, in contrast to his forebears such as Hurston, or even Frederick Douglass, Gates has no need to prove himself a cultured individual. Implicitly, Gates indicates the vastly improved position of African Americans in American intellectual life. Whereas Hurston, like Du Bois, asserted a claim to learning and refinement—to culture—because more conventional measures of success were denied, Gates, the renowned Harvard professor, is under no such pressure.

If Hurston can be criticized for a too-obvious desire for social climbing, then it is entirely fair to suggest that Gates strains too hard to climb back down, and this decisive difference undoubtedly reflects the objectively different social positions that African Americans have occupied across these generations. Nowhere is this difference clearer than in the conclusions of these memoirs. After dismissing racial solidarity as impossible, Hurston, good Boasian that she was, also dismisses the assumption that culture follows race. "My kinfolks and my 'skin-folks' are dearly loved," she asserts. "My circumference of everyday life is there. But I see their same virtues and vices everywhere I look." She then waxes about that great day when race matters not at all. Then, she dreams, "maybe all of us who do not have the good fortune to meet, or meet again, in this world, will meet at a barbecue." Compare that heavenly barbecue to Gates's wistful yearning for that last mill "pic-a-nic," made tragically obsolete, if not illegal, when the civil rights revolution "came crashing down upon the colored world of Piedmont," obliterating "its most beloved, and cementing, ritual. . . . Nobody wanted segregation, you understand; but nobody thought of this as segregation." Hurston dreams of an integrated barbecue to which she was never invited; Gates wants to return to a segregated picnic he can never have again. After all, "who in their right mind wanted to attend the mill picnic with the white people, when it meant shutting the colored one down?"[47]

If this is nostalgic, Gates still is confronting a disconcerting truth. The abundant defense mechanisms that African Americans built into their col-

lective way of life, wisely dependent on the strength of intermediary institutions of family, church, VFWs and black-run schools—even, we can concede, mill picnics—were undermined to the extent that the civil rights revolution worked its magic and African Americans became both structurally
assimilated and deracinated, just like the white ethnics. There are two very
important differences, nonetheless, between African Americans and their
ethnic fellows, between Gates and Tom Hayden. Hayden's Irishness is all
concoction. He may feel it every bit as intensely as though he were St.
Patrick or Gerry Adams, but it is still contrived. Gates and his peers are
dwelling in the midst of real, tangible memories, experiences as dearly held
and as powerful as the echo of a deceased parent's voice or the comfort of
their lap, memories that reside so hauntingly close to the surface that a smell,
a song, a turn of phrase can unleash tears in the most inappropriate places.

There is, additionally, the serious social problem of the incomplete revolution. Our racial cup remains half-empty, with far too many African American men institutionally assimilated only to the criminal justice system,
among other outstanding difficulties. While I'm convinced that our present
preoccupation with culture hardly helps us get to the remaining problems—
that in fact a genuine national commitment to universal education, to culture in the old-fashioned sense of learning and refinement, and affirmative
action in housing are the most practical solutions—it is not hard to understand an ongoing preoccupation with racial solidarity as a form of collective
self-protection. While such a mechanism is understandable for African
Americans, it is inexcusable for the likes of Tom Hayden, who, by contrast,
has to find oppression in assimilation rather than in some objective evidence
of Irish marginalization. Gates can still drive from Cambridge over to Roxbury to point to America's ongoing race-based failures; Hayden has to go to
Belfast, and even there has to confuse conflict with oppression in order to
achieve racial feeling. But at the same time, this social reality implies that
cultural nostalgia is the vain comfort of the comfortable, which is also to say
that while Gates's racial sensibility is legitimate as compared to Hayden's
phoniness, his own children would be well advised to grow out of the old
man's memories.

Whereas Hayden's newfound Irish nationalism resembles the embarrassing eagerness of the born again, there remains a moral imperative toward
racial justice that still beckons the black intellectual toward racial solidarity,
and in pursuing his obligations in this vein, Gates hit upon what must have
appeared initially to be a solution to Du Bois's dilemma. He writes in another
autobiographical piece, "Parable of the Talents," that he instinctively distrusted "the sort of institutions through which elites sustain themselves" and

fled Exeter as a teen because he found it so alienating; as an undergraduate at Yale, by contrast, he immersed himself in the growing black student contingent and thrived.[48] He apparently determined to repeat the Yale experience once appointed chair of Harvard's Department of African and African American Studies. There Gates proceeded to attract the best of the talented tenth, which came to include the renowned sociologist William Julius Wilson, the Ghanaian philosopher Kwame Anthony Appiah, and the most visible of black intellectuals, Cornel West. It was as though he expected to recreate Piedmont on a different plane at Harvard. In place of millworkers and preachers, there would be the best of academic minds; the VFW was spruced up a bit into the faculty club and scotch replaced draft beer. The worst of Cambridge snobbery, which most certainly would have been agonizing for the lone black faculty member, could give way to some real signifyin', as Gates and his colleagues reveled in the comfort of one another's company because each was black and each was brilliant. From here they would reclaim the black intellectual's dedication to racial uplift, hoping against hope to avoid the fate of the much-maligned black bourgeoisie. Was it not fated that such an effort would go for naught, as indeed it has, obviously failing to alleviate Gates's uneasiness with the world, amounting to an ineffectual wisp of a political effort, not even able, in the end, to hold its vaunted members together?

Any reasonable reflection on Gates's work in the last decade must insist on his willingness to face these questions of status and identity forthrightly, his nostalgia for village life notwithstanding. Even where it remains necessary to try to live up to the obligations of the talented tenth, the sociological reality is that the "black community" no longer exists. Du Bois's notion that educated people could and would rise to lead those lagging behind is just as fictional where the interests of the haves and have-nots vary to the point of incompatibility. All the appeals to cultural nationalism are self-delusory covers over the sociological chasm, "which no amount of kinte cloth or Kwanzaa celebrations will change. . . . The real crisis in black leadership," Gates concludes, "is that the very idea of black leadership is in crisis."[49]

If this is true for public figures, it is all the more true of intellectuals. Those in the crossover generation had to deal with the extreme pressures to be the ideologues of the race, credits to the race, mentors to the race—all at the same time. And it must be said that these pressures erupted not only from African Americans but from the intellectual establishment as well, which invested a great deal of optimism in the crossover generation to which it looked for solutions to the festering racial problems. This last created an odd situation in which the vast majority of established white intellectuals provided a pass to many black writers and artists—those, at least, who didn't get lumped into that strange category of the "black conservatives." Searching criticism was deemed impolite, and yet at the same time black writers and artists unleashed strenuous intellectual efforts to prove that they belonged to the thinking classes. Meanwhile, they had to accept the material rewards that accompanied Ivy League professorships, for to do so satisfied the long-standing equation of education with wealth among middle-class blacks. They had to maintain a common touch, if not an organic relationship to whatever was deemed to be authentically black, for to do any less was to be selfish or a traitor and would certainly destroy the individual's legitimacy as a spokesperson for the race. For a brief moment, this latter trick could be swung by writing academic defenses of pop music, especially rap, not only because it made the intellectuals sound hip but because the mainstream academy had come to accept the mass produced as authentic. The more it became clear that rap was just as empty as the rest of mass culture, the less effective even this strategy became, so that by the end of the decade, the black intellectuals who had put so much effort into meeting these swirling demands became exhausted, disenchanted, and thoroughly alienated, if not as yet discredited.

Gates's concession that the talented tenth cannot be all things to all people had to have the effect of liberating him from beneath that considerable pressure and might well have been a necessary effort in the preservation of sanity. His colleague, Cornel West, should have heeded Gates's example. With the exception of Toni Morrison and Gates, West was the most widely celebrated intellectual and surely the most visible. When he burst on the scene in the late 1980s, he was so unique, and so uniquely promising, that even such normally skeptical thinkers as Christopher Lasch lauded him as a bracing new voice. West seemed unburdened by race dogma and yet spoke vigorously, even heatedly, about the plight of poor blacks and the continuing effects of white supremacy. Unlike the civil rights establishment, he insisted on his radicalism, called for vast social programs and wealth redistribution and openly identified himself as a Social Democrat. A onetime student of the "postmodern" philosopher Richard Rorty, he dwelled in the unlikely world of intellectual history and formal philosophy and wrote about everything from John Dewey to Michael Jackson. In contrast to his mentor Rorty, who is utterly contemptuous of theological thought in spite of an illustrious Protestant pedigree, West enthusiastically proclaimed his Christian commitments. And he ended the 1990s by defending the traditional family at a time when few counterparts on the left dared do so. For all this, however, he gained fame mostly for his public presence; with his large physical frame adorned, in self-conscious imitation of Du Bois, in a three-piece suit, he unleashed a speaking style that combined a breadth of learning with the exuberance of the Baptist minister and the down-with-it style of a rap star.

Yet by the turn of the century, West found his reputation under attack. He became a favorite target of those strange folks at the *New Republic*, whose schizophrenic politics and snotty essays made them apt representatives of Clinton liberalism. An infamous hatchet job by the magazine's cultural critic, Leon Wieseltier, drew blood, in part because it contained more than a kernel of truth. Then, in a widely publicized confrontation that marked the unraveling of Gates's Harvard village, the university's new president, Lawrence Summers, accused West of forsaking real scholarship in favor of rather less-than-rigorous activities. Indignant, West fled Harvard for Princeton, proving, more than anything else, that he was just another academic prima donna and giving substance to Summers's charges. It hardly helped that West brought much of this trouble on himself by recording a CD and, worse still, shilling for Al Sharpton.

Because the hopes for him were so high, West might well be seen in retrospect to be the most disappointing thinker of this era. It would be unfair to judge him according to what others hoped he would become, except that he did much to cultivate those expectations. If we judge West and his thought simply on the terms that he held up for himself, he has to be reckoned a disappointment. But if this is the eventual assessment that awaits him, let it be said now that his shortcomings were not rooted in distraction, disingenuousness, or even in his inflated self-importance, but rather in his effort to be all things at once. He has his share of vanity, and that probably cost him. But his real vices were comparatively mild: He was too determined to prove himself master of everything, and the clearest result was that he never convincingly transcended any of the bodies of thought that he attempted to master. Everyone wanted a piece of him. Black student associations across the nation sought him as a speaker. Editors of collections of trendy essays, particularly ones with political pretensions, knew that a West contribution would automatically elevate a collection's profile. He knew full well that, as a Harvard professor, a regular on cable television public-affairs programs, a popular speaker, and a member of the crossover generation, he was expected to prove that a black man could do it all, and by all appearances he relished and nurtured those expectations. It must have been hard to be Cornel West.

Without dwelling on the details of the Summers controversy, it still ought to be said that the most striking thing about the case is that it focused almost entirely on West the public figure. It is fitting that this was so: West has taken his public career a good deal more seriously than his scholarly career in the last decade, and the consequence is that a strong hint of celebrity-seeking clings to him. He certainly has cultivated a very particular media image. He is not one to shun attention. Everything about him speaks of self-conscious inflation, down to his stump style. In promoting his CD, his Web site announces that "in all modesty, this project constitutes a watershed moment in musical history." After all, it combines the talents of a famous rap producer with "the oratorical passion and unmatched eloquence of Dr. Cornel West."[50] It might be interesting to see what an immodest promotion would proclaim. He writes in his self-edited *Cornel West Reader* that "I have great suspicion of autobiographical writing. So much of it reeks of self-indulgence and self-absorption."[51] If he means this, he must count himself among the most self-indulgent and self-absorbed of present-day writers, for his writing is filled with autobiographical references. Obviously, West is not shy, and if given to this sort of self-inflation, he can hardly complain when his media image takes on various lives of its own well beyond his control.

At the end of the day, what was lost entirely in the recent controversy was an evaluation of his thought, which is ultimately how any sort of intellectual, public or otherwise, should be judged. His defenders routinely call him one of the most important intellectuals of our time; his critics merely pass off his scholarship as postmodern nonsense. A broad reading of his body of publication over the last decade tends to confirm a bit of both. He has written passionately about contemporary problems; he has tried to distill his formal knowledge for public enlightenment. Yet the result is a body of work that is diffuse and shallow. In that withering piece in 1995, Leon Wieseltier observed that West is not a philosopher but "a cobbler of philosophies,"[52] and he was right. West has tried to synthesize every influence that has passed by him, which gives his writing the feel of someone trying to be both trendy and traditional at the same time. It can be taken as a sign of great intellectual curiosity and breadth that he has written about everything from Motown to Russian literature and classical antiquity. But very little of this writing has much weight to it. It is as though he were driven by a sense that he needed to prove himself, a sense that if he didn't read everything, master all bodies of systematic philosophy, and digest it all in written work, he would be seen as a mere affirmative action baby.

He was not nearly so prolific as his list of publications makes it seem. Several of his books were collaborations—*The Future of the Race* with Gates; *Breaking Bread* with bell hooks, *The War Against Parents* with Silvia Ann Hewlett—and others were collections of talks, brief essays, and interviews.[53] His most widely read book, *Race Matters*, was a slim volume intended to be accessible and not overly ponderous. It was not without its wisdom, nor without its faults, but it was not enough to carry a substantial philosophical statement. These all might be worthy pieces, each in its own way, and there certainly was a lot of work. But the fact remains that besides *Prophesy, Deliverance!* and *American Evasion of Philosophy*, both published in the 1980s as his career was just getting under way, West failed to produce a single sustained work of scholarship, much less a piece of systematic philosophy. Compare his output to that of Du Bois in his prime, which included not only a vast outpouring of polemical essays and cultural criticisms but important pieces of historical and sociological scholarship. Perhaps it is unfair to make such a comparison. After all, Du Bois was among the most prodigious writers of the century. But West has posed as Du Bois's heir and thus invites the comparison. Maybe the fairer measure is not against Du Bois but against other "public intellectuals," since that is what West also has claimed to be. In sheer output he was probably the equal of Lewis Mumford, Hannah Arendt, or C. Wright Mills, but unlike them he can boast of no single piece of sustained analysis or criticism or a piece of systematic philosophy, nothing of the importance of *The Pentagon of Power, The Human Condition,* or *The Power Elite*. Perhaps even this is unfair, but surely it is not unfair to compare him to contemporaries—Will Kymlicka, Charles Taylor, Michael Sandel, to name a few—who shared many of West's concerns and yet who managed to treat them systematically during the 1990s.

What if his work were taken as of a piece? With few exceptions, West's work leaves the impression of a writer almost obsessively trying to digest everything he has ever read. West is an incorrigible name-dropper, a strategy that seems to be intended as a way of demonstrating intellectual breadth as well as eclecticism but that typically results in undigested tidbits of mere references. Take as but one example the following: "My sense of the absurdity and incongruity of the world is closer to the Gnosticism of Valentius, Luira, or Monoimos," he writes in one of many recent autobiographical pieces. "My intellectual lineage goes more through Schopenhauer, Tolstoy, Rilke, Melville, Lorca, Kafka, Celan, Beckett, Soyinka, O'Neill, Kazantzakis, Morrison, and, above all, Chekhov. And, I should add . . . Brahm's *Requiem* and Coltrane's *A Love Supreme*."[54] One needn't doubt that West has mastered all these varied influences to wonder what purpose such a claim to pedigrees serves. We are all influenced by the things we read, often as much by the things we dislike as those we revere, but to draw them all up on lists without any substantive explanation of who they are and what they had to say amounts mostly to the writer's version of the three-piece suit, that is, to self-conscious pretentiousness. Bad enough in this form, the tendency to rustle up lists in order to criticize others is more troubling still. It is hard to see why we should have expected Du Bois to have shared West's tastes, and yet West scolds his predecessor for failing to deal with "Leo Tolstoy, Fyodor Dostoyevsky, Ivan Turgenev, Alexander Herzen, Lev Stestov, Anton Chekhov, or Franz Kafka, Max Brod, Kurt Tucholsky, Hermann Broch, Hugo Bergmann, or Karl Kraus."[55] It is doubtful that Du Bois would have revised his expectations for the talented tenth downward because he read *Oblomov*; it was another sort of Russian literature, in any event, that eventually attracted him.

This name-dropping is an unfortunate habit and a substitute for sustained analysis; it resembles as well his approach to philosophical systems. He plucks his way through bodies of thought to see what he can make use of, and though he does so with a critical method, he winds up with influences lined up in a row rather than synthesized. He is a pragmatist, and a Christian, a Marxist and a race man; he has called himself, variously, a prophetic pragmatist, a neo-Gramscian Marxist, and, most recently, a Chekhovian Christian. The result is not a new body of synthesized thought so much as a body of work explaining, endlessly, what he intends to think; he is forever telling his readers what his "prophetic pragmatism" is and never quite gets around to using that philosophy to give us an account of the world or a program of action. Few writers have ever been so self-conscious about forming a philosophy; few have been so laggard in the quest to have a philosophy formed.

This is to say that West has always been very systematic at attempting to construct a philosophy, and how he went about doing so suggests the complicated pressures working on him. A Rorty student, he wanted to be a formal philosopher; a member of the "postmodernist cohort," he sought to be engaged in the fashionable ideas of his time, a necessity for any up-and-coming professor. He was committed to social democracy and progressive politics of various sorts, and he remained committed to his racial obligations both to speak on behalf of and to live up to the expectations of African Americans. Each is a worthy and practical goal. Doing them all at once is an ambitious, but still possible, project. Doing them all at once beneath a philosophical mantle that synthesizes each is probably impossible. But it was all the more so for someone whose professional situation was such as to draw him increasingly away from any organic connection with the constituency he claimed to represent.

He deserves credit, at least, for the attempt to think about creating an overarching philosophy beneath which to collect his various efforts. It makes perfect sense that West would find pragmatism the most fitting foundation for his project. Aside from the blessing that Rorty extended to it, pragmatism carried the dual virtues of being recognized as a formal system of thought and of being extremely flexible. If anything is clear about West's *American Evasion of Philosophy*, it is that pragmatism, almost like culture, covers all bases. How else to go from Emerson, who obviously never heard the word, to Lionel Trilling, who most likely would have found his inclusion among West's American pragmatists puzzling, or to Reinhold Niebuhr, who would have considered it on the order of an accusation? Not only could he stretch pragmatism across time and individual differences but he also used it to find the right balance between philosophical humility and political commitment. "Its basic impulse," he wrote, "is a plebeian radicalism that fuels an antipatrician rebelliousness for the moral aim of . . . expanding democracy." Pragmatism was just the thing for the serious-minded progressive democrat. Pragmatism in West's hands became an absorptive thing with which he went about soaking up little pools of larger streams of thought. He could bring in a bit of Marx, a bit of Derrida and Foucault, anything that resonated among those various audiences he was expected to address.[56]

A philosophy of experience that sought a close connection with everyday life, pragmatism offered West a system with which he could be a philosopher and still claim ties to his roots. Pragmatism conferred a philosophical endorsement for whatever elements of the African American past West chose to put forward and allowed him to conceive the rather improbable philosophy of "prophetic pragmatism." West used the term to capture all of his influences while emphasizing the two most pronounced sources of inspiration—black Christianity and Dewey, respectively. The two sources do not have much in common, in spite of West's efforts to draw them together. If the two share anything at all, it is an instinct toward what might be called optimistic forbearance, a sense that one should reserve judgment against fellow humans in anticipation of personal and collective improvement. That the two share only this very general impulse is of little importance for West, however, because prophetic pragmatism is his version of Du Bois's maxim: It is formalized "twoness."

As he has described it, prophetic pragmatism begins as an attempt to salvage the best parts of African American life through evaluating black suffering in the face of the "absurd" and criticizing the varied black responses, all in hopes of "transforming" not only black life but America itself. It begins, in other words, in consideration of experience and thus acknowledges the central role of black folk culture, which inherently demanded attention to black music as "a countercultural practice with deep roots in modes of religious transcendence and political opposition." Jazz, soul, and rap amount, according to West, to a tradition of popular response to social conditions that at once carried forward the "spiritual-blues" tradition, reflected the contempo-

rary conditions of life, and posed future promises. The highbrow achievements of black artists are worthy of respect, not least the writing of Morrison,
Ellison, Baldwin, and others. On the whole, though, social conditions, West
maintained, have worked against genuinely great art, while the failure of
writers to connect with the popular imagination leaves popular musicians as
the most symbolic cultural actors. Without question, though, the most important black tradition is prophetic Christianity. The church has not only
been the single most important institution under community control, but
Christianity has been the most important structure of meaning for African
Americans; it is their cultural infrastructure. Beyond the consolation it
brings individuals in troubled times, prophetic Christianity has brought two
fundamental contributions to the black experience: "It confronts candidly
the tragic character of human history" and "elevates the notion of struggle,"
so that "to be a prophetic Afro-American Christian is to negate what is and
transform prevailing realities against the backdrop of the present historical
limits."[57]

Having patched together the inspirations for his synthesis of roles and systems, West laid out a game plan for becoming and remaining "an organic
public intellectual." And to a significant extent, he faced squarely the nature
of the difficulties entailed in that role for him. Intellectual life in America,
he has noted, has always been solitary, though today it is less solitary than relocated into the bureaucratic setting of the university. In this contemporary
setting, to be a black intellectual is nothing less than "an act of self-imposed
marginality." The anti-intellectualism of American society runs deep among
African Americans; whereas many white folks look at the intellectual life as
a sort of idle existence taken up by the harmlessly eccentric, African Americans have tended to see it as a means to middle-class status. "In good American fashion," West writes, "the Black community lauds those Black intellectuals who excel as political activists and cultural artists; the life of the
mind is viewed as neither possessing intrinsic virtues nor harboring emancipatory possibilities—solely short-term political gain and social status." As
the dominant institutions have been integrated, destroying autonomous
black institutions in the process, the paradoxical situation has arisen in
which there are more black academics than ever but fewer who "remain, in
some visible way, organically linked with Afro-American cultural life."
Where little real appreciation comes from their own communities and when
their bread and butter is doled out by universities, black intellectuals, according to West, are impaled on the horns of Du Bois's dilemma. They either
seek "success" by following the dreary path of professionalized academics or
they adopt an equally fruitless scorn for the "White intellectual world" and

accept self-exile to a world of narrow, race-obsessed discourse. The black community ignores both for the simple reason that "neither alternative has had a positive impact." The dismal consequence has been the decline "in both quantity and quality" of work by black intellectuals. West is quite right to note the underlying causes: "This is so primarily because of relatively greater Black integration into postindustrial capitalist America with its bureaucratized, elite universities, dull middlebrow colleges, and decaying high schools. . . . Needless to say, the predicament of the Black intellectual is inseparable from that of the Black community—especially the Black middle-class community—in American society. And only a fundamental transformation of American society can possibly change the situation."[58]

But here we get to the rub: How is that fundamental transformation to take place, and how could it possibly come out of Harvard or Princeton? In light of his late activities, it appears that West is convinced that change can come. It will come when "black culture workers," among whom are organic intellectuals such as himself, bring the radical claims of prophetic pragmatism to the consciousness of the black masses. "The repoliticizing of the black working poor and underclass," West insisted, "should focus primarily on the black cultural apparatus, especially the ideological form and content of black popular music." The culture workers—and surely West is thinking of himself here—have a special obligation to create the music, or thought in his case, to sustain and motivate a new activism.[59] It is obvious that those activities that got him into trouble at Harvard fall under this injunction, and that, accordingly, his own "cultural work" is aimed at keeping him "organically connected" to working folks as he climbs down from the ivory tower and dreams of leading the revolution. By doing his cultural work, he can be Harvard and Harlem at the same time.

Whatever one thinks of West, it has to be admitted in all fairness that there is a real logic at work here, one, moreover, that guards West against charges that he is a mere charlatan. Clearly he actually believes that prophetic pragmatism disseminated through the mass media can effect fundamental change by taking command of culture. In this sense, West would have been dishonest if he hadn't cut his CD or delivered those innumerable addresses or joined Tavis Smiley as a cultural critic; failing to do so would have exposed him as just another academic pretender to radicalism.

The problem, ultimately, is not that he has been shirking his formal scholarship or teaching duties or that he is too radical for Harvard. The underlying obstacle to his hopes is that he turns out to be an entirely conventional thinker who, for all his critical posturing, dogmatically accepts the prevailing notion of culture as the main realm of social conflict. West has argued quite rightly that popular culture is a necessary field of study for anyone interested in African American history, since that is where "Black people have left their imprint and fundamentally made a difference." But it is a very different thing to say this and to say as well that mass-produced music is worthy of ennobling as culture simply because it is produced by African Americans, much less that mass-produced music can possibly have a liberating effect. Like most of his white contemporaries, West is far too ready to look upon mass culture kindly and ignore its gross materialism. Like others, he is far too ready to stretch the concept of culture wherever necessary, as in insisting, for example, that "rap is unique because it combines the black preacher and the black music tradition,"[60] a claim that, as we have seen, at least Wynton Marsalis disputes. Similarly, he embraces the larger delusion that "contesting" images is the "culture worker's" main contribution to liberation. Indeed the job of the postmodern "black cultural worker," he insists, is to "constitute and sustain discursive and institutional networks that deconstruct earlier modern black strategies for identity formation, demystify power relations that incorporate class, patriarchal and homophobic biases and construct more multivalent and multidimensional responses that articulate the complexity and diversity of black practices."[61]

This conception of culture permits West to ignore many disconcerting things. It allows him to ignore the vast changes in the nature of African American cultural forms that have come with integration; it allows him to ignore how deeply the marketplace, which is, after all, one of his main targets, has corrupted the popular arts. It further allows him to ignore how far removed he is from his organic sources of culture, in part because the forms of culture he is fond of—soul, R & B, and now rap—are themselves now inorganic. Most disturbing, the delusions of cultural struggle allow him—and this is even more true of Gates—to turn cultural work into big money. When it comes down to it, he has to measure the benevolent influence of his CD by its sales; meanwhile, he and Gates have launched their other ventures, including a coffeetable book, *The African American Century*, a teacher's guide to African American history promoted by Coca-Cola, and an effort to sell black history pamphlets with McDonald's meals. And while Gates pushes his *Africana Encarta* with Bill Gates, West has opted for a role in upcoming films.[62] They are, as the business types would say, achieving synergy between Afro-American studies and multinationals. Somehow I don't think Gramsci would approve.

More than anything else, it is sad to see what Cornel West has done to himself. It portends badly, but not for Afro-American studies or African Americans themselves. If anything, these business dealings suggest how marketable both are, which is to say how thoroughly assimilated both are. West's case is sad, rather, for what it tells us about the fate of the intellect in contemporary life. Where a once-promising figure with many angles going for him could fall into such foolishness, we have as good an indication as any that the mass media destroys all it touches. West's case gives us evidence that even the intellectual is now commodified and that the marketplace that he so often decried has probably breached the last barrier of seriousness in American life, the last intermediary institution capable of resisting leveling and homogenization.

Notes

1. Harold Cruse, *The Crisis of the Negro Intellectual* (New York, 1967), 13–14.

2. Hollinger, *Postethnic America: Beyond Multiculturalism* (New York, 1995), 36.

3. Robert F. Lowie, *Are We Civilized? Human Culture in Perspective* (New York, 1929), 294.

4. Franz Boas, *The Mind of Primitive Man*, rev. ed. (New York, 1983), 37; Boas, "Modern Populations of America," Proceedings of the 19th International Congress of Americanists (December 1915), and Boas, "Race and Progress," Presidential Address to the American Association for the Advancement of Science, Pasadena, June 15, 1931, both reprinted in Boas, *Race, Language and Culture* (New York, 1940), 19–20, 3, respectively; Boas, "Race and Nationality," *Everybody's Magazine* (November 1914), reprinted in *International Conciliation* 86 (January 1915): 5–8; and Boas, ed., *General Anthropology* (New York, 1938), 104–105.

5. Boas, *Mind of Primitive Man*, rev. ed., 73, 86–87, 102.

6. Ibid., 153, 172–73.

7. Linda Chavez, "Demystifying Multiculturalism," *National Review* 46 (February 21, 1994): 29–30.

8. Molefi Kete Asante, *The Afrocentric Idea* (Philadelphia, 1987), 9.

9. Ibid., 10, 48.

10. W. E. B. Du Bois, *The Souls of Black Folk* (1903; reprint, New York, 1994), 5.

11. David Levering Lewis, *W. E. B. Du Bois: Biography of a Race* (New York, 1993), 162–70. On Crummell and Du Bois, see also Kwame Anthony Appiah, *In My Father's House: Africa in the Philosophy of Culture* (New York, 1992), 20–24, 28–35.

12. W. E. B. Du Bois, "The Conservation of Races," in American Negro Academy, *Occasional Papers* (1897), reprinted in David Levering Lewis, ed., *W. E. B. Du Bois: A Reader* (New York, 1995), 22–23. Appiah, *In My Father's House*, 34.

13. Appiah, *In My Father's House*, 21–22. Du Bois lists these "artificial criteria" in "Separation and Self-Respect," *The Crisis* (March 1934), reprinted in Lewis, ed., *W. E. B. Du Bois: A Reader*, 559.

14. Lewis, *W. E. B. Du Bois: Biography of a Race*, 351–352.

15. W. E. B. Du Bois, "What is Civilization? Africa's Answer," *Forum* (February 1925), reprinted in Meyer Weinberg, ed., *W.E.B. Du Bois: A Reader* (New York, 1970), 374–81.

16. See W. E. B. Du Bois, "A Negro Nation within the Nation," *Current History* 42 (June 1935), reprinted in Lewis, ed., *W.E.B. Du Bois: A Reader*, 566; and "Criteria of Negro Art," *The Crisis* (October 1926); reprinted in Lewis, ed., *W.E.B. Du Bois: A Reader*, 513.

17. See David Levering Lewis's treatment of this issue in *W. E. B. Du Bois: Biography of a Race*, 259–73.

18. Du Bois, "Separation and Self-Respect," 559.

19. Du Bois, *Souls of Black Folk*, 66.

20. Lewis, *W. E. B. Du Bois: Biography of a Race*, 272.

21. Du Bois, *Souls of Black Folk*, 35.

22. Ibid., 64–67.

23. Ibid., 193.

24. Du Bois, "Criteria of Negro Art," 510.

25. Ibid., 5.

26. W. E. B. Du Bois, *The Autobiography of W. E. B. Du Bois: A Soliloquy on Viewing My Life from the Last Decade of Its First Century* (New York, 1968), 393.

27. David Levering Lewis, *W. E. B. Du Bois: The Fight for Equality and the American Century, 1919–1963* (New York, 2000), 550, 554.

28. Du Bois, "A Negro Nation within the Nation," 565.

29. Henry Louis Gates, Jr., *Colored People: A Memoir* (New York, 1994), 20–25.

30. Harold Cruse, *The Crisis of the Negro Intellectual* (New York, 1967), 83–85, 88.

31. Cornel West, *Race Matters* (Boston, 1993), 14.

32. Russell Simmons and Nelson George, *Life and Def: Sex, Drugs, and God* (New York, 2001), xii, 9, 4; Ellis Cashmore, *The Black Culture Industry* (London, 1997), 158–60.

33. Simmons, *Life and Def*, 6.

34. Todd Boyd, *Am I Black Enough For You? Popular Culture from the 'Hood and Beyond* (Bloomington, Ind., 1997), 78.

35. Cashmore, *Black Culture Industry*, 155.

36. Simmons, *Life and Def*, 59.

37. Ibid., 70, 61.

38. Wynton Marsalis on "The Hip-Hop Generation," *All Things Considered*, National Public Radio, June 2, 2002.

39. John McWhorter, *Losing the Race: Self-Sabotage in Black America* (New York, 2000), 27–29.

40. bell hooks, *Yearning: Race, Gender, and Cultural Politics* (Boston, 1990), 33–35.

41. bell hooks, *Bone Black: Memories of Girlhood* (New York, 1996), 4, 154–56.

42. Zora Neale Hurston, *Dust Tracks on a Road: An Autobiography* (1942; reprint, New York, 1969), 11.

43. Gates, *Colored People*, 12.

44. Hurston, *Dust Tracks*, 157–58; Gates, *Colored People*, 69.

45. Hurston, *Dust Tracks*, 155, 157; Gates, *Colored People*, 101.

46. Henry Louis Gates, Jr., "Parable of the Talents," in Henry Louis Gates, Jr. and Cornel West, *The Future of the Race* (New York, 1996), 11–12.

47. Hurston, *Dust Tracks*, 293–94; Gates, *Colored People*, 213, 211.

48. Gates, "Parable of the Talents," 14–15.

49. Ibid., 37–38.

50. See the CD promotion at www.cornelwest.com.

51. Cornel West, ed., *The Cornel West Reader* (New York, 1999), 1.

52. Leon Wieseltier, "All and Nothing at All," *New Republic* 212 (March 6, 1995): 34.

53. See his *Prophetic Fragments* (Grand Rapids, Mich., 1988); *Prophetic Thought in Postmodern Times* (Monroe, Maine, 1993); *Prophetic Reflections: Notes on Race and Power in America* (Monroe, Maine, 1993).

54. West, ed., *The Cornel West Reader*, xvii.

55. Cornel West, "Black Strivings in a Twilight Civilization," in Gates and West, *Future of the Race*, 76.

56. Cornel West, *American Evasion of Philosophy: A Genealogy of Pragmatism* (Madison, Wis., 1989), 5.

57. Cornel West, "On Afro-American Popular Music: From Bebop to Rap," *Le Monde Diplomatique* (November 1983), reprinted in West, *Prophetic Fragments*, 177–87; on the prophetic tradition, see West, *Prophesy Deliverance! An Afro-American Revolutionary Christianity* (Philadelphia, 1982), 19–20.

58. Cornel West, "The Dilemma of the Black Intellectual," in Cornel West and bell hooks, *Breaking Bread: Insurgent Black Intellectual Life* (Boston, 1991), 135, 137.

59. Cornel West, *Keeping Faith: Philosophy and Race in America* (New York, 1993), 289.

60. "The Political Intellectual," an interview with Anders Stephanson, in West, ed., *The Cornel West Reader*, 288; also "On Afro-American Popular Music: From Bebop to Rap," 177–87.

61. Cornel West, "The New Cultural Politics of Difference," reprinted in West, ed., *Cornel West Reader*, 131.

62. Thulani Davis, "Spinning Race at Harvard: The Business Behind the Gates-West Power Play," *Village Voice* (January 22, 2002), 39.

CHAPTER SIX

~

How the Left Got Cultured

There is no clearer proof of the ascendancy of cultural determinism over materialism than what has happened to the Western Left since the 1960s. Among political progressives, the conviction that culture constitutes the main battleground of conflict and, therefore, the realm in which liberation is to be etched indisputably has come to dominate. Whereas the mid-century generation fought wild battles over Stalinism and Trotskyism, and even the moderates were passionately committed to trade unionism and convinced of capitalism's grave material flaws, the generation that followed shifted its ground first toward debates over values and ethics and eventually came to the general conclusions, following Marcuse and Fanon, that oppression is mostly a matter of mind, which is to say culture.

This is hardly news. During the 1960s, so goes the well-worn interpretation, baby-boom radicals confronted the competing pressures of the civil rights movement, the war in Vietnam, and the bureaucratization of trade unionism at home and socialist regimes abroad. Old-line Marxism was too stiff to account for this welter of political and social realities, not least in its more or less complete indifference to racism and sexism; the "labor metaphysic," which focused on material inequities, was obsolete in a society where the working class was living in the suburbs, driving Torinos and Camaros, and spending their ample leisure time in front of the television. Radical minorities—African Americans, feminists, gays and lesbians—all began to proffer new and even startling insights about how the cultural system worked to create damaging stereotypes and about the ideological systems that kept oppression in place. Meanwhile progressives grew increasingly indifferent to the hard work of political and economic change, to coalition-building and patient organizing, to the practical compromises that gradually make a movement tangibly effective. In this new incarnation, progressives appeared to be convinced that liberation required a culture war, as opposed to either a class war or, for that matter, political conflict.

It was inevitable that such a strategy would spell political disaster for the Left. As many writers have argued, the more progressives tried to fight in the realm of culture, the more they relinquished any influence in the political and economic realms. American politics moved firmly to the right beginning in 1980, and even through the Clinton administration, Gingrich Republicanism set the tone of national debates to which Clinton progressives constantly adjusted. Meanwhile, the state houses and governorships, where so much of the grain of American politics is sown, grew increasingly conservative; as Michael Tomasky notes, Republicans took control of both houses of Congress in the 1994 off-year elections and dominated on the state and local levels, taking thirty governorships and more than half of all state legislative chambers.[1] Given the secure hold of pro-market conservatism on all the real levers of power, the Left's descent into culture can only be regarded as a historic failure, a massive miscalculation at best and, more honestly, a true failure of will.

So obvious that the point needs no elaborate defense, the collapse of the Left tells us a good deal about the nature of culture. It tells us that culture, in fact, is not power. If it were, progressivism would be dominant today, since progressives control the humanities and the arts and loom large in the creative mechanisms of the entertainment industry. The widespread presence of progressives in the cultural apparatus has not dented conservative control of the state and the economy. Many of the most vigorously asserted progressive verities—that cultural diversity is alive and well, that unhampered behavioral freedom and freedom of expression are the ends of the good society—correspond to the interests of contemporary capitalism, so that there is a certain amount of collusion between the culture makers and the economic system they pretend to oppose. This unwitting collusion aside, their cultural turn rendered progressives politically impotent because, in contrast to the central dogma today, culture and power are less and less related. By making culture into material for buying and selling, consumerism sucks it of any meaningful political importance. All that the culture industries, and by extension capitalism itself, need to keep afloat are customers, not ideologies. It does no good to fight over culture when culture itself has been gutted of substance.

This contention runs afoul of much that progressives have come to believe about culture in the last two decades. Convinced that culture is power, they seized hold of analytical systems, particularly that of Antonio Gramsci, that do not apply very well to the contemporary situation. Radicals embraced Gramsci enthusiastically because he elevated culture to a level of importance in Marxist analysis, but they managed to turn an enormously insightful approach to thinking about social systems into casual, routinely delivered claims that oppressed people can stand their ground and even subvert their oppression by whipping up a ritual and a song. The overuse of Gramsci corresponded directly to the inflation of culture itself; hegemony, by 1990, became one of the most overused concepts on the Left. The incessant invocation of Gramsci obscured a difficult truth about the current state of matters: Gramsci insisted, at bottom, that ruling classes rule by creating belief systems that keep the masses grudgingly obedient; but while they busied themselves seeing how that worked historically, the contemporary Left failed to see that contemporary consumerism imposes no system at all beyond the lowest common denominator of choice.

If we recall that at its best, culture results from the struggle to distinguish the human from the natural, then the Left bears an important relationship to culture properly understood. That essential cultural struggle is keenest where nature impinges most tightly, and, by definition, the Western Left has been most concerned with elevating struggling people from want, which is, when boiled down, the essential compensation that culture provides. We have, then, in the contemporary Left's descent into culture, a crystalline example of our paradoxical situation. The more progressives inflated the importance of culture, giving it a world-changing power that it cannot have, the less genuine impact they have had. The less culture mattered to the day-to-day functioning of state and economy, the more vigorously progressives inflated the boundaries of culture, hopelessly diluting the term to the point of meaninglessness. It should not go without notice that the cultural turn has also corresponded to the time when progressives themselves have, by and large, become increasingly comfortable and therefore detached from any struggle with nature. The fate of the Left demonstrates that culture broken from any clear sense of humanity's limitations is no culture at all.

Culture as Self-Defense

It was not disingenuousness that took the Left to culture. Rather, coming to terms with culture was an indispensable tactical move after World War II, one necessary to the survival of progressive politics of any sort. The spectacular success of the Western economies through the 1950s made it impossible for a reasonable person to believe that capitalism was in its death throes and the advent of a socialist order immanent, though these presumptions were matters of common sense a mere twenty years earlier. The bureaucratization of the Soviet state and its attendant moral corruption, meanwhile, made one question whether a socialist order, immanent or otherwise, could ever be a good thing. The success of capitalism was especially destructive to Marxist dogma because it managed to spread material well-being in unprecedented ways, thanks to trade unionism and the social compact of the welfare state. It simply could not be plausibly argued that the working class was being ground down in misery; any honest person would have to admit that capitalism came closer than socialism to creating the workers' paradise. Unless Marxism could be rethought, the whole radical gig was up.

As the industrial world reached a state of what intellectuals took to calling an "age of post-scarcity," radicals faced enormous analytical problems. Coming to terms with prosperity logically gave rise to questions about the historic role of the working class. If workers were materially satisfied, why would they be revolutionary? A momentous issue, it gave rise to a variety of positions through the mid-1960s. The easiest way to dispatch the problem, and the most familiar, came out of the nascent student movement and was stated plainly enough in the Port Huron Statement. Especially to the extent that they accepted the leadership of bureaucratized labor, the students charged, workers had essentially forfeited their historic roles in exchange for consumer goods. In the age of abundance, the revolutionary student would replace the proletariat.

A second and theoretically more substantive position emerged from different angles and held that the new revolutionary vanguard would emerge from those people who were essentially marginalized from the system of production broadly understood. Sophisticated theorists, most notably Herbert Marcuse and Daniel Bell, understood that the system of production now included not just the mass production of goods on the factory floor but the dissemination of those goods. Bell called this system the "post-industrial society"; Marcuse simply called it capitalism. In Marcuse's famous formulations, the only source of resistance to the all-consuming nature of consumer capitalism rested among those people who had completely removed themselves from the system and engaged in "the great refusal." Following Bell, Christopher Lasch, whose thinking in the 1960s and early 1970s was far closer to the emerging cultural radicals than his eventual reputation would have one believe, speculated that postindustrial society would create "new classes of marginal and technologically superfluous people who make up an increasingly alienated and subversive force."[2]

The speculation that scattered groups of marginalized people would constitute the new vanguard underlay the emerging attraction of racial minorities, sexual radicals, and Third World anti-colonialists. Pick a marginalized people, and they became the new breed of revolutionary, characterized not by their relation to the system of production but by their removal from it. Obviously, this theoretical twist undergirded the increasing prestige of black nationalists, gay and lesbian activists, and feminists on the Left, but it also raised questions about where revolutionary impulses would emanate from. If the struggle over work ceased to generate radicalism, then revolutionary demands would have to emerge out of those parts of marginal lives that were detached and different. Because people were marginalized for different reasons—race, gender, sexual orientation—their demands would logically be drawn from different sources. While the origins of the much-decried fragmentation of the Left reside here, it is more important to note that the point of struggle, which previously was understood to be on the factory floor, was spun out into the subjective worlds of those who claimed to be marginalized. Where was the terrain of battle here? What, precisely, was to be fought over? The struggle could not be for "inclusion" to end their marginalization because, after all, that marginalization had to be the constant wellspring of radical energy. As long as workers worked, they might be expected to continue to struggle for control; the new theoretical assumption brewing here could only be that nursing continued differences was essential to radicalism. But how to define what constituted difference? Unleashed from concrete, material considerations, the definition of difference and the accompanying expectations of how differences might be maintained could be gathered only beneath the accommodating mantle of culture.

This convenient bend toward seeing culture as the new battleground for revolutionary activity gained strength through several other theoretical twists. If the age of postscarcity had removed the main cause of radicalism from the shop floor, it was necessary to ask where the new sources of repression lay. Here again Marcuse offered the most elaborate and influential answer when he argued that material prosperity had been gained at the expense of real freedom. To him, mass production of consumer goods sated the material needs of most people but shifted the basis of control and repression away from work and to the more insidious, more subtle ground of mass culture. Mass culture, he insisted, was designed to breed the assumption of the good life into people while flattening out their subversive instincts. The genius of consumer capitalism was that it packaged and sold those very needs, sex especially, that inspired radical action. By offering its pallid substitutes in abundance, consumer society created an all-encompassing delusion of satisfaction. The system of domination had turned its energies to producing culture, first, because of the growing need of the affluent society to establish ever-more-ingenuous methods of repression and, second, because the realm of culture contained and nurtured the rebellious instincts traditionally expressed through art. By substituting television for genuine art, mass culture "moronized" people and destroyed the subversive potentials of beauty. By titillating the masses with glossy sex and initiating the false "sexual revolution," mass culture erased the interior drive toward true sexual freedom and polymorphous perversity. More than that: By relaxing sexual taboos and discarding strictures against obscenity, mass culture destroyed guilt and shame. "Thus we are faced with the contradiction," Marcuse wrote, "that the liberalization of sexuality provides an instinctual basis for the repressive and aggressive power of the affluent society."[3]

With the sublime all but eliminated, the inhabitants of mass culture lived a flattened, barren, "one-dimensional existence," in which the simple capacity to imagine a radically different world was obliterated. The "one-dimensional man" completely identified with the world around him because all the barriers to total administration, all the protected havens in which individuals might cultivate genuine autonomy, had been breached.[4] In a phrase, this social order, which blended illusory freedom with total administration, rested on "repressive tolerance." In tolerating art, anti-art, and pseudo-art, mass culture blunted the "radical impact of art" and "swallowed up" the "protest of art against the established reality." "Art stands against history," Marcuse insisted, "for art subjects reality to laws other than the established ones."[5]

Marcuse's influence in the 1960s was always a bit strange, as many commentators noted at the time. A stiff, severe German expatriate whose writing was turgid, not to say inaccessible, Marcuse nonetheless became radical chic in the mid-1960s, gaining the admiration of radical students who probably understood him badly and would have disowned him if they had seen his main point—a mismatch made in heaven. Timing, if nothing else, explains the relationship. In One Dimensional Man and a heated essay, "Repressive Tolerance," which appeared in 1965, Marcuse posed an uncompromisingly bleak assessment of democratic societies that corresponded perfectly with the deepening sense in the New Left that the establishment was collapsing into utter madness. Marcuse brought a certain radical prestige with him, as did Franz Fanon, whose Wretched of the Earth also appeared in English in 1965 and was equally uncompromising in condemning Western capitalism; both Fanon and Marcuse, it is worth noting, conceived of oppression and its radical opposition in psychological terms. Marcuse indicted the tolerant liberal leaders of Western institutions at just the moment when Vietnam and the student rebellion erupted. He explained in sophisticated terms what the middle-class radicals of the day badly yearned to hear: that their rejection of middle-class morals and their cultural and psychic liberation were legitimately radical and that the social order beckoned new agents of revolutionary change, including students. Marcuse reworked Marxism's concern with political economy through Freud and into a theory of psychological and cultural liberation and appealed to the period's radicals who were bent on cultural and not economic rebellion.

Marcuse's star fell quickly once it became clear that he considered those things that many of the young radicals enjoyed, such as rock music, as just so many parts of the all-encompassing system of repression. But his contribution to the late-century Left remains clear. As much as anyone, Marcuse lent theoretical power to the cultural turn. Whether one believed that mass culture was good or bad, the point of emphasis on the Left had surely shifted away, it might be said, from the shop floor to shopping. And whatever else is said about the Left's turn, it was a necessary response to the most basic nature of contemporary capitalism, which, after all, has flourished in the last half-century by replacing culture with entertainment and leisure. Leisure activities constitute the largest markets and, therefore, the most important products of consumer capitalism, and failing to take note of this would have been a self-exile into oblivion.

The Gramsci Fetish

These theoretical twists might have gone a long way toward preserving a left-wing analysis of contemporary society, but they could not save Marxism. Given the larger political and economic developments of the last twenty years, it is doubtful that Marxism of any conventional sort could have survived, save among those gristled old-timers, museum relics really, who show up now and again at local book discussions or college-sponsored talks stammering about class warfare. This is true at least of Marxism as an active political ideology. By contrast, it deserves to survive as a meaningful form of historical analysis, every bit as accurate in its apprehension of how capital and technology work in contemporary capitalism as when *Das Capital* was published. In any event, the acceptance of those various bits of postindustrial theory undid Marxism by replacing the point of production with culture as the core of conflict. No one could make this shift and still claim to be a Marxist—unless, that is, one discovered Antonio Gramsci.

Here is one of the most remarkable cases of a theory rising up out of utter obscurity because it happened to meet the intellectual needs of people living in an age the originator of the theory could scarcely have imagined. Hardly known outside of Italy during his lifetime and essentially ignored by party-line thinkers through mid-century, Gramsci became the darling of radical intellectuals by the 1980s and so popular by 1990 that the term "hegemony" had entered the language of both the humanities and the social sciences. Gramsci was not "rediscovered": He was practically nonexistent until the New Left began to translate and read him.

There are many reasons for Gramsci's unearthing. Historian Jackson Lears suggested in a 1985 essay that Gramsci was a moral inspiration to "young intellectuals on the Left" because of his "resistance to Mussolini" and "his stress on the role of individual action and thought in history."[6] If this is true for Lears himself, it generally is a dubious claim, given the indifference to Gramsci's life in the vast majority of invocations of his theories; it is much more likely that young radicals took to Gramsci because he wasn't boring. A still more cynical explanation would be that Gramsci gave university intellectuals a reason to believe that they could be revolutionaries and comfortably tenured at the same time. Gramsci, after all, claimed that intellectuals had an important vanguard function to play, a claim that had to have a powerful attraction to those who, at an earlier point in their lives, believed that university students might fulfill that role. Gramsci, to be blunt, flattered them.

This is not to gainsay the serious analytical value—the truths—of Gramsci's speculations. Gramsci was inspiring largely because a casual familiarity with his main piece of work, *The Prison Notebooks*, potentially opened up a whole new realm of history to Marxist analysis, and that realm was culture. The deep reason why Antonio Gramsci was unearthed was because the Age of Culture needed him. Lears's defense of Gramsci suggests as much. By rejecting the economic determinism of the party line, Lears insisted, Gramsci "points us toward cultural definitions of race, ethnicity, and gender." The concept of cultural hegemony at once widened the definition of who wields power in society by seeing "parents, preachers, teachers, journalists" and others as participants in creating the values and habits that sustain domination. Gramsci's concept of hegemony, according to Lears, suggests that the real power of ruling-class domination "may well be in the realm of culture." It is no surprise that Lears proceeded here to recommend a "linguistic turn" in cultural and intellectual history.[7]

It is true that Gramsci saved Marxism from the encrusted, anti-human dogma it had become by mid-century. He was prescient about much, particularly so about the fundamental importance of intellectuals both to modern capitalism and to revolutionary movements. He rightly saw that without ideas, movements go nowhere. Personally attentive to the social position of southern Italian peasants, he was willing to consider the place of groups other than workers in social change, another quality that suited him well for discovery after 1960. And he demonstrated an unusual sensitivity toward the changes in modern capitalism that included the hyperrationalization of mass production and the rise of the corporation. All of these virtues recommended Gramsci.

But there is a vast difference between saying that Gramsci reenergized radical history and Marxist thought, on the one hand, and that he reenergized Western radicalism itself. Gramsci can no more be lifted out of the historical context of this moment in time than can any other sort of thinking. The uncomfortable fact is that the more the intellectuals have analyzed cultural hegemony, the less real political effect their radicalism has had. No one would be more disappointed over such a turn of events than Gramsci himself, given his lifelong emphasis on political action. It is time to ask what has gone wrong.

Gramsci's concept of hegemony grew out of his entirely accurate understanding of the nature of modern bourgeois society in which the state grew increasingly bureaucratic and complex and, in so doing, collected around civil society. Essentially, Gramsci claimed that ruling classes do not always, or even primarily, rule through the barrel of the gun, however much brute force might rest in the background. Instead they create ideological structures, such as education systems, that promote sets of values and convictions that conform to their political and economic interests. These values and beliefs are successful to the degree to which they are persuasive and take some account of reality even as they obscure the real workings of power in a society. "Subaltern groups" come to accept hegemonic values partly out of the normal human tendency toward quiescence and partly because such values become embedded as common sense. By accepting the values of their overlords, the subalterns become complicit in their own oppression. The real genius of this arrangement, as Perry Anderson wrote, was that the strength of hegemonic values rested on "a belief by the masses that *they exercise an ultimate self-determination* within the existing social order," especially in bourgeois democracies. At its most succinct, then, hegemony is where "coercion [is] . . . ingenuously combined with persuasion and consent."[8]

The utility of such a concept as an analytical tool is immediately apparent, since it permits the radical scholar to relate everything from church history to popular philosophy to the base of power. The whole superstructure, dutifully ignored by conventional Marxists, was in effect opened up to searching analysis and criticism. The concept allowed radicals to claim, as Perry Anderson did in one of the earliest deployments of Gramsci in English, that "power in advanced capitalist societies is polycentric" and resides in a "configuration" of institutions, economic structures, ideas, and, for that matter, history itself.[9]

But it would hardly do for radical intellectuals to accept a system of thought that only allowed for the study of working-class quiescence. The essence of Gramsci's dialectic—arguably the central concern of his work—was the conviction that because the dominant values ran against their material interests, subaltern groups were instinctively uneasy and potentially always ripe to be weaned away from hegemonic ideals. That turning away did not depend on some crisis, such as a severe depression or war; the process was at once more subtle and more difficult. The work of building a "counter-hegemonic" consciousness required a steady effort to reorient the masses by introducing theory into common sense and slowly drawing potential converts "to a higher conception of life." By tying revolutionary ideas to simple common sense, radical intellectuals avoided breaking with the masses, even while trying to show how much common sense is simply "inherited from the past and uncritically absorbed." The result was to be a synthesis that critically understood the practical problems of the masses and offered alternatives that had "real value"; in this way a new "cultural and social bloc" could emerge to challenge the dominant class.[10]

This process absolutely required an intellectual vanguard, an elite ideally drawn out of the particular groups whose consciousness needed to be raised. It is clear from his discussion of how ideas and practice were to meet that Gramsci's scheme depended on, as he wrote, "the creation of an *elite* of intellectuals." What is more, that creation is itself a process, one bound to be "long, difficult, full of contradictions, advances and retreats, dispersals and regroupings, in which the loyalty of the masses is often sorely tried." Thorny as it is, the process is a wide one, because it was to include the gradual elevation of the masses "to higher circles of culture"; cultural refinement, meanwhile, would ensure the emergence of "outstanding individuals" who could exercise moral and intellectual leadership effectively because of their subaltern roots. The foremost problem was that the intellectuals occasionally might outpace those whom they needed to lead and gaps would develop that obliged the intellectuals to slow down and reestablish the relationship between the leaders and the led.[11]

So far, so good: Gramsci seemed ideally suited to the temperament of the New Left. The problems began, however, in the rush to apply Gramscian thought without considering the political context in which he worked. It was possible to look at the theory of cultural hegemony and believe that the radical intellectual could execute a revolutionary strategy by concentrating on values. But for Gramsci, those intellectuals were always party members, not university scholars. Modern political parties in general—and of course he always had the Communist Party in mind—were responsible for recruiting individuals from subaltern groups. With theoretical positions already set, the party cultivated the intellectual, who in turn added the practical concerns and day-to-day struggles of the people to the party's agenda; in this way, party structures were the essential mechanism of counterhegemony, "the crucibles," Gramsci wrote, "where the unification of theory and practice . . . takes place." When recurring gaps threatened the unity between the intellectuals and the masses, it was up to the party to impose an "iron discipline on the intellectuals so that they do not exceed certain limits of differentiation."[12]

Given the complete evaporation of the Communist Party in the West, it may seem like a silly point to suggest that those who have borrowed from him over the last generation ought to keep in mind Gramsci's fundamental political commitments. Still, at the very least, it is odd that so few want to remember that he was a Communist. This selective memory fits hand in glove with selective applications of Gramscian thought and reveals some of the essential causes of the contemporary Left's political default. No one wants to be associated with so moribund an institution as the Communist Party anymore—but few want to recommend an alternative institution to serve the functions that Gramsci saw for the party. The absence of institutional alternatives is in part a consequence not of laziness on the part of radicals but of the constant absorption and assimilation of organic communities into the system of consumer capitalism. The great historic blocs that Gramsci was concerned with, particularly the working class and the peasantry, no longer exist in any coherent form in the West; nor, at least for any length of time, do any other substantial organic communities. Structural assimilation and the spread of consumerism have absorbed them—as Gramsci's theory would indicate—and won their consent. It is very difficult to see where alternative values can come from. In this sense, Gramsci's own theory gives us abundant reason to fear that bourgeois hegemony is, as far as we can see, nearly absolute.

Where are the organic intellectuals today? Over the last half-century, it is easy to point to a few people who fit that role. Martin Luther King, Jr., as Cornel West long has claimed, measured up to the Gramscian demands. He was very much a son of the constituency that he led, and yet, educated in the north and deeply influenced by philosophies (including Marxism) that were foreign to that constituency, he reconnected with the most vital practical needs of his people while bringing them cosmopolitan ideas fused into a political strategy. His constituency certainly must be considered a historic bloc. Keep in mind as well that King put together a party organization in the Southern Christian Leadership Council. There are no Kings among African Americans today, but that is because African Americans are no longer a historic bloc in the sense that Gramsci and his fellow Marxists thought of such things, and as such, if theory matters, it would be unreasonable to expect organic intellectuals to step forward. There have been other genuine leaders in the King mold—one thinks of Cesar Chavez or Harvey Milk. But what is striking about them is that they both emerged from and appealed to communities with distinct moral-ethical sensibilities, communities, moreover, that had a certain geographical integrity and that, at the moment when these two emerged, were completely marginalized. There are no more Chavezes and Milks for the same reason that there are no more Martin Luther King, Jrs.: Those historic blocs no longer exist.

The most important quality of organic intellectuals is that their lives are irreducibly political. That so much recent Gramscian analysis forgets that the whole purpose of the intellectual should be political and that culture was ultimately just a superstructural avenue leading toward political change runs back to the indifference to his communist commitments. By seeing all subaltern cultural activity as somehow political because it challenges conventional morality or ethics, the latter-day Gramscians ignore altogether that the basic goal of the revolutionary is the seizure of power. As early as 1976, Perry Anderson noted the tendency to confuse cultural activity with political change. "Once bourgeois power in the West is primarily attributed to cultural hegemony," Anderson warned, "the acquisition of this hegemony would mean effective assumption by the working class of the 'direction of society' without the seizure and transformation of State power, in a painless transition to socialism; in other words, of Fabianism. Gramsci himself, of course, never drew this conclusion."[13]

Where the hard and gradual work of organizing revolution is dreamed away and the Left becomes willingly content with "cultural resistance," the best radicals can hope for is directionless, feeble, and scattered opposition to the state of things. And there is another exacting price to pay, for as concrete political action gives way to cultural resistance as the main goal of radical activity, the whole notion of process gets discarded as well. Almost no one on the Left speaks any longer about the "withering away of the state" or the impending proletarian uprising, and if these things have turned out to be historical myths, they nonetheless indicated the radicals' self-confidence, which in turn often inspired and sustained action. "Praxis" became an oft-heard word among the Gramscians of the 1980s and 1990s, invoked for its own sake; in contrast, to Gramsci, praxis was supposed to describe a consistent series of deeds. But, then, revolutionary action is hard. At some point, it requires violence. People get arrested. They get beaten. They get killed. Challenging hegemony through "cultural resistance" entails none of these dreadful things.

Just as Gramsci's emphasis on practical action was invoked in inverse relation to the extent of radical activism, so too the corruption of his vision into a theoretical version of cultural agency reflects a doleful lack of radical vision. Say what you will about the Old Left: They acted as revolutionaries because they had faith in their ideological narrative, which understood history as moving from stage to stage. However ham-handed that narrative seems to us in these jaded days, it was a source of inspiration and hope. There is no narrative in cultural determinism. The subalterns already possess what the cultural dogmatists want them to have: rootedness and agency. Granted, the typical historical analysis has the group in question absorbing the hegemonic values and changing them to suit their interests, and there is a dialectic to that. But it leads to nothing beyond that cultural synthesis because it doesn't need to. The end, which apparently is the exertion of cultural agency, is already achieved within the act of cultural absorption and subversion. And in this sense, there is no narrative and, accordingly, no source of inspiration and hope. No wonder there is so little practical action.

It is probably true, as Perry Anderson thought, that the tendency to confuse cultural activism with political change was a temptation partly rooted in Gramsci's own slipperiness. But what always anchored Gramsci, and what tended to anchor the earliest Gramscian pieces of the New Left Review radicals, was their materialism. "There is no doubt," Gramsci himself wrote, "that although hegemony is ethical-political, it must also be economic, must necessarily be based on the decisive function exercised by the leading group in the decisive nucleus of economic activity. . . . It thereby achieves not only a unity of economic and political aims, but also intellectual and moral unity."[14] If one thinks of the first great works of history written with Gramsci's influence, E. P. Thompson's Making of the British Working Class or Eugene Genovese's Roll, Jordan, Roll, one sees a similar steadfast materialism that systematically related cultural elements to the material realities of class formation and power. My point here is not that the more recent Gramscian intellectuals have been phony radicals or, perhaps worse, Fabians, but that the fundamental cause of the political failure of radical intellectual will rests in the immersion into merely cultural analysis, which traps us all into its broad and slithery net and leaves us with a general paradigm that is completely ill suited to meaningful political action. The concept of cultural hegemony was inherently vulnerable to corruption by the dogma of cultural agency, and what originally was intended as a sophisticated program for revolutionary consciousness-raising devolved into self-satisfied proclamations that the subversions of consumer culture amounted to substantive challenges to the status quo.

It is telling about the dangers of playing with culture that Gramsci has endured the same thoughtless expansion as the concept itself. Those who have strained to keep his thought relevant in the midst of the steady expansion of cultural studies have stretched it to cover all things. As David Harris writes in his examination of the intellectuals associated with the Birmingham Centre for Contemporary Cultural Studies, who pioneered in the application of Gramsci to the advocacy of so-called popular culture, "pretty well everything can be explained by the term hegemony."[15] There is ample evidence to confirm Harris's point. John Hargreaves, invoking Gramsci, tells us that sport is culture, and culture is power. "The fundamental importance of culture can be appreciated if we bear in mind that social relations, as such, of whatever kind, are culturally constituted, in the sense that they embody signifying practices . . . through which social agents generate ways of giving meaning to their experience. . . . Put another way: there would be no experience without culture." Put another way: Culture is everything. And the most likely sort of reasoning to follow such a broad rendering is the declining persuasiveness of an argument built on such a cheapened foundation. Nowhere has this trap been so unwittingly and yet so plainly stated than in Florencia E. Mallon's 1995 study of post-colonial Mexico and Peru. "I have found it necessary to go beyond equating hegemony with a belief in, or incorporation of, the dominant ideology," she boasts. "Hegemony is a set of nested, continuous processes through which power and meaning are contested, legitimated, and redefined at all levels of society. According to this definition, hegemony is hegemonic process: it can and does exist everywhere at all times."[16] Cast in this manner, hegemony becomes a tautology.

The best corrective to this conceptual inflation might be found in Gramsci himself. It is hard to imagine Gramsci, who insisted that the intellectuals' task was in part to educate the masses into higher forms of culture, engaging in "media studies" or seeing the football match as a site of serious conflict. Indeed, in a biting piece directed at "weak and colourless intellectualism," he warned against "seeing culture as encyclopaedic knowledge. . . . This is not culture, but pedantry. . . . Culture is something quite different. It is organization, discipline of one's inner self. . . . It is the attainment of a higher awareness, with the aid of which one succeeds in understanding one's own historical value."[17]

It is difficult to resist the temptation to suggest that the intellectuals who have recently spoken in his name return to read Gramsci closely again. But it is beside the point—and also a form of pedantry these days—to accuse the radical intellectuals of "weak and colorless intellectualism." There is a much larger problem afoot, and that is that in contemporary society the concept of hegemony was doomed to yield diminishing returns. Whether one sees the most humdrum activity as an instance of resistance or capitulation, in both cases the trivial is elevated to a plane of importance it does not deserve. Maybe there is an element of the political in everything, but that does not mean that everything is of equal political weight or that everything has a measure of political importance. It is closer to the truth to say that the vast majority of what falls under the category of entertainment is fundamentally meaningless; it creates neither Marcuse's "narcotized" morons nor the subversive consumers of the cultural populists. It creates nothing of consequence. Like the mass-produced food that is loaded with calories without nutritional value, mass entertainment simply is vapid; much as junk food fills the belly with nothing, mass entertainment merely fills time.

Radical intellectuals would do well to rethink Gramsci in light of this dilution and overexpansion. The masterworks of Gramscian scholarship, such as Genovese's *Roll, Jordan, Roll*, remain not only immensely informative but entirely persuasive—much, in fact, as I find Gramsci himself. But because the very nature of culture has changed so drastically from his time to ours, I am no longer sure that the concept of cultural hegemony can be applied except as a method of historical inquiry—and even then only with much greater care than seems to be the case today. Given the formidable economic and political apparatus that is in place in the West, and most of all in the United States, it is possible that the powers that be do not need to forge a hegemonic consensus through culture. At some basic level, of course, there is a general consensus among Americans about how the system is supposed to work. But in those fundamental premises, which amount to little more than a widespread agreement that the more "choice" people have, the better, everything from malls to education to reproductive rights are themselves least common denominators rather than systematic values. The dogma of choice is in complete harmony with consumerism, but the important point is that it takes so little work on the part of those in power to promote such a value. The sort of cultural regimentation that was necessary to bourgeois order during the industrial era no longer is necessary. Teachers, preachers, and pundits do not parrot a class-based party line, nor is Homer

Simpson on the vanguard of revolution because he ridicules the supposedly dominant concepts of masculine fatherhood.

Because the contemporary ruling class no longer really cares what sort of values are promoted within consumerism—other than that of spending and buying—they make "counterhegemonic cultural practices" all but impossible. It is impossible to "counter" what is not there. The only way to oppose consumerism is to resist consuming culture, which would rely on the recreation of a craft-based vision of society and, along with that, a renewed commitment to a stern conception of culture as the pursuit of excellent work. I will return to this point in my concluding remarks, but here let me note the obvious and say that the contemporary Left clearly has no desire to renew such a commitment. Instead, even the most theoretically rigorous continue to think that cultural radicalism can arise within consumerism. They continue to apply Gramsci, as Chantal Mouffe and Ernesto Laclau did in their influential *Hegemony and Socialist Strategy* in 1985, to the contemporary social order in bids to defend that proposition. Indeed, this closely reasoned book represents the end point of the Gramsci fetish, for the authors carry the argument from the old economic determinism through Gramsci and to a position that rejects as obsolete any commitment to working-class radicalism. The authors argue that Gramsci played a pivotal role in undermining conventional Marxist materialism and, more important, legitimized the present-day search for new vanguard groups by insisting on revolution as the result of alliances between various blocs of subalterns rather than merely through the class struggle. The problem with Gramsci, they continue, was that his instinctive Leninism prevented him from escaping the conviction that radicalism had to be tied to productive relations, and consequently the working class remained for him the essential revolutionary group.

Gramsci, accordingly, cannot be taken too literally in a society where the working class is neither homogenous nor hard pressed, and it is at this point that Mouffe and Laclau venture their prescriptions for updating and therefore salvaging the concept of hegemony. As they see it, the expansion of the profit motive and the accompanying state regulatory apparatus into every nook and cranny of society has created a variety of new groups of subordinate people whose positions in relation to capitalism are just as important as the working class's once was. The expansion of the apparatus of control, far from rendering Gramsci obsolete, only means that "the tensions inherent in the concept of hegemony are also inherent in every political practice and, strictly speaking, every social practice."[18] Here again we see the irresistible temptation to inflate the concept, and for them it leads to the argument that the arena of consumption, now ubiquitous, replaces the realm of work as the site of struggle. For there, the system's attempt to regulate all aspects of life has created "new social movements" that resist their own respective situations. The only common denominator of these movements is "their differentiation from workers' struggles." The new struggles are to be waged within the "media-based culture," which, to be sure, exerts pressure to conform to dominant values but which also "contains powerful elements for the subversion of inequalities." By presenting consumption as an activity that all should aspire to and can engage in, consumer society promotes an ideal of a "democratic consumer culture" that, dialectically, sets off demands for real equality, "as was the case in the United States," so they implausibly claim, "with the struggle of the black movement for civil rights."[19]

Supposedly, Mouffe and Laclau envision a struggle where the assertion of "antagonisms" allows different groups to assert their own collective self-definitions within the structure of consumption. To a point, this has been happening, and I am perfectly prepared to agree with their contention that where it does, as in the case of feminism and gay rights, it expands the ideal of democracy. But the inclusion of women in the political and economic sphere, the final collapse of the patriarchal family, and the public acceptance of homosexuality have all been a matter of general indifference to those who inhabit the most powerful corporations—some of whom, it hardly needs to be said, are women and gays. These gains have made real improvements in people's lives, but they have also served to expand the hold of consumer values for two reasons: first, because the more people are in the public realm, the more consumers there are to exploit; and, second, because this consumer democracy functions on the preeminent ideal of choice. While Americans want an abundance of choice, those values do not seem to apply to the political or economic realms, where they are apparently content, respectively, with two major parties of microscopic differences and the dominance of immense corporations. It is not unreasonable to think that the abundance of choice in the cultural realm reinforces the absence of meaningful choice elsewhere. But the crucial point is that culture acts to reinforce the economic and political status quo not because the latter drives the former but because culture, ideologically speaking, can be left more or less to function on its own. I am not saying that culture is irrelevant but that it no longer carries the ideological importance that it had in other bourgeois epochs and that the concept of hegemony, accordingly, is outdated. In this regard, we might have to face a still more distressing reality. If the cultural turn was utterly essential to the survival of the postwar Left, then the obsolescence of Gramsci may also signal the obsolescence of the Left itself.

Progressive Politics as a Captive to Culture

One can make an argument—as Michael Berube, if I understand him correctly, has—that the foremost problem with the American Left is not its commitment to cultural politics but rather its capitulation on matters of concrete policy. Perhaps the failure of political will grows from its apparent pessimism in the face of the Right's stranglehold in politics and economics. Berube even credits the Right with dominating intellectual life as well. He sees successful Gramscian intellectuals all over the place; regrettably, they are the likes of Rush Limbaugh, Dinesh D'Souza, Charles Murray, and other right-wing ideologues. In his view, the crucial problem for the Left has been that when cultural radicals talk about everyday life, they seem to forget that everyday life should, in a just world, include "school breakfast programs, disability law, [and] the minimum wage." Berube seems to think that the Left needs better arguments, or, more precisely, that it needs to turn its cultural analysis into more pointed demands for concrete policy. "It is deeply disturbing to me," Berube writes, "that there is so much skepticism and outright disdain, among the academic Left, directed at the proposal that intellectual work in cultural studies should seek to have an impact on the mundane and quotidian world of public policy."[20]

I sympathize with Berube's sentiment here, but I find the continued insistence that "cultural studies" of any sort can be translated into concrete progressive policies bewildering. As soon as a defense of rap celebrities turns into an argument for school lunches or public day care, it ceases to be "cultural." The sooner progressives give up altogether on the notion that culture is where power rests, the sooner they will get back to the business of politics. When the two become conflated, trouble follows. Indeed, I want to point to two recent instances in which progressives have tried to base concrete policy on notions of culture, with poor results.

These cautionary tales begin with Lyndon Baines Johnson's War on Poverty. Well-known in its outlines, Johnson's domestic "war" turned out to be the apogee of the welfare state in America, the last time that the federal government committed to bureaucratic expansion in the cause of social welfare outlays. Present-day scholarship on the historic value of the War on Poverty is mixed: Some historians have lauded it as a necessary commitment to the dual goals of racial justice and economic equality; others have insisted that by extending dependency it actually worsened the social calamity of the inner city and created the urban black underclass. As a matter of influencing policy, clearly the latter argument has prevailed, given the dismantling of the welfare system.

My own view is that the War on Poverty was laudable in purpose but poorly designed. It was too hastily created as part of Johnson's determination to throw largess at as many places at once, and it was underfunded. Any real improvements in urban areas would have required much larger outlays, which Johnson avoided because he was determined to fight the war in Vietnam without raising taxes. It was impossible to have both guns and butter, and the nation would have been considerably better off had Johnson opted for butter rather than guns. I have always found the most persuasive critics of the War on Poverty to have been Johnson's contemporaries, Martin Luther King, Jr., A. Philip Randolph, and Bayard Rustin, who were proposing just such a shift in national priorities at the time of King's assassination in 1968.

On the face of it, the War on Poverty was easy to justify and explain. The administration's mantra, as Sargent Shriver, head of the Office of Economic Opportunity, liked to put it, was that the programs were giving the poor "a hand up, not a hand out." There were to be job programs (the Job Corps), educational benefits (Head Start), and nutritional programs (school lunches, Food Stamps), all of which were designed to give poor folks the basis from which they could work their way out of poverty. Johnson and Shriver thought of the program as the best of both worlds: The federal government would use its resources to help poor people realize the age-old American dream of self-reliance and independence. Perfectly reasonable on its face, the War on Poverty suffered from a fatal internal flaw in that the programs were largely designed to affect the so-called culture of poverty that trapped poor people. And the culture of poverty, strange to say, was not the same as poverty itself.

The convoluted manner in which this concept entered policymaking is one of those strange episodes, which recur with amusing regularity in Washington, in which an ivory-tower idea is seized upon by an administration and applied to a favorite cause without much consideration of the practical differences between nice-sounding thoughts and practical application. The conviction that there were certain universal behaviors characteristic of poor people, that those behaviors were passed down as a culture, and that poverty therefore reproduced itself gave rise to concrete policies designed to alter behavior rather than address the basic causes of poverty. The socioeconomic problems that the United States faced were complicated, to be sure, and required the assimilation of unskilled migrants from the rural South, Appalachia, Puerto Rico, and Mexico into a industrial setting that was already well on its way to a postindustrial service economy. Providing low-end jobs was the most sensible approach to addressing poverty and could have been accomplished through extensive public works programs, ones perhaps aimed at low-cost housing construction or other projects in inner cities, thereby addressing several urgent needs at once. A determined progressive might have argued for redistributive taxation and, needless to say, the redirection of funds from Vietnam to domestic uses. Once mid-level progressives in the Kennedy-Johnson administrations reconceived of poverty as cultural, however, such straightforward approaches were passed over for programs that sounded more innovative.

The culture-of-poverty concept was the brainchild of the anthropologist Oscar Lewis, whose extensive postwar studies of poor Mexican and Puerto Rican families constituted a novel sort of ethnography. Lewis's place in the discipline was a bit strange. He was not a charter member of the Boasian circle with Mead, Benedict, and Herskovits. It is not clear that he had the taste for traditional anthropological fieldwork. He wound up studying in Mexico because North America already had been "done"; once there, he moved from studying rural communities to studying Mexico City slums. He justified the shift by defining the cultural distinctiveness of his subjects, so he applied the standard professional definition of culture to poor families and began to extrapolate from there. Thus "poverty and its associated traits" were seen as a "culture, . . . with its own structure and rationale, as a way of life which is passed down from generation to generation along family lines."[21] It is curious that he chose neither religion nor ethnicity as a basis for his construction. Why not, for example, follow members of a distinct Indian group from the countryside into the city and examine the consequences of migration? His early fieldwork had been among rural Indians, after all, and given the extensive rural-to-urban movement that engulfed Mexico City after World War II, it could not have been too difficult to manage such a study. Almost surely his decision to focus on poverty as the defining element of his subjects' lives was a political one, a result of his sensitivity to the issue. But the decision inherently confused an economic condition as a cultural one.

According to Lewis, because the culture of poverty was essentially a strategy of adaptation to difficult circumstances, it could not be seen merely as "a matter of economic deprivation." Rather, "it is also something positive and provides some rewards without which the poor could hardly carry on." In describing the numerous traits involved, Lewis was hard pressed to describe many that were positive, and those that were came through his minute descriptions of his subjects' everyday lives—their decency and affection toward one another, their neighborliness, their guarded optimism for their children against the backdrop of generalized despair. Generally, though, it was as if Lewis thought he was doing the poor a favor simply by saying that the traits that defined their behavior constituted a way of life with its "own modalities and distinctive social and psychological consequences for its members." In truth, the major structures of the culture of poverty were actually anti-structures. The poor enjoyed no "effective participation and integration . . . in the major institutions of the larger society." Social organization beyond "the nuclear and extended family" bedeviled them, though a tentative sense of community could develop in the midst of slums, especially where the neighborhoods were physically demarcated (as many Latin American slums are) from surrounding neighborhoods. Even there, family life was unstable; male abandonment was frequent, "free unions or consensual marriages" appeared, and children largely were unprotected. Individuals were beset with a sense of helplessness and isolation reinforced by a series of psychological maladies—"weak ego structure, confusion of sexual identification, a lack of impulse control . . . and a high tolerance for psychological pathology of all sorts." The poor were provincial, narrow in mind and experience, with little knowledge and less care for things outside their pitiful existence. Given so many debilitating traits, it might be said by way of summing up that "the poverty of culture is one of the crucial aspects of the culture of poverty."[22]

But this wordplay begs the question: Why, then, talk about it as a "culture?" When some of his critics insisted that he really was talking about a "subculture" rather than a culture, he waved off the objection with an answer that hardly foreshadowed analytical precision. It was "technically more accurate" to use the term subculture, he conceded, but he insisted on the shorter term "because my books were intended for a wide audience." Besides, subculture suggested inferiority, whereas the more generic term "would convey a sense of worth, dignity, and the existence of pattern in the lives of the very poor." Apparently he believed that his subjects would take more offense at being reduced to a "subculture" than at actually being poor. In the end, Lewis assumed that "any careful reader" could see that "I was describing a model of a subculture and not of a culture."[23]

In any case, Lewis was less interested in using the concept of culture with precision than in distinguishing, he wrote, "between poverty and the culture of poverty." The distinction is difficult to see. "Low wages, chronic unemployment and underemployment lead to low income, lack of property ownership, absence of savings, absence of food reserves in the house, and a chronic shortage of cash," he observed. One would think this was a fair definition of economic poverty. But it wasn't the pinching grind of such a life that caught his attention; want alone was not the issue. Rather, want discouraged literacy, membership in unions and political parties, or use of "banks, hospitals, department stores, museums or art galleries." Thoroughly marginalized, the poor were generally cynical about mainstream values and hostile toward the public symbols of the social order, the police, the courts, and so forth.[24]

The concept was not without its virtues. It arguably provided a sound basis for urban anthropology. More important, the concept that poor people shared a culture contained potential breadth. If there were "common adaptations to common problems," as Lewis wrote, it was possible to conduct "cross-national studies." The model could be laid down as a template that would detect universal attributes in groups as apparently distinct as Mexicans, Puerto Ricans, and African Americans; it would also be possible to note local differences. This same breadth, moreover, underlay Lewis's intention to undertake comparative studies between "class-stratified, highly individuated, capitalistic society" and socialist states such as Cuba, where Lewis expected to find the poor unleashed from their cultural bondage—materially deprived, perhaps, but culturally rich—because of their participation in the socialist state's civic life.[25] As he put it: "When the poor become class-conscious or active members of trade-union organizations, or when they adopt an internationalist outlook on the world, they are no longer part of the culture of poverty, although they may still be desperately poor." Political organization and movement was perhaps the best solution to the perpetuation of the culture of poverty. After all, "it may be more important to offer the poor . . . a genuine revolutionary ideology rather than the promise of material goods. . . . It is conceivable that some countries can, without materially increasing the standards of living, eliminate the culture of poverty . . . by changing the value systems and attitudes of the people so they no longer feel marginal—so they begin to feel that it is their country, their institutions, their government, and their leadership."[26]

The political utility of this last point, when applied to the United States, is clear. If the solution to the culture of poverty was political organization and psychological adjustment, this immediately implied that redistributive agendas, so difficult to execute against the entrenched opposition of the wealthy, could be ignored. Organizing the poor was the answer, along with offering some social work and psychological counseling. Not that Democratic politicians fell over themselves to gain a hearing with Oscar Lewis. If anything, Lyndon Johnson most likely would have thrown the culture-of-poverty bureaucrats out on their ears had he known what they were thinking.

Instead, the idea took a much more circuitous route to influence. It awaited popularization, which it received in a crucial way in Michael Harrington's widely influential *The Other America* (1962). Harrington had intended his book as a direct counter to John Kenneth Galbraith's 1957 work,

The Affluent Society, in which the Harvard economist all but dismissed poverty as a minor problem that effected isolated pockets of American life and could be addressed most directly through migration out of poor regions. Harrington, by contrast, harkened back to the memory of Franklin Roosevelt's 1936 campaign and announced that roughly one-third of the nation, between forty and fifty million Americans, were poor.

The Other America was a pathbreaking book in many ways. For one thing, it exploded liberal complacency and helped mobilize the nation's conscience for the better part of a decade. A lifelong Social Democrat, Harrington accurately diagnosed the consequences of postindustrial capitalism even as those consequences were still in the womb. He warned that the technological revolution would lead to widespread deindustrialization and unemployment; most of those out of work would either never work again or be forced to take seasonal or part-time employment in the service sector with low pay, no benefits, and no union protection. What Galbraith saw as "pockets" of poverty, Harrington saw as enormous structural flaws that impoverished huge swaths of American life—the coal and steel regions of Pennsylvania, all of Appalachia and the rural South, the entire agricultural sector, and inner cities. These were not mere pockets.

Given the size of "the other America," perhaps Harrington believed that it must have a culture all its own. If Oscar Lewis could claim as much about his Mexican families, there was no obvious reason why Harrington couldn't make the claim about America's poor. After all, like their Mexican counterparts, America's poor were institutionally marginalized; family life was often unstable and casual. Like Lewis, Harrington highlighted the centrality of the slum in reinforcing the attributes of the culture of poverty. In contrast to the ethnic slums of the early century, which nourished "the culture of aspiration," the postwar slums bred despair, hopelessness, and frustration and thwarted the development of community sensibilities. These conditions gave rise to a pathological "psychology of the poor," a "twisted spirit," he called it, where stress and anxiety created an accelerated incidence of mental illness that as often as not led to self-destruction or antisocial violence." In short, "poverty in America forms a culture, a way of life and feeling, that makes it a whole."[27]

It is hard to see here, however, the elements of culture properly understood. Continuity and permanence, essential to cultural transmission, were nonexistent. So were the other principal elements of culture. As with Lewis, Harrington's "culture of poverty" had no institutional ballast. It was an anti-culture. Nothing, in fact, made this a culture, properly speaking, other than Harrington's insistence that poverty was a way of life.

So the question is obvious: Why culture? It is not as though Oscar Lewis's work had become widely known in 1962. If anything, it was Harrington who made Lewis's career, rather than vice versa. If the concept had any clear virtue, it was its flexibility, for it allowed Harrington to collect under one term the many different sorts of people he defined as poor: inner-city black youth, the aged, the technologically displaced, California migrant workers, the Appalachians stuck back in the hollers. It was a good way to understand that poverty was a condition that carried with it a host of effects, including family instability, mental illness, drug and alcohol addictions, criminality, and violence.

This flexibility brought with it the considerable vices of abstraction and confusion. Harrington, as his biographer Maurice Isserman has pointed out, held to an essentially materialist understanding of poverty. The "other Americans," Isserman writes, were beset "by lack of income, not by cultural traits or behaviors that, presumably, could be exchanged for others." Instinctively, Harrington must have recognized the fundamentally economic nature of poverty; his prescriptions, such as an ambitious program for low-cost housing construction, spoke to the concrete and the material rather than to values or behaviors. Isserman writes: "Clearly, what Michael meant to ask was, 'How did these people come to be poor?' . . . instead of 'How did they come to the culture of poverty?'"[28] Yet Harrington also argued that it wouldn't be enough to stick with the old methods of the welfare state, in part because the modern poor resided outside of the nation's institutional life and were therefore ill represented when public largess was distributed. Logically, new programs had to include mental health counseling, drug-rehabilitation programs, and the like—much, it might be added, as Oscar Lewis had maintained. The solution had to be both comprehensive, including everything from low-cost housing to educational and mental health aid, and designed to "help them so they can help themselves."[29]

The best explanation for Harrington's use of the concept was that he hoped that deploying a trendy idea would yield political effects. Taking hold of an emerging concept, however, yoked Harrington's effort to the fate of that widening tendency to rethink everything through cultural claims. In a way, Harrington's designation of the poor as another cultural group was similar to Herbert Gans's designation of Boston's poor Italians as a distinct culture; or, to be more accurate, the very concept of the culture of poverty resembled the increasingly frequent application of culture to ethnic groups. No matter how strong Harrington's materialism was, describing the poor in almost the same way the social sciences were describing ethnic groups detracted from the fundamental observation that poverty was an economic condition imposed by the inherent inequalities of capitalism. This blurry formulation at once inflated the concept of culture and diluted the problem of poverty. The poor wound up being thought of as outsiders, as a group unto themselves, a certain number of whom wanted to remain isolated in their "culture." Isolating poverty somewhere outside the normal functioning of capitalism amounted to an intellectual marginalization of the poor, a rather ironic end for thinkers whose first good instincts were to remind their affluent fellow citizens about the poor they still had with them.

In the short term at least, Harrington's political instincts were on the mark. Kennedy administration policymakers were smitten with trendy ideas of all sorts, and in domestic policy circles, culture was all the rage. Indeed the first—and only—social initiative launched during Kennedy's tenure, the infamous juvenile delinquency program, was based on the thesis of Richard Cloward and Lloyd Ohlin's influential *Delinquency and Opportunity*, a book that closely resembled Oscar Lewis's work by claiming that juvenile delinquents inhabited subcultures through which mainstream values were filtered and subverted. Harrington's prescriptions had two other enormous benefits, as far as policymakers were concerned. First, its logic would lead to all sorts of new innovative programs, which meant new bureaucracies. Second, it avoided the unpleasantries of class conflict, particularly demands for corporate responsibility and progressive taxation. Nurturing the poor out of the culture of poverty really didn't demand serious wealth redistribution. No wonder Walter Heller, Kennedy's main economic advisor, was enamored of it: "The moment I heard about it," Heller said, "it became part of my thinking."[30] And the thinking by fall 1963 had accumulated around the concept of "community action," which was a catchall phrase that included locally administered mental health, juvenile outreach, and educational programs.

Kennedy was murdered before settling on any anti-poverty program, so it fell to Lyndon Johnson to push efforts forward. Always more interested in domestic matters than Kennedy, Johnson immediately looked to launch his historic wave of social programs. When Heller explained that they had been working toward an anti-poverty program but had not yet settled on a politically feasible plan, Johnson provided enthusiastic encouragement.[31] Still, it is one of the lingering mysteries of his presidency why Johnson, an old-fashioned New Dealer to the core, let a culture-based program go forward. As Nicholas Lemann tells the story, Johnson and his Texas aides were instinctively suspicious of Heller's plans because they were all so vague. But the Kennedy intellectuals had decided that community action was the only way to approach the problem—all the vaunted social scientists told them so—and Johnson must have feared their ridicule if he disagreed. So he set into motion the War on Poverty and appointed Kennedy in-law Sargent Shriver to lead the assault on the basis of community action. Shriver put together a task force to draw up the collection of programs that would fall under the Economic Opportunity Act and be administered by his new bureaucracy, and for advice he took counsel from, among others, Oscar Lewis and Michael Harrington. The result was a piece of legislation that called for over one billion dollars to fund a series of locally run, diffuse services aimed primarily at inner-city blacks. This was far less money than was necessary for a sincere effort, but beyond that, the money was spent largely to fund programs, not people; what jobs were created were social service or bureaucratic jobs, positions largely out of the reach of those people who were supposed to benefit. Even as he signed the bill, Lemann writes, Johnson probably did not fully understand what he had created.[32]

Ill conceived from beginning to end, the War on Poverty quickly devolved into an unmitigated political disaster. Many community action programs appeared to have had the exact effect that Lewis's theory anticipated: By helping the poor to organize on the local level, the programs encouraged opposition to urban political machines, all of which were Democratic. But then, it was never clear that the "poor" were actually organized; for the most part, those who came to control local programs tended to be people who were either already interested in political action or were, in a few cases, simply charlatans who thrust themselves into agencies for the purpose of sharing in the federal kitty. It is true that the creation of new bureaucratic jobs helped to improve employment conditions for some, particularly African Americans, but otherwise they produced nothing substantial in the way of basic economic improvement for the bulk of the poor. If anything, the plight of the urban poor worsened over the ensuing years, not because, as many on the right claim, federal programs indulged them in their natural improvidence—this claim, in fact, is merely the culture-of-poverty thesis turned on its head—but because those federal programs did nothing to alleviate the main cause of poverty, the absence of decent-paying jobs.

The blunder of community action is not completely unrelated to the other cautionary tale about applying culture to problems whose roots lay in other realms, namely, affirmative action. Whatever the legal and bureaucratic reasons for the evolution of affirmative action programs, the failure of the War on Poverty to redress economic imbalances between whites and racial minorities made affirmative action all the more necessary. Against the backdrop of Johnson's domestic "war," affirmative action can itself be seen as a jobs program, the skeletal remains of what ought to have been a forthright effort to ensure full employment. It is possible that many of the standard criticisms of affirmative action might have been blunted had the effort to improve the material well-being of African Americans been cast as part of a broader effort at economic justice, which could have included, among other things, a guaranteed-income plan of some sort that applied universally.

Inevitably during the 1960s, liberal politics and material reality entwined anti-poverty efforts with civil rights, a cause which also has suffered from culture creep. There has never been more than one practical way to realize something near to justice in civil rights, and that way is, like it or not, through the integration of minorities into the institutional mainstream. In a society built on bureaucracies, doing right by once-marginalized minority groups means immersing them in structures that inherently reduce human differences by imposing standardized rules and routines. And as I have argued, that necessity destroys any genuine cultural diversity.

From the first, however, culture provided a convenient and largely painless way to avoid this hard truth. Integration became a dirty word among the radicalized younger civil rights activists of the late 1960s, who, disillusioned with Martin Luther King's dream of the beloved community, began to float various nationalist schemes. These visions were always pipe dreams, when they weren't downright foolish, and never appealed to more than a handful of radicals. It didn't take long before the energies being spent on hopes for black independence, or even the more modest hope for economic self-determination, were converted into cultural nationalism. In an aesthetic sense, this was a very good thing, for it excited a wave of poetry, art, and literature that included Toni Morrison's first novels. But in a political sense, the move toward culture was a comparatively painless way to assert a sense of independence while capitulating to the dominant economic structure of contemporary America.

White progressives, meanwhile, continued to assume that integration was the principal goal in any pursuit of racial justice, which put them at odds momentarily with black radicals. The reconciliation of white and black progressives awaited Justice Lewis Powell's controlling decision in *University of California v Bakke*, which invoked "diversity" for the first time. Probably more than anything else, the Powell opinion made it possible for progressives to adopt the delusion that minorities could be assimilated into the nation's bureaucratic order without sacrificing their way of life. What this means is that the concept of diversity as it has been applied to bureaucratic inclusion is an unintended construct of legal reasoning in search of a compromise, and as such never contained at its origins any coherent notion of what human diversity is. The concept has proved both resilient and workable precisely because it is so ill defined, and this virtue has immunized diversity from any really searching intellectual scrutiny ever since. The concept of cultural diversity in the service of bureaucratic inclusion has proved itself to be a serviceable obfuscation.

Any faith in cultural diversity was only a dim element in the *Bakke* decision. Powell himself was a moderately conservative jurist, a southerner who somewhat reluctantly had come to recognize racial integration as necessary to preserving social order. Going into *Bakke*, he was determined to preserve affirmative action while also circumscribing its reach and extent. Compulsory quotas offended him. He saw no good reason to widen affirmative action to groups with no historic claim as victims of discrimination or to groups whose members consistently succeeded in spite of discrimination. Partly because he was a southern gentleman, so his biographer speculates, he retained vestiges of white paternalism for blacks and sought to confine affirmative action efforts to them. To make programs available to African Americans while denying them to other groups, Powell insisted that the strictest standard of judicial scrutiny be employed to judge whether discrimination requiring remedy had occurred. Finally, he believed that affirmative action should not be permanent.[33]

To pull off this feat of moderation, Powell famously resorted to a series of close distinctions glued together with the concept of diversity. There was an important difference, he maintained, between a goal and a quota; there was a subtle but notable difference between using race as a "preference" and using it as a mandate. Because university admissions always had been settled on qualities other than pure test scores, race could legitimately be included among many other ingredients. These distinctions then were bound together beneath the nebulous notion that the state's compelling interest in affirmative action admissions rested on the general importance of a heterogeneous student body, which presumably was necessary to the educational mission of the university.

As John C. Jeffries tells the story, Powell got the idea from his clerk, Robert Comfort, whom he entrusted to compose an early draft of a *Bakke* opinion. While poring over his research material, Comfort came across Harvard's early 1970s admissions guide, which justified its preferences with the magic word: "Fifteen years or twenty years ago . . . diversity meant students from California, New York, and Massachusetts; city dwellers and farm boys; violinists, painters and football players. . . . [Today] a black student can usually bring something that a white student cannot offer."[34] Comfort and Powell were not attracted to the idea of diversity as such but rather to Harvard's use of race as one criteria among many that figured into any given admissions decision. Powell ultimately rested his argument on just this point when he held that ethnic diversity was not a strong enough interest to justify the selection of students on that basis alone. Rather "the diversity that furthers a compelling state interest encompasses a far broader array of qualifications and characteristics, of which racial or ethnic origin is but a single, though important, element." Because the goal of diversity was supposed to be that students from different backgrounds shared their varied experiences for the general edification, it actually ran against that interest to "insulat[e] each category of applicants with certain desired qualifications from competition with all other applicants."[35] Diversity, evidently, was just mushy enough to suit Powell's moderating purposes.

In negotiating between quotas and the dismantling of all affirmative action programs, the Powell decision was a marvel of careful moderation. Immediately it pleased almost no one; in the intervening years it provided the defense, as historian Bernard Schwartz has argued, for well-conceived programs and in a sense saved affirmative action.[36] Now that the Court has reaffirmed Powell in *Grutter v Bollinger*, it is clear that Schwartz is right. *Grutter* also means that the vague moderation of the Powell decision has constitutional imprimatur for at least the next quarter-century.

The two important cases from the University of Michigan brought before the Court in spring 2003, *Gratz v Bollinger* and *Grutter v Bollinger*, provided an opportunity to clarify what diversity means, and yet the many arguments raised on behalf of the university tended mostly to demonstrate how vapid the concept is, while those marshaled on behalf of the plaintiffs avoided asking the most fundamental questions. The Court ruled in favor of the plaintiff in *Gratz*, because the undergraduate process awarded a specific (and not inconsiderable) number of points to applicants from designated racial and ethnic backgrounds and smacked too clearly of a quota system. The law school won in *Grutter*, by contrast, because in its admission process race and ethnicity were merely two among many other "soft variables" that contributed to the candidate's overall profile. In *Grutter*, the majority decided not to alter the Powell decision and to maintain the conviction that "student body diversity" was a compelling state interest in university admissions. The plaintiffs' attorneys spent much energy arguing that any use of race violated individual rights and otherwise maintained that racial diversity was not compelling. The university—and ultimately Justice O'Connor's opinion—insisted that diversity was a compelling enough interest that it trumps individual rights. This claim rests on the assumption that racial and ethnic backgrounds translate directly and inevitably into significant experiential differences. But no one bothered to ask the simpleton's question: Is there such a thing as diversity?

This certainly wasn't a question that the university cared to raise. Rather, its numerous briefs included the work of Patricia Gurin, chair of the psychology department, which was taken as surefire evidence of diversity's necessity to the educational mission. [37] Gurin argues that interacting across racial lines is a good in itself, for it improves students by forcing them to confront unfamiliar situations. Doing so, she claims, fosters "deep and complex thinking"; students working in heterogeneous groups "show greater potential for critical thinking." Confronting "multiple points of view" are prerequisites for creating future leaders who will "accept diversity, negotiate conflicts, and form coalitions . . . in an increasingly heterogeneous and complex society." Gurin calls this willingness to accept diversity the "capacity for democracy" and contends that "racial diversity experiences in college" have an empirically demonstrable effect in creating that capacity. Logically, then, racial preferences in admissions are necessary to the future of democracy itself. That would pretty well take care of the matter of compelling state interest.[38]

According to Gurin, these positive "democracy outcomes" depend on an ample mixing of three different types of "campus experience variables." "Structural diversity" applies to the actual ethno-racial mix on campus and is particularly important for African Americans, who apparently succeed best when they are able to sustain close relationships with others of the same race; hence a critical mass of fellows is important to the general success of African American students. The second form, "classroom diversity," comes from multicultural curricula where courses are designed to foster "knowledge about diverse groups." Finally, "informal interactional diversity," in which students mix more or less on their own in dorms, coffee shops, study sessions, and the like, contributes still further to learning.[39]

The most important "outcome" is that students who benefit from these three forms of diversity remain committed to "living and working in a diverse society" well after leaving college. Her "democracy outcomes" measure the degree to which postgraduates "understand and consider the multiple perspectives that are inherent in a diverse environment," deal with conflicts that grow from diversity, and "appreciate the common values and integrative forces that incorporate these differences in the pursuit of the broader common good." Unlike previous studies, hers followed students into their postgraduate social lives and considered their residential and career choices as well as their perspectives on how college had prepared them for the real world.[40] It is not surprising that Gurin found that those students exposed to healthy doses of her three forms of diversity displayed empirically verifiable positive results in their democracy outcomes after graduation. Across the board, students from all ethnic and racial groups showed strong results four and nine years after graduation.

Gurin's argument is strange. It is stacked, for one thing—a good example of how easily social scientists can manipulate argument beneath a veneer of empiricism. To some extent, Gurin's entire study rests on something close to tautology: Students who are immersed in the diversity dogma while in school remain devoted to the diversity dogma for a decade or so. More important, her views of both democracy and knowledge are self serving. To her, a democrat is that person who embraces the dogma, while a "complex" thinker is one who does the same. I have no doubt that a willingness to act across racial and ethnic lines contributes to the common good, and a broad willingness to do so is a virtue. The point, however, is that Gurin's definition of democracy is crafted to meet the circumstances of the case and certainly is a narrow and idiosyncratic one. If she had included among her "democracy outcomes" a detailed comprehension of the Bill of Rights or the ability to control the basic elements of work lives, ethnic studies courses most likely would have been utterly irrelevant. She never breaks the students down into majors, so we cannot know whether it is up to the humanities to save democracy or whether those who major in engineering, business, biology, and math have some hope that they too might become good citizens.

A potent argument can be made that the humanities provide the best vehicle for generating college graduates who are more than just white-collar corporate automatons. But Gurin's view of knowledge, like her definition of democracy, is narrowly self-serving. She is curiously indifferent to the cultivation of basic intellectual skills. Her "complex thinking" does not include the cultivation of the difficult skills of writing and self-expression. She even dismisses grade point average, which would seem to be a fairly easy way to measure student success, as a reliable measure of the value of diversity education; because "African American students who had taken the most diversity courses earned somewhat lower grades" while Latino students earned higher ones and the grades of white students showed little effect, it was best to forget that measure.[41] Otherwise, Gurin's conception of knowledge is entirely instrumental. The purpose of college education in her scheme is to produce graduates who take diversity into the real world, much as engineers and MBAs carry their newly acquired but narrow knowledge away from Ann Arbor.

The most distressing part of her entire project is that she equates critical thinking with embracing the diversity dogma. All humanists want to foster critical thought. But critical thought ought to be measured by intellectual independence and originality, not by whether a student accepts the word that the profs. hand down as gospel. Any self-respecting college student these days of whatever background ought to reject the assumption that group diversity is a perpetual force to which we all must bow, and any honest assessment of critical thinking would give extra points to the student who dared make such a counterclaim in the face of professorial censure. Nor is this point irrelevant to democracy, for the best democrats are always the best iconoclasts.

In a sense, what Gurin would like to see are students who turn out to be conforming nonconformists, people who buck the assumptions of racial security that their parents' generation held to. And there is no harm in that. But what she and her peers are seeking is not a world of diversity. The whole purpose of shaping universities in the way they have in mind is to bring on racial integration, not just on campus but through society generally. Theirs would be a great service, which deserves to be spoken about openly and defended forthrightly. Gurin concludes with this point, yet in a way that ought to leave her readers scratching their heads: "Diversity experiences during college had impressive effects on the extent to which graduates in the national study were living racially or ethnically integrated lives. . . . This confirms that the long-term pattern of segregation noted by many social scientists can be broken by diversity experiences during college."[42] Here we are again at the best of both worlds: In Patricia Gurin's world, diversity promises integration.

Other self-evident contradictions appeared in the Court's ruling. Justice O'Connor gave heed to two very different lines of argument from the university. First, she accepted at face value the claim that race equates to cultural difference and hence to different perspectives that would add learning value. She reiterated the lower court's opinion that "the greatest possible variety of backgrounds" yields "cross-racial understanding" and classrooms that are "livelier, more spirited, and simply more enlightening and interesting." In addition to this reasoning, O'Connor accepted the university's claim that a "critical mass" of minority students was necessary, not, as Patricia Gurin might have suggested, because African American students need to find refuge among their own but on the grounds that having enough minority students relieved all of them of the pressure to stand as examples of their respective race. A critical mass makes it possible for minority students to be themselves, and in so doing, it breaks down generalized stereotypes by proving that there is "a variety of viewpoints among minority students."[43] As Justice Breyer suggested when, during oral arguments, he mulled over the critical-mass claim, it would be of educational value in itself for white students to meet a black student who was rich, Republican, and came to Michigan from Exeter.[44] On the one hand, then, the university claims that race equates to unique group-based perspectives; on the other, it claims that there is no single "minority" viewpoint. The latter view assumes that there is no uniform minority experience; but then the whole argument for diversity as a compelling interest—to convey the minority experience to those who know nothing about it—teeters. For that matter, the unquestioned assumption that there is such a thing as diversity, as distinguished from individual differences, becomes problematic.

The only thing that can save it is the argument that race still matters. "Just as growing up in a particular region or having particular professional experiences is likely to affect an individual's views," O'Connor wrote, "so too is one's own, unique experience of being a racial minority in a society, like our own, in which race unfortunately still matters."[45] In so claiming, O'Connor sidled up to affirmative action defenders such as Ronald Dworkin, who maintains flatly that "the experience of a black person in American society is special, and cannot be duplicated by the experience of a white person of similar economic and social background."[46]

But it is precisely this claim that can no longer be taken for granted. When Justice Powell wrote in 1978, it was indisputably true that the life experience of an African American, regardless of economic circumstances, was significantly different from that of a white peer. But with each passing year, as our homogenizing social system works its leveling, the life experiences of suburban kids—the very population most likely to wind up as Michigan applicants—collapse into numbing similarity regardless of race. It is a measure of how detached from the younger generation Dworkin, O'Connor, and their colleagues are that they continue to assume that what was true in 1978 remains so today. It hasn't dawned on them that the African American child of professional parents living in suburban America has life experiences that are not appreciably different from that of the Asian American kid or the Caucasian kid in the same circumstances. Surely, family lore is different; perhaps religious ties as well. But these are minor variations, as I've argued, that grow less discernible all the time. Indeed one of the unspoken oddities of O'Connor's opinion is the argument that the use of race as a "soft variable" in admissions decisions is no different from the use of any other such variable: legacy status, athletic or artistic ability, regional roots, and so forth. Race, even the most ardent mainstream supporters of affirmative action implicitly admit, is just another individual idiosyncrasy.

If race still matters in the way that diversity advocates claim—that America's racial injustices continue to block the path of minority advancement—if indeed minority children continue to endure life experiences substantially different from those they are likely to meet at the nation's elite colleges, this condition of difference is a matter of class-based isolation. The children of

America's urban and social catastrophes are disproportionately African American, and we owe them strenuous efforts to improve their education, housing, and job opportunities, efforts far greater than affirmative action programs. Even here, I would quarrel with the claim that the life experiences of the black working class are appreciably different from that of the white working class today. In both cases, institutional disintegration, joblessness, and lousy schools are the controlling features; like Oscar Lewis's marginalized Mexicans, they tend to be profoundly provincial, not to say narcissistic, and dwell in generalized ugliness—they inhabit, in other words, an anti-culture.

Two good arguments remain on behalf of affirmative-action efforts. The first is simply that universities, as distinct institutions with their own integrity, have the right to set their own admissions standards, as long as those standards do not clearly violate the Fourteenth Amendment. Surely Justice O'Connor was right to see the law school admissions policy in this light.[47] The second valid argument remains the same one Justice Thurgood Marshall made in his vigorous opinion in *Bakke*, in which he insisted on the fundamental importance of racial justice through remediation of specific historical wrongs. Marshall based his opinion on the undeniable injustices done by preventing African Americans from joining the institutional mainstream of American society and claimed that by any reasonable measure of social success, the effects of officially sanctioned racism still burdened blacks. "The dream of America as the melting pot has not been realized by Negroes," Marshall scolded his colleagues during a flurry of memoranda on the case. "Either the Negro did not get into the pot, or he did not get melted down."[48] While Powell was reportedly shocked when Marshall contended that it would take a century to remedy past discrimination,[49] at least there was something measurable in Marshall's vision. If affirmative action programs in college admissions were justified because of the continuing economic disparity between blacks and whites—as they should be—then their relevance can be measured through a straightforward application of income and wealth data.

The diversity argument, however, permits no such clarity of measurement, for it is impossible to know when and if enough diversity has been achieved or, more to the point, when diversity has served its purpose. What is clear is that the sorts of affirmative action policies at issue in *Grutter* have no effect at all on the remaining economic disparities between African Americans and others. Broadly speaking, affirmative action programs, particularly those designed to erase outright discrimination in hiring, doubtless have been key to the expanding black middle class. But it is impossible to agree with Ronald Dworkin that policies such as Michigan's constitute "our best weapon" against racial inequality.[50] If this is our best weapon, then we are surely doomed. For it is clear that their commitment to diversity has not helped the nation's elite colleges and universities improve the lot of economically deprived minorities—a point that Justice Thomas drove home in his dissent in *Grutter*. Indeed, on the heels of the *Grutter* decision came a study from the Century Foundation that vividly revealed the great shortcoming of this approach to social justice. Seventy-four percent of students at nearly 150 of the nation's most exclusive colleges and universities hail from the top 25 percent of the income hierarchy. A minuscule 3 percent have risen from the most disadvantaged quarter. Blacks and Hispanics are still underrepresented, but not nearly to the extent that poor kids are.[51]

If these numbers are true, then clearly the whole commitment to diversity in the university becomes nothing more than an exercise in intraclass fraternization. Let us be honest about what diversity in this guise represents. It has nothing to do with preserving or honoring any substantial human diversity and is secondary at best as a solution to the nation's most pressing social ills. Its purpose is to ensure the racial heterogeneity of America's professional-bureaucratic class. Much of Michigan's argument frankly admitted as much. That racial and ethnic considerations were necessary to ensuring that the nation's future leaders "look like America" was the punctuating claim. Particularly because law schools so often tend to be the first step in prominent political careers, it is necessary, so the argument went, that Michigan and other elite institutions invited racial heterogeneity. Justice O'Connor noted that "a handful" of "highly selective law schools" trained one-quarter of the U.S. Senate as well as a large proportion of the federal bench. Consequently, she wrote: "In order to cultivate a set of leaders with legitimacy in the eyes of the citizenry it is necessary that the path to leadership be visibly open to talented and qualified individuals of every race and ethnicity." And though they smacked of mock populism, the dissents of Justices Thomas and Scalia rested on the perfectly legitimate observation that Michigan's real interest lay, as Scalia put it, "in maintaining a 'prestige' law school whose normal admissions standards disproportionately exclude blacks and other minorities. If that is a compelling state interest," he concluded, "everything is."[52] Meanwhile, scores of supporting briefs flooded the Court from a who's who of American public and private bureaucracies. O'Connor pointed to their briefs and reiterated the dogma that "the skills needed in today's increasingly global marketplace can only be developed through exposure to widely diverse people, cultures, ideas, and viewpoints."[53]

O'Connor, following Powell to the end, ruled in the university's favor in *Grutter* because the law school's standards did not set any numerical standards that could be taken as quotas, and even here, like Powell, she insisted that any consideration of race be subjected to the strictest scrutiny with an eye toward limiting the duration of affirmative action. Another twenty-five years ought to do, she concluded.

The odds are that she is being naive. The essence of the diversity argument, which she bought in its entirety, is that considerations of race are not tied to historic claims, much less to evidence of discrimination; diversity is not remedial. Rather, it is an educational good now and in itself a compelling state interest. Given that economic globalization is unlikely to reverse, given that the nation's ruling class is likely to become more racially and ethnically heterogeneous, it is difficult to see how the diversity argument, now established as constitutional common sense, will have less force in the future. In twenty five years, the nation's ruling class—its university leaders, its federal judges, its corporate executives—will have that much deeper an investment in globalization, and insofar as the logic provides the foundation for their power, they are not likely to surrender that process because of the qualms of a former Supreme Court justice.

Because of *Grutter*, America's professional and bureaucratic leadership—its ruling class—will become increasingly heterogeneous. Let there be no doubt: There is a substantial historic justice being done here. That the nation's corridors of power are to be opened to racial minorities addresses the nation's original sin. It is just that the "coloring" of the ruling class ought not to be mistaken as cultural diversity; over a brief time, this new "set of leaders" will align their thinking, bury their differences, and rule over a society still beset by class differences, institutional decay, and cultural bankruptcy. It will be in their compelling interest to do so.

The Problem of Freedom in an Age of Liberation

The simultaneous rise of culture and demise of the Left cannot have been mere coincidence. Though historians will argue cause and effect for another century, there already are plenty of writers who have linked the Left's retreat into "identity politics" and "culture wars" directly to its undeniable impotence. Wise people—Todd Gitlin, Jean Bethke Elshtain, Russell Jacoby, Richard Rorty, Cornel West at his finest, and Michael Lind, among others—have in various ways insisted that the Left's cultural tendencies amounted, at the least, to a grand distraction, a squandering of abundant energy and great good faith. We do not, as of yet, have enough historical perspective to comprehend the whole reason behind the Left's ruination. But as we gain some distance, we might well come to understand that a much longer historical trajectory is involved than these contemporary laments suggest, and that trajectory might well join the rise of culture and the demise of the Left as related developments.

The two are tied together, perhaps irrevocably so, within the broader stream of economic and technological change. Culture in the deepest sense was a function of humanity's dependence on nature; the will to create and refine is rooted in the struggle to transcend a merely biological existence. Culture is an implicit acknowledgement of human frailty, an unspoken recognition of our ultimate inability to best nature in the ways that matter most. The will to culture includes a yearning to break nature's bondage yet recognizes that such a break is impossible, and it accepts the creation of useless objects as compensation for nature's ultimate supremacy. The guiding purpose of the modern Left historically was to struggle against the material improvidence of industrial capitalism and insist that people deserve conditions that at least allow them to envision a future above starvation. To the extent that the Left's fundamental purpose was to make it possible for human beings to be something more than cogs in a wheel or mere turners of wrenches, just to that extent the Left shared an underlying sensibility with the will to culture. The deepest connection between the Left and culture rests not in the revolutionary potential of art, the passion of the artist for free expression, or, as the cultural populists like to think, the mutual opposition of activist and consumer to snobbery. Rather, the sympathy between the two lies in a mutual appreciation of the tension between biological need and the yearning to have something more in life.

In the last forty years, the emergence of a technological order in the developed world capable of producing such material abundance that its inhabitants no longer worry about satisfying basic biological needs greatly unsettled both the Left and the substance of culture. Not only was the starvation struggle conquered in the United States, but the obligation to drudgery was overcome as well. With these conquests came lengthening longevity rates, vastly increased leisure activities (if not necessarily more leisure time), and an ever-mounting accumulation of stuff—what sociologist David Riesman once called a "surfeit of goods." How could these not be good things, when what they replaced was a life that was short, nasty, and brutal?

Nothing comes without costs, however, and the consequence of postindustrial abundance was that it resolved the ancient tension between nature and humanity's instinctive desire to transcend nature. In one fell swoop, abundance removed the sources of material discontent on which the Left always fed and weakened the yearning for refinement that held nature and the will to culture in proper tension. Abundance made the Left obsolete and rendered culture irrelevant.

This two-part destructiveness of abundance manifested itself in powerful ways at just that moment when the Left began its flirtation with culture— that is, in the late 1950s and early 1960s. As we have seen, the Left had no choice but to acknowledge capitalism's material successes and rethink the essentials of radicalism. One result of that rethinking—which on its face seems barely tangential to the rise of culture—was the increasing tendency to embrace technology, particularly in the workplace, as an agent of human improvement that might be harnessed for progressive change. We might recall Tom Hayden's one great piece of writing, the Port Huron Statement, which devoted a section to the paradox of automation, the then-current term for the computerization of work:

> While automation is creating social dislocation of a stunning kind, it paradoxically is imparting the opportunity for men the world around to rise in dignity from their knees. The dominant optimistic economic fact of this epoch is that fewer hands are needed now in actual production. . . . The world could be fed, poverty abolished, the great public needs could be met, the brutish world of Darwinian scarcity could be brushed away, all men could have more time to pursue their leisure, drudgery in work could be cut to a minimum, [and] education could become more of a continuing process for all people.[54]

In many quarters, similar optimism celebrated the end of toil, the final liberation not only from the assembly line but from labor itself. This was the theoretical hope that Marcuse hung on; this was the moment when Marx's *Grundrisse*, with its hints about a final liberation from work issuing from the technological dialectic of capitalism, assumed popularity on the Left. This was the point at which American sociology began to shift its attention from the alienated in mass society to ethnicity and cultural agency. This was the moment when both the Left and the will to refinement gave way beneath a massive acquiescence to technologically generated material abundance.

As the Port Huron Statement indicates, automation only seemed unrelated to culture at first glance. Those who looked a bit more closely began to think that it had everything to do with culture. After all, if people were liberated from toil, they could reasonably be expected to pursue more genteel interests. They would have the time—and what is infinitely more important, the psychic energy, to say nothing of the money—to indulge their many interests. They could spend time reading up on Civil War history and even running around the Virginia and Pennsylvania countryside, as thousands of men and women do today, dressed in blue and gray, reenacting the drama of national catastrophe. Surely, if given a chance, they might learn an instrument, take up woodworking, gardening, or any one of a hundred crafts. They needn't become armchair philosophers or highfalutin' opera lovers, though they'd be free to do those things; they could go fishing or hunting or bird-watching or remodel their homes again and again. They might become more active in church, the PTA, or a dozen other voluntary associations; they might revive civil society. They might go bowling—in a league organized by their union, church, or local Red Cross. These were the hopes of the Left on the cusp of its descent into culture, and they deserve our respect, for they were neither trivial nor improbable.

What the Left failed to appreciate at that crucial moment was that the will to refinement and cultivation, the process of which was implicit in these hopes for education of all sorts as a "continuing process," in the words of the Port Huron Statement, depended on the tension between scarcity and transcendence that automation destroyed. The working class, along with everyone else, was liberated from toil, but it was liberation into a technological environment in which no one had good reason to exert themselves. It became far easier to purchase the products of abundance than to trouble ourselves about making our own; distanced from nature's imperiousness, the citizens of the developed world were no longer burdened by tensions that needed to be resolved through creative work. It was no coincidence that as one stream of left-wing thought was increasingly inclined to celebrate automation, another was increasingly inclined to renounce the will to cultivation and celebrate, in the cause of "popular culture," tastelessness.

Nor was it coincidental that the assimilation ideal came under ridicule at the same time. In no small way, the compulsion behind assimilation always had been the bourgeois demand for an orderly and compliant working class. Abundance, by contrast, was built not on the backs of workers but out of the wallets of consumers—a truth that Hayden and his precocious peers at Port Huron seemed to be groping toward. The postindustrial economic ruling class was able to abdicate its cultural dominance because of abundance. There was a huge payoff. Acting as social role models and involving themselves in the moral order of a society is hard work. The corporate class and its political allies today have been able to hold and extend their power while giving up all that stuff about "taste," "culture," and "breeding." The postindustrial ruling class understands, in ways that the intellectuals have not quite fathomed, that cultural imperiousness is very much like outright imperialism: Why bother with all the hassles of domination when all you really want is to generate consumption power? There is no reason for the present economic ruling class to demand that black kids "act white" when the Phil Knights of the world can take their money by indulging them in their "authenticity"—and the same thing goes, of course, for every other identity group. Cultural rule under such circumstances is downright counterproductive. It is bad business.

In light of the abdication of the cultural ruling class, the main end of the contemporary Left, human freedom, becomes harder and harder to discern. If there is no active will to class rule, no clear will to power, it becomes difficult to know what we are to seek freedom from. The temptation in recent years has been to treat freedom much like culture and demand free reign for every urge, every subjective instinct, every word or expression. We have come to the point where the direct oppression of fellow human beings has become so remote in the developed world that otherwise sane people, apparently deprived of any substantial injustice against which to unleash the energies of their indignation, have seriously claimed that animals have political rights. As with abundance, it would be inconceivable to suggest that the passing of outright human oppression is unfortunate. Nonetheless, our understanding of freedom in the West has always been linked to our understanding of slavery; without the latter, the former gradually becomes indefinable, and the tendency is to begin applying it to more and more circumstances. The only possible outcome of that expansion is to render this fundamental concept meaningless.

In this sense, freedom also shares much with culture. Neither is an absolute condition. Both gain their substance from being tethered to their opposites—slavery in the case of freedom and nature in the case of culture. Their beauty arises not out of their capacity to extract us from those tyrannies but rather out of the human engagement against them.

Notes

1. Michael Tomasky, *Left for Dead: The Life, Death, and Possible Resurrection of Progressive Politics in America* (New York, 1996), 5.

2. Christopher Lasch, "Toward a Theory of Post-Industrial Society," in *Politics in the Post-Welfare State: Responses to the New Individualism*, ed. M. Donald Hancock and Gideon Sjoberg (New York, 1972): 38–39.

3. Herbert Marcuse, *An Essay on Liberation* (Boston, 1969), 8–9.

4. Herbert Marcuse, *One Dimensional Man* (Boston, 1964), 10.

5. Herbert Marcuse, "Repressive Tolerance," in Robert Paul Wolff, Barrington Moore, Jr., and Herbert Marcuse, *A Critique of Pure Tolerance* (Boston, 1965): 88–91.

6. T. J. Jackson Lears, "The Concept of Cultural Hegemony: Problems and Possibilities," *American Historical Review* 90 (June 1985): 567.

7. Ibid., 571–72.

8. Perry Anderson, "The Antinomies of Antonio Gramsci," *New Left Review* 100 (Winter 1976/77): 30; Antonio Gramsci, *Selections from the Prison Notebooks*, ed. Quinton Hoare and Geoffrey Nowell Smith (New York, 1971), 310.

9. Perry Anderson, "Origins of the Present Crisis," in Perry Anderson and Robin Blackburn, *Towards Socialism* (Ithaca, N.Y., 1965), 41–42. Anderson elsewhere claims, probably correctly, that he and his British colleagues at the *New Left Review* were the "first anywhere outside Italy . . . to make deliberate and systematic use of Gramsci's theoretical canon." "The Antinomies of Antonio Gramsci," 6–7.

10. Gramsci, *Prison Notebooks*, 332–33, 330.

11. Ibid., 334–35.

12. Ibid., 335, 331.

13. Anderson, "Antinomies of Antonio Gramsci," 46.

14. Gramsci quoted in ibid., 19.

15. David Harris, *From Class Struggle to the Politics of Pleasure: The Effects of Gramscianism on Cultural Studies* (London, 1992), 152.

16. John Hargreaves, *Sport, Power, and Culture: A Social and Historical Analysis of Popular Sports in Britain* (Cambridge, Eng., 1986), 8–9; Florencia E. Mallon, *Peasant and Nation: The Making of Postcolonial Mexico and Peru* (Berkeley, Calif., 1995), 6.

17. Antonio Gramsci, *Selections from the Political Writings, 1910–1920*, ed. Quintin Hoare et al. (London, 1977), 11–13.

18. Chantal Mouffe and Ernesto Laclau, *Hegemony and Socialist Strategy: Towards a Radical Democratic Politics*, trans. Winston Moore and Paul Cammack (London, 1985), 88.

19. Ibid., 159, 164.

20. Michael Berube, *The Employment of English: Theory, Jobs, and the Future of Literary Studies* (New York, 1998), 219.

21. Oscar Lewis, *La Vida: A Puerto Rican Family in the Culture of Poverty—San Juan and New York* (New York, 1966), xliii; and Oscar Lewis, "The Culture of Poverty," in *Explosive Forces in Latin America*, ed. John T. TePaske and Sydney Nettleton Fisher (Columbus, Ohio, 1964), 150.

22. Lewis, *La Vida*, xlv–xlviii, lii; and Lewis, "The Culture of Poverty," 152–53.

23. Lewis, *La Vida*, xliii; and Oscar Lewis, *Anthropological Essays* (New York, 1970), x.

24. Lewis, *La Vida*, xlii, xlvi.

25. Ibid., xliv; Lewis, "The Culture of Poverty," 159.

26. Lewis, *La Vida*, xlviii.

27. Michael Harrington, *The Other America: Poverty in the United States* (New York, 1962), 80, 143, 150–51, 128–29, 159–60.

28. Maurice Isserman, *The Other American: The Life of Michael Harrington* (New York, 2000), 215–16.

29. Ibid., 171, 162.

30. Nicholas Lemann, *The Promised Land: The Great Black Migration and How It Changed America* (New York, 1991), 133.

31. Ibid., 141.

32. Ibid., 156.

33. John C. Jeffries, Jr., *Justice Lewis F. Powell, Jr.* (New York, 1994), 468–86.

34. Ibid., 475.

35. *Regents of the Univ. of Cal. v Bakke*, 438 U.S. 265 (1978).

36. Bernard Schwartz, *Behind Bakke: Affirmative Action and the Supreme Court* (New York, 1988).

37. Material relating to the university's case can be found at http://www.umich .edu/~urel/admissions/legal/expert/.

38. Expert Report of Patricia Gurin, "Theoretical Foundations for the Effect of Diversity," available online at http://www.umich.edu/~urel/admissions/legal/expert/ theor.html.

39. Expert Report of Patricia Gurin, "Conceptual Model of the Impact of Diversity," available online at http://www.umich.edu/~urel/admissions/legal/expert/ model.html.

40. Expert Report of Patricia Gurin, "The Studies: Method and Measures," available online at http://www.umich.edu/~urel/admissions/legal/expert/studies.html.

41. Expert Report of Patricia Gurin, "Empirical Results From the Analyses Conducted for this Litigation," available online at http://www.umich.edu/~urel/admissions/ legal/expert/empir.html.

42. Ibid.

43. *Grutter v Bollinger*, 539 US (2003).

44. Breyer is paraphrased in Ronald Dworkin, "The Court and the University," *New York Review of Books* 50 (May 15, 2003): 11.

45. *Grutter v Bollinger*.

46. Dworkin, "The Court and the University," 11.

47. Jeffrey Rosen made something of this point in his admirably judicious assessment of *Grutter*, "Light Footprint," *New Republic* (July 7–14, 2003): 16–18.

48. Schwartz, *Behind Bakke*, 128.

49. Jeffries, *Justice Lewis F. Powell, Jr.*, 487.

50. Dworkin, "The Court and the University," 15.

51. Anthony P. Carnevale and Stephen J. Rose, *Socioeconomic Status, Race/Ethnicity, and Selective College Admissions* (New York, 2003).

52. *Grutter v Bollinger*.

53. Ibid.

54. "The Port Huron Statement," reprinted in James Miller, *Democracy Is in the Streets: From Port Huron to the Siege of Chicago* (New York, 1987), 342.

CHAPTER SEVEN

~

The Virtues of Cosmopolitanism, Complexity, and Taste

It has been nearly fifty years since Raymond Williams elevated the concept of culture in *Culture and Society*. In that book, Williams argued that in an increasingly democratic world, where imperialism was crumbling and the working class firmly established, the Arnoldian notion of culture ought to give way to the more generous conception of culture as "a way of life." A broadened conception of culture, he expected, would be both befitting and beneficial in contemporary times.

Williams's hopes, rather like Du Bois's, have been dashed, and it is time to rethink his argument. There is no cultural ruling class left, strictly speaking, though the economic and political ruling class is alive and well. Where political and economic elites have discovered that they can rule without insisting on class-based cultural standards—indeed that their interests are best served by the absence of such standards—the critique of snobbery becomes mere evasion. The only cultural standard of our day is whatever sells, and to the small degree that art has any political purpose, its power to effect change, or even to rattle the status quo, is enormously diminished. It is equally clear that culture as a way of life has lost its democratic character. Williams's hope that the broader anthropological conception of culture contained the democratic spirit relied on the assumption that the working class enjoyed a large degree of autonomy, the sort of social space adequate to the formulation of distinct values and the preservation of unique traditions that could then be imparted upward. But such autonomy cannot be taken for granted any longer, and today it exists mostly in the minds of romantics who have bought into academic notions of "agency."

We would do much better today to champion a vigorous cosmopolitanism that draws its inspiration from distinct but bygone ways of life while committing itself to new forms of cultural expression judged by strict standards of well-done work. We should abandon the false comforts of provincialism and pull ourselves up from the lazy notion that buying things is the only skill a person needs. Such an effort at cultural reclamation inherently returns to the virtues of our two traditions of cultural thought, to a clear-headed anthropological understanding of what it takes to maintain cultural integrity and to a sensible aesthetic that, once again, takes the cultivation of skill seriously. Doing so will not reverse the counterrevolution that the Right has sprung in the last generation, but it might remind progressives that culture is not the same as economic and political power and set them free to reengage those realms in ways that might return the Left to relevance.

Our present way of life, founded as it is on the relentless cycle of consumption that revolves around sites of mass production now arranged globally, is inherently hostile to culture in both its aesthetic and anthropological senses. It is of utmost importance, however, that we not slight one tradition in favor of another—there is no one way to think about culture. That contemporary capitalism is mutually destructive of culture in both its meanings indicates that the two traditions are deeply related and suggests that both, in their own way, tap into elemental human yearnings that apparently run so counter to the workings of the present order that they must be systematically repressed or quenched through false satisfactions. As streams in our intellectual history, they have always been entwined. Their profound companionship rests on a mutual devotion to the ideal of permanence—on the creation of durable objects, on the one hand, and the replication of collective ways of life, on the other—and this mutual devotion assures their simultaneous annihilation today. Even as we renew an understanding of each tradition and learn to recognize how we invoke one or the other at any given time, there is no salvaging one or the other separately.

If we are to repair any of the democratic nature of the anthropological conception of culture as a way of life, we have to begin with the realistic understanding that almost all people prefer material improvement to cultural preservation. But that they must surrender the latter to obtain the former is as much a political as a cultural matter. Economic globalization has taken place out of a system of mass production of consumer goods undertaken beneath the control of private corporations, and there is no rule that says that this is how things must be. Demands for the socialized control of the means of production now sound ridiculously obsolete. But perhaps the socialization of the means of production is now more relevant than ever. It is not impossible that Marx was ultimately right to think that capitalism would have to dominate the entire world before its contradictions catch up with it. If this sounds a bit too quixotic, I offer it here to make a point: The now-global system of capitalist mass production can be stymied, but not through "cultural resistance." It can be shaped toward democratic ends only through politicized labor resistance. Even then a more democratic system of global economics would not help preserve the material integrity of different ways of life. A socialized, or at least more just, system of contemporary production would still pull people out of the provinces. No one in their right mind is willing to call for the sort of thorough separation of peoples necessary to strict cultural integrity, and it wouldn't be possible in any case. Things have come too far, there has been far too much cultural dissolution, to recover anything more than romantic isolation. Ultimately, there is a vast difference between democratization and cultural integrity.

It would well serve the understanding of culture as a way of life to absorb the wisdom of the contemporary anti-globalization movement. For the most part, those involved in this loose-knit assortment of activists understand that they can't call Disney or Nike back from Asia, lest the workers who have been pulled into subcontractors' factories find themselves both uprooted and unemployed. It is probably better that global workers be employed, even if only indirectly, by American-based multinationals, because at least companies such as Nike can be held up to public scrutiny here and embarrassed to the point of conceding to decent labor standards. Democratizing the global workplace beyond that requires international labor standards that could only be established, if not somehow enforced, through comprehensive treaties under United Nations supervision and conceived along the same lines as environmental accords and weapons-proliferation agreements. Short of such accords, old-fashioned protectionism can be effective. Protectionism raises wages and protects local forms of production; it serves workers at the expense of consumers. It is effective because it remains based in the nation-state, which is still the only determining political structure we have. Of course, the free traders insist that a wave of protectionism would hurt everyone. But protectionism designed on a producer's ethic could be carefully selective and used to promote unique local, culturally specific forms of production while defying the multinationals. In this way, the best work of specific societies can be reinforced and, to some degree, traditions, local knowledge, and distinct ways of life might be partly sustained.

The situation in international agriculture actually holds one of the more pointed illustrations of how regulated trade connects to local ways of life. U.S. officials regularly pound out their demands for open agricultural markets by ridiculing, for instance, the European opposition to genetically engineered food. U.S. trade representatives have every interest in turning the ongoing rift with much of the rest of the world over this issue into just another trade dispute, akin to quarrels about steel or automobiles. Meanwhile, the most common argument from the opponents of such products revolves around the potential health risks of largely unproven technologies. Yet the health emphasis is the weakest argument against genetic modification, because on the whole the scientists will make sure the stuff is reasonably safe. The real importance of the clash over genetically engineered foods rests in the revealing way agricultural technology undermines localized forms of production. The expanded use of modified seed corresponds directly to the interests of U.S.-based corporate giants such as Monsanto, who control the patents. Monsanto's short-term interests are in the expanded use of modified seeds, and to the extent that U.S. trade representatives succeed in making that possible, obviously to that same extent local farmers from India to England lose that much control over the character of their work. In the long term, the use of modified seeds designed to resist weather, disease, and pests would give those farmers who use them a competitive advantage over those who don't; farmers who resist the technology sooner or later will lose out, and with them go whatever local methods of production they sought to maintain, not to mention the web of human relationships, bonds of family and community, that typically revolve around localized agriculture. The long-term result of genetically modified agriculture will be the slow but steady destruction of distinct local ways of life—and it is no coincidence that it will reduce biological diversity as well.

Opposition to the homogenization of agriculture has to take the shape of political activism with an eye on how economic power works in the real world, and it is both admirable and refreshing that activist groups such as Food First rarely resort to the concept of culture in their literature. In such groups we see the reverse of the diversity paradox: The less anti-globalization activists emphasize culture, the more likely they are to act in ways that support cultural diversity. Culture, so to speak, benefits from benign neglect. This paradox also means that the real heroes of cultural diversity are not Iris Young or Sandra Day O'Connor—or, for that matter, the university presidents who put out their diversity plans while also presiding over institutions that may well be doing some of the basic research in genetic modification. The real heroes of cultural diversity are people such as Jose Bove, the charismatic French farmer who vandalized a McDonald's that was under construction in southern France in the late 1990s. Bove used his arrest and subsequent trial as a stage for protest against U.S. trade policies specifically and globalization generally. While he criticized the power of multinationals and insisted that mass-produced food inherently undermined small farmers, he also railed against mass-produced food for creating *la malbouffe,* bad food.[1] It has taken a French sheep farmer to reconnect culture as a way of life to culture as good taste.

Within the United States, the anti-globalization movement and the various anti-consumer impulses that show themselves in Buy Nothing Day and advocacy of frugal living testify to those ineradicable repositories of American common sense. Anything that obstructs consumerism can be a boon to culture. We might even refashion blue laws and sumptuary laws. It hardly needs to be said that these sorts of laws were always reactionary, the first based on religious demands for respecting the Sabbath and the latter to keep the lower classes from imitating the upper classes. But the practical effect of both remains valuable. We would only need to redefine their social meaning. Why shouldn't all stores shut down one day a week? We can remove the whole business about respecting the Sabbath and still remind ourselves that people shouldn't have to work on weekends, New Year's Day, or the Fourth of July. And it would be simple enough to manipulate the class basis of sumptuary laws. Why not a law prohibiting anyone who makes over, say, $50,000 a year from owning or using a car that gets less than fifty miles per gallon?

If there is a noticeable failing among present-day anti-consumerists, it is that they show insufficient attention to the importance of how work is properly done, a shortcoming that could be remedied by returning to the earlier wisdoms of those late-nineteenth-century republican movements in America, the Grange and the Farmers' Alliance. These movements never routinely invoked "culture" except in its oldest meaning of agricultural production; their participants understood that relinquishing control over the production of life's basic items was the first important step into the so-called cash nexus and that that was the beginning of the end of the farmers' independence.

But the best starting point for an intelligent opposition to the state of things might well be William Morris, the enormously important critic of nineteenth-century industrial England. Raymond Williams saw Morris as "the pivotal figure" in English cultural argument because he was very much a Victorian romantic and yet, as a dedicated socialist, he looked ahead to the democratization of culture that Williams was hoping for. Williams seized on Morris as a figure of such importance primarily because, whatever he had to say about art and culture, Morris was intensely political; an advocate of nuts-and-bolts improvements in the living conditions of the working class, Morris was more than a misty-eyed chaser after a lost past. For our purposes, when keen material want in the United States is uncommon and labor has been generally degraded into retail sales and menial health care jobs, it is not Morris's practical socialism that we would profit from—though that could hardly hurt—so much as his constant attention to the fundamental relationship between how work is done and the quality of culture.[2]

Morris should be obligatory reading for anyone who invokes the term "culture" today, above all for anyone who claims to be interested in cultural studies. The honest contemporary reader would find that Morris was neither a Victorian snob nor a mere armchair socialist. His archopponent among intellectuals was Arnold, whom he associated with the effort to sequester culture among a cultivated few. Suspicious of the very word—Morris often put "culture" within quotation marks to indicate his doubts about its common usage— he was convinced that even people of perfect good faith, "men of the highest aspirations towards Art" who were "deeply convinced of the necessity to civilization of surrounding men's lives with beauty," were doomed to fail as long as they were willing to accommodate themselves to industrial society. Particularly before the rise of "modern Socialism," he wrote, surely with Arnold in mind, "almost all intelligent people" were "contented with the civilization of this century . . . and saw nothing to do but to perfect the said civilization by getting rid of a few ridiculous survivals of the barbarous ages." These Whig aesthetes, Morris wrote, unwilling to condemn the system as a whole but earnestly determined to save art, were "as helpless in spite of their culture and their genius as if they were just so many over-worked shoemakers."[3]

Morris was no more a hopeless romantic than he was a snob. As he once put it, he was "luckier than many others of artistic perceptions" in that he was no "mere railer against 'progress'" nor an aesthete who squandered "time and energy in any of the numerous schemes by which the quasi-artistic . . . hope to make art grow when it no longer has any root."[4] He was perfectly ready to acknowledge the two great historic achievements of nineteenth-century Britain: the firm establishment of principles of political freedom and the technological genius of industrial society. These two achievements were not directly associated in his mind, and it was, of course, the second that drew his energetic criticism. But even at that he was never a technophobe. Machines that eliminated burdensome labor were healthy things, he maintained, as long as the people who worked them were not forced to do so for another's gain, since free people would recognize at what point the machine was abusing the art of the work in hand.[5] Morris's dialectic acknowledged the political and economic gains of his time but held that the latter particularly were realized at the unacceptable cost of all that mattered most to the human need for beauty.

Morris understood that the fundamentals of culture were rooted in humanity's engagement with nature, which, he observed, compels labor: "Nature does not give us our livelihood gratis; we must win it by toil of some sort or degree." Labor was not only necessary to survival, it was the prerequisite to restful leisure as well, for unless work were sufficiently arduous, leisure would lose its meaning. The question for him was whether that necessary toil was pleasurable or "a mere curse, a burden to life." Work worth doing yielded "the hope of pleasure in rest, the hope of pleasure in our using what it makes, and the hope of pleasure in our daily creative skills."[6] Pleasurable labor, simply put, exercised the will to culture, and for Morris, art was at the center of that expression.

Clearly, in light of his dismissal of the bourgeois strategy of preserving art in "the carefully guarded interiors of our aesthetic drawing rooms,"[7] Morris's conception of art inherently had to be a broad one. Art was that product of the "creative skills" that endures; presaging Arendt, he maintained that "all works of art . . . have the property of becoming venerable amidst decay."[8] By this, he meant far more than the masterpiece painting or sculpture. Much of his life was given to the "lesser arts," a term that carried no disapprobation in his mind, for the sorts of activities that permitted the application of "daily creative skills" could not be severed from the greater arts. While he dedicated himself to furniture-making, bookbinding, and other crafts, he also held in high esteem the daily art of interior design, committed as it was to coaxing beauty from the run-of-the-mill objects that made up life's routine. In so doing, interior design took as "the chief part of its alliance with nature . . . to sharpen our dulled sense in this matter" and thereby "to give people pleasure in the things they must perforce *use*."[9]

Not the least corruption that attended the rise of industrial capitalism was the division it created between the fine and the practical arts. But this corruption was not only, or even primarily, aesthetic. True, by burying England in a "mountain of rubbish," industrial capitalism indisputably made the world a much uglier place. But the decline of art, he became convinced, was a consequence of the degradation of labor, and for this reason Morris the aesthete had no choice but to become Morris the socialist. As his convictions moved in this direction, he embraced the socialist condemnation of class division. But his aesthetic concerns were never far from the surface. While he reserved his greatest indignation for the extreme poverty and wretchedness of the humblest among the working class, he held that industrialism had destroyed pleasurable labor for everyone. The middle classes liked to boast of how hardworking they were. But for merchants and capitalists work meant cutthroat competition, while for "engineers who have to make the machines . . . down

to the hapless clerks who sit in the wholesale exchange . . . and the shopmen"
who sell the mass-produced goods retail, work had become a meaningless
burden. Meanwhile, the bulk of the middle class generally produced nothing
and relied on workers to generate the superficial luxuries to which they tied
their status. Morris's prescription for the good society encompassed all these
concerns: work worth doing, ample and comfortable lodgings, a world that
was orderly and beautiful, and time for leisure.[10]

Perhaps so generous a world is out of reach for us today. Morris's thinking
might translate poorly in a day when the humblest among the working class
now commonly perform such toil as refitting diapers on physically decrepit
nursing-home patients who have lost control of their bowels. But Morris is
not obsolete, at least not theoretically, because he leads us to ask just where
that nurses' aide is to get solace and compensation for her necessary toil. One
answer drawn from the present misconceptions of culture would have her
seek recompense in consumption. Morris anticipated that argument and
rightly dismissed it—another indication of how far-sighted he was—on the
grounds that the combination of degraded work and the proliferation of
cheap goods dissolved away any lasting benefit from mere consumption. Indeed the worker in a consumer society was "doubly grieved," "compelled to
labour joylessly at making the poison which the . . . system compels him to
buy." Even necessary toil had access to compensatory pleasures in the preindustrial age, but under capitalism, instead of laboring to live, we "live to
labour."[11]

If Morris's vision can still be bracing and his outrage compelling, it is fair
to doubt that his thought would have much resonance today. It isn't only
that the nurses' aide all too often has accepted the proposition that there is
pleasure in consumption. More deeply, in the sort of service jobs common to
the "new economy" there is no logical connection between the task being
done and a previous, more satisfying form of work. The nineteenth-century
factory worker at least could make the imaginative leap from the assembly
line to the independent workshop; even today the memory of alternative
methods of work lingers in the process of mechanical production. No such
connection exists, however, for the worker who serves rather than makes.

It may well be that rather than generating animosity over how work is
done and then rippling outward into class consciousness, the dislocations of
our time, though not different in nature from those of Morris, resonate in
ethnic and racial sensibilities, which these days might rest closest to the surface. Where the labor-based issue of production animated Westerners in the
last century for clear historical reasons, perhaps racial and ethnic consciousness is the most tangible connection between the average person and a dig-

nified cultural past. For all the muddleheadedness surrounding cultural diversity, multiculturalism clearly taps into a lively predisposition. Whatever its abundant faults, the diversity rhetoric might yet contain the one best source of creative renewal for our time, if for no other reason than that racial and ethnic consciousness seems to carry the most meaning for contemporary Americans. Whereas Morris tapped into the living memories of workers who had grown up under another form of production and for whom the independent control of the means of production was therefore far more than just radical fancy, multiculturalism taps into memories of ways of life that are in the process of disappearing but remain in the vivid presence of grandparents and the knowledge of roots in another place.

Yet in its present form, multiculturalism serves mostly to preserve those memories behind the false protection of bureaucratic existence, and, consequently, the cultural determinists of our time occupy a historical place eerily similar to the snobs of the late-nineteenth-century bourgeoisie, who vainly hoped to preserve the best that was thought and said in museums. And so we find ourselves in the exact opposite situation from that which Raymond Williams confronted in the 1950s. Williams had enormous sympathy for the aesthetic project of the nineteenth-century aesthetes but believed that without sufficient attention to the cultural sensibilities of the working class, their efforts to keep beauty alive were merely "regressive." So now with racial and ethnic sensibilities. Looking to the past for inspiration, looking to our varied histories as repositories of ways of life deserving of respect, is necessary to a good society, and yet to see in ancestry anything more than a source of inspiration is to dwell in the same narrow regressive mentality that Arnold and his fellow Romantics nursed 150 years ago. Cultural strategies based on once-marginalized ways of life can no more rescue genuine culture than the strategy of the snobs a century ago could save art.

So the question for us is this: What sort of intellectual and cultural strategies—as distinguished from practical economic and political ones—might we embrace in order to restore the integrity of our concepts of culture?

Cultural progress at this point can begin only with the inspiration of diversity. Beyond that, improvement must come through the development of a cultural cosmopolitanism. It is time to jettison the provincial mentality of the culture wars and identity politics and to mature beyond manufactured parochialisms. Let me say again—because I believe it so strongly—that it cannot be a matter of choice whether and to what degree to wrap oneself in the ancestral garb. On the matter of identity, one can only be regressive or cosmopolitan. Cultural cosmopolitanism requires maturity beyond the provincial mentality as a prerequisite to appreciating the virtues of older ways of life; it is necessary to be emancipated from one's own tradition in order to appreciate the beauty generated in others. The goal should be to make use of the best of every way of life as a contribution to the universal store of human culture, an end that should not be mistaken as a relativistic acceptance of diversity as a good in itself.

Rather than envisioning a polyglot of choice as the indication of healthy diversity, cultural cosmopolitanism seeks social complexity. Understanding that the best alternative to mass society is neither the consumer bonanza nor racial and ethnic rigidity, the cosmopolitan is willing to live in a world in which different realms and distinct institutions run according to their own logics. Churches, schools, family and kin networks, and certainly universities serve different functions and ought to contain their own truths. They reinforce each other not by their similarity, much less their homogeneity, and not even because they complement one another. In a complex human environment, different institutions satisfy different human needs and reinforce one another only indirectly through their mutual solidity. The state serves political purposes and in a democracy must run on principles of strict equality and individual rights. The family, by contrast, nurtures and socializes children and bonds kin groups across generations; it is not a democracy and ought not to be asked to function according to rules necessary to the political realm. Churches mediate between their congregants and the spiritual world, and they too should function toward that end.

This sort of complexity, which can never be absolute, would be very hard for Americans to develop. Though Western Europeans have been steadily surrendering their sense of complexity, most other peoples continue to respect institutional distinctions. It is no surprise that Americans are the least capable of doing so. In a society that long ago had the distinctions between the private and public erased, where no intimacy is tolerated or respected, in which institutional integrity probably has never been so strong as in other places, people are ill disposed to develop the basic respect for institutional differences necessary to a properly balanced world. All sides of the culture wars exhibit a pronounced impulse toward leveling institutional differences by trying to force the values of one area of life into another. For progressives, this tendency typically leads to demands that the essential values of liberal politics, namely individual freedom and equality before the law, dictate the functioning of the intermediary realm as well. Catholics are ridiculed for not ordaining women as priests, while Protestant churches are nearing a deep point of crisis over gay rights. Meanwhile, religious conservatives seem increasingly bent on dissolving the separation of church and state. Free market conservatives insist that the market model works its magic everywhere, including education and health care, which civilized people understand to be matters of public obligation. So obviously opposite in intent, these efforts just as obviously reveal the same drive toward homogenization.

The great virtue of a complex society is that it restores the strength of those social bulwarks that provide refuges from deracination. Only institutions with their distinct functions intact and capable of generating and preserving anti-consumerist values provide hope for sustaining cultural diversity. Only in such refuges can people gather with enough room to develop and extend unique ways of life. Given the long road we have already traveled, it is doubtful that even institutional solidity will save or promote the sort of racial and ethnic diversity that multiculturalists advocate. But it would provide the setting for the generation of newer solidarities that might have enough strength to carry people from one generation to the next and, in this sense, sustain culture as a way of life.

Knowing that both the aesthetic and the anthropological traditions share a history and live and die together, the cultural cosmopolitan has to salvage both. If restoring social bulwarks might help foster distinct ways of life, the answer to nurturing the aesthetic is also close to hand. Just as a complex society accommodates institutional distinctions in order, among other things, to sustain a range of important values, so the arts and crafts might be reconstructed on the basis of that most discredited of old values, taste, understood as the cultivation of a refined sense of work well done. Taste, widely apprehended, would be one of the most formidable obstacles to cultural homogenization, because it is the opposite of the consumer mentality. Taste spurns fashion as transitory and manipulative. It recommends devotion to those things that last and carry meaning beyond their utility. It knows mere entertainment for what it is, a way to spend time occasionally, as we all need to do. In the cultural arsenal of a cosmopolitan, taste makes it possible to appreciate the varied sources of excellence, from whatever tradition, and confirms Kant's belief that beauty can be found in both the diverse and the universal. In contrast to Kant, however, the standards of the cosmopolitan have to rest not in the eyes of the beholder, much less the eyes of the consumer, but in the hands of the producer. Taste must begin with a direct question: Is it well-made? For the one thing that cannot be mass produced is the well-made object, and taste seeks that object out. This is why advocating taste is the most radical of propositions.

What remains is to consider the most elemental problem of culture in our time. We are far removed from nature and therefore from the tension between our dependence on the natural world and our yearning to escape to immortality. If this tension was responsible for generating the will to culture in the first place, its contemporary disappearance leaves us no source for reclaiming the essentials of culture. Perhaps the source of a revived creative will might be located in the tension between the desire for material comfort and the tacit acknowledgment that material comfort cannot compensate for the absence of a meaningful way of life. In a world carried well beyond nature's grip, we might find the tension necessary to the healthy process of cultural creation in exactly this inescapable reality: We like our material ease and yet understand, to our distress, its consequences. In place of imperious nature, we confront a technological and economic system that in many ways is just as capricious, just as domineering, and against which we legitimately yearn to distance ourselves. Recall Freud's reflections in *Civilization and Its Discontents* concerning the paradox of technology's capacity to improve material conditions while straining basic human sensibilities: "If there had been no railway to conquer distances, my child would never have left his native town and I should need no telephone to hear his voice; if traveling across the ocean by ship had not been introduced, my friend would not have embarked on his sea-voyage and I should not need a cable to relieve my anxiety about him. . . . What good to us is a long life if it is difficult and barren of joys, and if it is so full of misery that we can only welcome death as a deliverer?"[12]

Freud's hope was that modern humanity would come to terms with this paradoxical strain and that doing so would yield a certain creative maturity. The hope remains. The cosmopolitanism through which that hope might be fulfilled would be reflected in a modest tyranny built on a complex way of life and an aesthetic of craftsmanship. It would give us a means for limiting the reach of deracinating forces and help root us in a place bound not by the potentially violent insularities of race or religion but by parameters of institutional integrity and the standards of taste. A regime of complexity and taste would oblige us to consume less and to take more responsibility for the material elements of our own lives, which ought in turn to restore a lived respect for the values and rituals of earlier times. Yet it would give latitude for creative energies now squandered in our restless pursuit of goods or wasted in search of bygone pasts. We would not have the best of both worlds. But we might be able to create a single decent one, where everyone has access to basic material necessities and yet where traditions are given their due through our most skilled engagement with them, the end of which must be to pass them on to those who follow. In such a world, we might yet cheat death.

Notes

1. Jon Henley, "Flip Flop," *New Republic* 222 (January 3, 2000): 24.

2. Raymond Williams, *Culture and Society* (New York, 1958), 161. In his massive biography of Morris, E. P. Thompson also gives great weight to the arts and crafts pioneer's practical political activity. See Thompson, *William Morris: Romantic to Revolutionary* (London, 1955).

3. William Morris, "Art and Socialism," in *The Collected Works of William Morris* (New York, 1915), XXIII: 198; "How I Became a Socialist," in ibid., 279.

4. Morris, "How I Became a Socialist," 281.

5. William Morris, "The Aims of Art," in *The Collected Works of William Morris*, XIII: 86–87.

6. William Morris, "Useful Work v. Useless Toil," in *The Collected Works of William Morris*, XIII: 98–100.

7. Morris, "The Aims of Art," 91.

8. Morris, "Art and Socialism," 196.

9. William Morris, "The Lesser Arts," in *The Collected Works of William Morris*, XXII: 3–5; Thompson, *William Morris*, 93–109.

10. Morris, "Art and Socialism," 195, 209–11; Morris, "Useful Work v. Useless Toil," 101–102.

11. Morris, "Art and Socialism," 197; Morris, "Useful Work v. Useless Toil," 105.

12. Sigmund Freud, *Civilization and Its Discontents* (1930; reprint, New York, 1989), 40.

Index

~

About the Author

David Steigerwald is associate professor of history at Ohio State University, Marion. He is the author of *Wilsonian Idealism in America* and *The Sixties and the End of Modern America*.